Kinde Pitty and Brave Scorn

Thy *Satyres* short, too soone we them o'relooke.

Thomas Freeman, "To John Dunne," in *Runne, and a Great Cast* (1614)

so eminent a Divine as Dr. *Donne*, seem'd a proof with what Indignation and Contempt a Christian may treat Vice or Folly, in ever so low, or ever so high a Station.

Alexander Pope, "Advertisement" to *The First Satire of the second Book of Horace Imitated* (1733)

. . . plain DONNE in honest vengeance rose,
. . . 'midst an age of puns and pedants . . . ,
With genuine sense, and *Roman* strength of thought.

John Brown, "An Essay on Satire," in *A Collection of Poems by Several Hands* (1748)

these Satires are inestimable.

A. B. Grosart, "Preface" to *The Complete Poems of John Donne, D. D.* (1872–73)

Kinde Pitty and Brave Scorn

JOHN DONNE'S *SATYRES*

M. THOMAS HESTER

Duke University Press   Durham, N.C.   1982

8532204

Library of Congress Cataloging in Publication Data

Hester, M. Thomas.
   Kinde pitty and brave scorn.

   Bibliography: p.
   Includes index.
      1. Donne, John, 1572–1631—Criticism and
interpretation. 2. Satire, English—History
and criticism. I. Title.
PR2248.H46 1982   821'.3   82–9571
ISBN 0–8223–0480–5   AACR2

To Grace, for love and light

CONTENTS

ACKNOWLEDGMENTS

Rare poems ask rare friends.

Ben Jonson, "To Lucy, Countesse of Bedford, with
M. Donne's *Saytres*"

My own struggles *about*, *and about* the *huge hill* of Donne's *Satyres* have been
greatly aided and supported by many friends, colleagues, and organizations.
My great debt to the *mindes indeavours* of the community of scholars is indicated in my notes and bibliography. It is difficult to single out a few members
of my Department, since so many of them have offered constructive criticisms, encouragement, and support; I wish to thank Robert Young, Antony
Harrison, Polly Williams, Jack Durant, Phil Blank, John Wall, Larry Champion, and Walter Meyers, who were willing to read a chapter once again, to
help with another note, or to listen to yet one more version of a passage.
Barbara Baines, Harry West, and Mike Reynolds have been *rare friends* indeed, willing to share their time with Donne and me, to listen and to help in
so many ways. Gratitude is extended also to the National Endowment for
the Humanities, the NCSU Faculty Research Fund, and the Department of
English Administration for funds and release time to continue this study.
The library staffs at NCSU (especially the cheerfully helpful members of
the Interlibrary Loan Department), at Duke University's Perkins Library, at
the Folger Shakespeare Library, and at The British Library were always
helpful and considerate. For her patience with me and with Elizabethan
spelling, I thank Charlene Turner, who typed the many drafts. Some of the
chapters and parts of chapters of this study first appeared in professional
journals; for their informative suggestions and for permission to reprint, I
thank *Studies in English Literature*, *Genre*, *Texas Studies in Literature and Language*, *English Language Notes*, *Papers on Language and Literature*, and *Renaissance
Papers*. The editors at Duke University Press, especially Ashbel G. Brice,
John Menapace, Myrna Jackson, and Anne Poole were especially gracious,
helpful, and considerate to me, and I thank them for their attention and care.

Three persons must be especially thanked for their support and critical
helpfulness during the preparation of this study: Aubrey L. Williams, who
always provides a model of charity, patience, and excellence; A. Leigh
DeNeef, whose critical acumen, *right* reading, and abiding friendship have
helped make this a better study than it was when he first saw it; and Grace,
who made it all possible and worthwhile.

MTH
22 July 1981

Kinde Pitty and Brave Scorn

"Zeal" as Satire

The imagination . . . is always at the end of an era.

Wallace Stevens, "The Noble Rider and the Sound
of Words"

our end is now approached neere,
Our dayes accomplish'd are, this the last day.

Donne, *The Lamentations of Jeremy, for the most part
according to Tremelius*

Despite the judgment of Ben Jonson and Alexander Pope that Donne's five
Satyres are among "his best things,"[1] with the notable exception of the third
Satyre they are among his most neglected pieces. Even the third poem has
received almost as much attention for the insight it supposedly provides
about the poet's conversion (or apostasy) as for its intrinsic literary merit.
One might rely on a critical cliché and contend that such a situation is surprising or unfathomable, but except for the fourth *Satyre* such neglect is
understandable, given the extreme obscurity the poems manifest. We do
have an excellent edition of the poems by W. Milgate, and several recent
essays have begun to focus on Donne's considerable achievement in these
poems. However, the *Satyres* as a whole have never received the critical attention given to the *Songs and Sonets*, the *Anniversaries*, and the *Elegies*, even
though it has been pointed out frequently how those poems display the poet's
mastery of satire.[2] This study aims to redirect attention to the excellences of
Donne's earliest achievement in this mode by examining the satiric strategies
of these poems, individually and as a unit, within the historical and literary
contexts of their composition. When viewed from this vantage, they reveal
much about Donne's early poetic and his concomitant moral-aesthetic perspective on late Elizabethan morals and manners. Much too sophisticated to
be apprentice pieces or early experiments, they disclose how, early in his

career, Donne successfully met aesthetic, poetic, and moral problems and shed much light on his own opinion of his duty as Christian poet, fallen man, and religious devotee. Unique transformations of the norms and forms of formal verse satire, Donne's *Satyres* offer a unified, sequential examination of the problems of Christian satire, a creative shaping (or re-shaping) of the generic, conventional, intellectual, and biographical materials available to Donne in the 1590s.

One of the commonplaces of Donne criticism has been the emphasis on Donne the innovator and initiator—Donne the first metaphysical poet, the first Renaissance meditative poet, the first formal verse satirist.[3] Such no-menclature provides a valuable starting point for any analysis of his achieve-ment. Indeed, it is central to this study of Donne as the most important and most original of the English formal verse satirists. But there is another Donne, another feature of his historical and personal situation to which at-tention should be directed. This is the position of Donne *at the end*—at the end of the sixteenth century, of one phase of Christian humanism, of a move-ment of English literary history. In fact, if we accept Jonson's evaluation, Donne had "written all his best pieces err he was 25 years old"[4]—by 1598, the most probable date of composition for *Satyre V.* Such an end-of-the-age figure is well known to Donne readers, of course, as the English Elijah of the *Anniversaries* who saw the "new Philosophy cal[ling] all in doubt" and "all cohaerence gone" from the "old world" of morality and value.[5] The concern of this study is with the first appearance in his poems of this jeremiadic "Trumpet," with Donne's first "invasion [of] this great Office" in the *Satyres*, those poems that belong chronologically, thematically, and, with the sudden reversal of his fortunes because of his marriage, biographically to the end of the century and to the end of one phase of Donne's career. This poet—or at least his persona, that "artful fabrication"[6] who speaks the poet's poetic truths—is the figure who envisions the decay and destruction of order and value. Certainly he is always a Christian figure, acknowledging "the need and value of loving the imperfect and incomplete" and conceding that man is "necessarily finite, lacks omniscience, and therefore must fail in most of his endeavours"; Donne's satirist never loses sight of that eternal "cosmic toler-ance for admitted failure [which] allows us to be comparably merciful to those who fail as we do."[7] But this self-conscious awareness of his own fallen nature only reinforces his awareness of the precarious position of man in a providential universe, which is accentuated by his position at the end—at the end of the "golden age," at the end of the century, at the end of what many of his contemporaries insisted were "the last dayes."[8] The search for and creation of a voice appropriate to such conditions is one of the central impulses of the *Satyres*.

Apocalyptic and millenarian fears and hopes abound at the end of centu-ries;[9] but this fact, and our ability to turn such phenomena into historical commonplaces, cannot detract from the sincerity and urgency of the men and women who lived and wrote during such "last dayes." In a sense, in fact, the warnings and predictions of the soothsayers at the end of the sixteenth century were accurate—if not in the apocalyptic or literal terms in which they were evoked, at least in terms of the development and directions of English art and civilization. The end was the beginning, the end of the golden age, the start of another period of magnificent creativity and art. And Donne's *Satyres*, like Donne himself at the time of their creation, at the end of his education and the beginning of his brief political career, stand on the cusp. The first English imitations of the ancient genre, the *Satyres*, by capturing the spirit, themes, and tensions—the rich complexities of that unique age of beginnings and endings, births and deaths—show Donne making his (poetic) beginning by focusing on the (apocalyptic) ending. To appreciate fully the stances, tensions, and generic complexities essential to these five poems, we must start at the end—at the end of the sixteenth century and the climate of opinion in which they were written. It is there that we find the bases for the genre and the persona Donne creates in the *Satyres*.

As recent criticism has confirmed, one of the cardinal rhetorical principles that the Renaissance inherited from the classics was the concept of decorum. Even the satire of the Renaissance, that genre least commented upon in the critical documents of the age, is better understood by cognizance of what the satirist understood "decencie demanded" or allowed of him.[10] Alvin Kernan has documented, for example, the influence of one doctrine of decorum on English "savage" satire at the end of the sixteenth century; Annabel Patterson has suggested yet another.[11] But Donne's poems, the most original, the "most consistent and ordered"[12] verse satire of the period, seem little indebted to either of these concepts. There was, however, a broader and less exclusive concept of satirical decorum available to the Renaissance Christian satirist, a view of the requirements of the satirist that satisfied both the general rhetorical principles of verse satire and the ethical prescriptions of late sixteenth-century England.

This older and more comprehensive view of the features and limitations of the satirist was sanctioned by biblical example, patristic commentary, and sixteenth-century homiletic and critical opinion. It was verified, in fact, by the "first formal definition of satire in English literature,"[13] Thomas Drant's preface to his 1566 translation of Horace's *Satires*. Although this definition repeats in part the etymological confusion of *satira-satyros* that Kernan sees as the foundation of the "cankered muse" of Renaissance satire, Drant's defense of his inclusion of both the *Satires* of Horace and the *Lamentations* of Jeremiah in the same volume acknowledges the concept of satirical decorum that Donne's *Satyres* most fully enact. Both authors depict the satirist as a Christian "rebuker" whose earliest precedents were the Old Testament Prophets. And in accordance with the central rhetorical principle of *laus et vituperatio*,[14] which Drant attempted to satisfy by offering the "chiding" of Horace with the "wayling" of Jeremiah, Donne's five poems provide a dramatic integration of these two concepts through their portrait of the satirist's gradual realization of the *ethos* his age identified as that of the Prophets. To this view of the satirist as a "zealous" prophet Donne's poems seem most fully indebted. Just as Donne, like Herbert, Crashaw, Vaughan, and Traherne after him, turns to the words, voices, themes, and stances of the biblical poets in his *Holy Sonnets* and *Divine Poems*, so he turns to biblical aesthetics in his earliest poetic creations in order to formulate a spokesman appropriate to the times in which he lived and wrote.

It is important to remember, at the same time, that the *Satyres* are imitations of the Latin genre. Most appraisals have quite correctly focused on them as the first example of "a sustained 'imitation' of the Latin genre"[15] in English literature. Certainly, the exasperated indignation of Juvenal's "difficile est saturam non scribere" is echoed throughout the *Satyres*, and the rough asperity of Persius and the exhortative irony of Horace find their complements in the paradoxical encounters of Donne's persona with knaves and fools, as well as in his conversational style. Central throughout the *Satyres* is the adaptation, redaction, and accommodation of specific tenets and stances of Roman satire.[16] Nevertheless, the speaker of these poems is not simply a Juvenalian "railer" in Elizabethan garb who modernizes the situations of Horace in the tones of Persius. He achieves a balance, an integration, to use his own words, of "Kinde pitty" and "brave scorn" (III, 1) not found in the Latin originals.

Sidney, Puttenham, and Wilson characterize the earliest Christian poets as prophets. And Renaissance documents concerned more specifically with satire—the annotations and *Artes poeticae* of Fabrini, Estienne, Robortellus, and Correa,[17] for example—note specific analogies between the styles, techniques, and themes of the Roman satirists and biblical poets, especially the Old Testament Prophets. In the same way, the features of Donne's satirist in the *Satyres* accord with the Christian "zeal" that contemporary and traditional documents described as fundamental to the "satire" of the Prophets, and which they recommend in those times of "heinous enormities."[18] Donne's five poems portray the satirist's instruction in the necessity, justice, and limitations (the decorum) of such zeal to the satirist in an "Age of rusty iron" (V, 35) and to fallen man in a providential universe.

Although often overshadowed temporarily by responses to military victories, sectarian disputes, or political intrigues, "it is not too much to say," Roy Battenhouse points out, "that the doctrine of divine Providence was the chief apologetic interest" of the sixteenth century.[19] A single persistent and typically Elizabethan theory of Providence is difficult to formulate, however, except that it delineated God's attributes of Mercy and Justice in His continuing connection with His creation.[20] At the end of the century, while acknowledging and agreeing that God's Justice is the "fullness" of his Mercy, influential voices insisted that a fuller understanding of and response to God's wrathful justice was necessitated by the alarming state of English manners and morality.[21] Thomas Beard, for example, observed in his *Theatre of Gods Judgements* that "the greatest part of men dreame upon mercie, mercie and never thinke upon *justice* and *judgement* . . . so that the worlde everie day groweth worse and worse."[22] Stephan Batman set forth his *Chronicle of Doome, or Warning to Gods Judgement*, he said, "thereby to give my country the occasion to beware of some monstrous plague to follow, than shapes of former view have expressed, unless some *speedie remedie* is found in time accceptable to God."[23] "These are the laste dayes of dolor and heavinesse," lamented that barometer of public opinion, Thomas Nashe, "wherein the Lord is known by executing *judgement*."[24]

Donne's friend, John King, voiced a similar warning in his description of England in the 1590s as "a seeded garden of sinne" comparable to Sodom and Gomorrah. "These are the laste dayes," he urged, "so if we begge of God for anything, let us begge for mercie, for *justice* surely he owes us."[25] This allusion is, of course, a commonplace of homiletic discourse; but it is reiterated with persistence and volume by writers as diverse as Adam Hill, Timothy Timme, Thomas Playfere, Thomas Drant, Tobias Bland, Henry Bedel, and James Bisse, as well as by the late Elizabethan bishops and the Catholic recusant apologists.[26] It becomes nearly the watchword of the last two decades of the sixteenth century in England. Although often opposing each other in political and doctrinal controversies, these spokesmen generally agreed on the precarious spiritual condition of the nation. Bishop King's appraisal of the years 1593–94 (the probable date of composition of Donne's first two *Satyres*) is typical:

> The Lorde hath bowed the heaven, & come down amongst us with more tokens and earnests of his *wrath* intended, than the agedst man of our lande is able to account of so small a time. . . . The anger of the clouds hathe been pored down upon our heads . . . the aire threatened our miseries with a blazing starre; the pillars of the earthe tottered [and] the arrowes of a woefull pestilence have been caste abroad in all quarters of our realme . . . ; treasons against our Queene and Countrie wee have knowne maine and mightie . . . ; our expectations and comfort so fayled us in Fraunce. . . .

The calamities of the day impart, he asserted, that "it is *highest* time to forsake highest wickednesse" for "God seeth and overseeth at all times the untamed madness of the wicked [and] *the time is near* when he will turne them backe when their sinnes are ripe and his *wrath* thoroughly incensed."[27]

The apocalyptic tenor of these speakers is not novel to Christian apologetics and complaint; its lines of indictment against luxury, ambition, and pride were common to native complaint.[28] What is peculiar about these voices of alarm is their volume and the real sense of urgency and fear they convey. That their worst apprehensions did not transpire and that the material extravagance about which they protested can be explained as reactions to the "growing spirit of capitalism"[29] should not distort the essential fact that many concerned and influential Elizabethans at the end of the century felt that England, the nation John Foxe had shown to be "God's elect," had so misused the gifts of God's grace that His terrible and thorough judgment was imminent unless immediate reformation was achieved. However strongly the age earlier may have believed itself another golden age, and in spite of momentary exuberances over naval or political victories,[30] warnings about impending doom and destruction temper English thought at the end of the century.

In search for remedies to forestall the doom, many in the age turned, quite naturally, to biblical guidances and examples.[31] In their appeals for a more spirited assault against sin, what they concluded was needed immediately was the "godly zeal" of Old Testament Prophets, those exemplars whose "loving anger" was sanctified by the actions of Christ against the money-lenders and witnessed by the epistles of St. Paul. "The world is come to such a dissolute liberty and negligent forgetting of God," Bishop Pilkington decried, "that men sleeping in sin need not so much a whip to drive any out of church . . . but they need a great deal of whips to drive them thither."[32] The bishop's prescription corresponds to the zeal recommended by the later writers and preachers of the period. Although not all these writers used this specific term, their recommendations essentially agreed with Thomas Becon's definition in the seventh homily of the authoritative *Book of Homilies*. "Zeal," he said, is *"anger meddled with and mixed with love*; as when the loving father is angry with the child for doing amiss, he doth it not because he hateth his son, but in doing so he signifieth his fatherly love towards him; willing by that that he shall do no more, but endeavour to better. For when the child is thus chidden or beaten, he taketh heed that he doth not so again, for fear of a more grievous punishment."[33]

The most popular preacher of the time, Henry Smith, sounded the same note, concluding that England's "sicknesse" is "a lacke of zeale,"[34] just as Bishop John Jewel earlier had forecast that God's preachers would become beasts and "their flocks scattered" because of a lack of zeal.[35] "In God's cause no man must yield or be patient," Bishop Sandys concurred, "for the best that can be said of a state, a king, or a man is that they are eaten up by God's *zeal*." These "stray sheep" must "be *constrained* towards God . . . for the rod in the hand of the pastor is as necessary as the staff, yea, perhaps more, because they are more whom fear doth constraine, than whom love doth allure to become virtuous. . . . It is not sufficient to mislike sinne," Sandys concluded, "one must proceed against it, *zealous* in God's cause . . . possessing *vehement love*."[36] In these "last days," Smith urged, "godly zeal" is man's only recourse in order to avert God's wrathful judgment and to earn His mercy: "for God is pleased with *zeal*, as men are pleased with love."[37] And Smith, like Jewel, Sandys, Pilkington, and John King, pointed specifically to the Prophets, St. Paul, and Christ in the Temple as biblical witnesses to the sanctity and need for such "zeal" at the present.

Preachers such as Adam Hill, Thomas White, Thomas Tyrer, Anthony Anderson, and Thomas Drant answered these pleas with some of the most vitriolic sermons ever preached.[38] "Because you are full of olde festered wounds," Arthur Dent explained, "you must have Corasive Salves, for that is best for you and the speediest way to recover your health; and for as much as you be rough Horses, you must have a Rough Rider; and for harde knobbie timber; must have harde wedges, and strokes with a bettle."[39] Such sermons were not necessarily expanding the possibilities of the genre, nor breaking with traditional Christian ideas about the proper uses of anger and harshness; the popular manuals of sacred rhetoric of the day sanctioned such fervor. Keckermann, for example, listed the use of harsh and reproving language figures as one of the rhetorical tools of the preacher; and Hyperius of Marbury defended such sermons in his discussion of the "correction sermon" by using the Prophets as example. This type of sermon, he explained, is "that wherein the corrupt manners of men are reproved & chastised. *Esay* cap. 28 inveigheth bitterly against the excesses and superfluitie of the Jews. The same prophet cap. 58 condemneth the weightly works of the hypocrites."[40]

This profusion of "zealous" sermons was not the only response to the prescription for the age when attention turned to the exemplary methods of the Prophets. In the first Englishing of the *Satires* of Horace, Drant offered a complement to his own activities in the pulpit. In his 1566 edition of the *Satires* and *Ars Poetica* he included the *Lamentations* of Jeremiah, complete with an explanation of the similar features and values of Latin "satyrs" and prophetic "waylings." The classical satirist, he explained, "was excellent good in his time, a much zelous controller of sinnes, but chiefly one that with sharp satyres and cutting quippes, could displaie and disease a glosser." Drant used the term *zelous* to describe the Latin poet, but he dismissed him with the conclusion that he was only a great reformer "in his time." He then turned his attention to the Prophet: "The holy Prophete *Jeremie* dyd rufully, and waylingly lamente the deepe and massie enormities of the tymes, and earnestly prognosticate and forspeake the sorie and sower consequences that came after, and sauce with teares the hard plagues that had gone before." In a conclusion that reiterates the critical and homiletic defenses of zeal, Drant then explained why he offers both the "cutting quippes" of Horace and the "rueful . . . teares" of Jeremiah in one volume: "Therefore as it is mete for a man rather to wepe then to iest: and not indecent for a prophane writer to be iesting, and merie spoken: I have brought to passe that the plaintive Prophete *Jeremie* should wepe at synne: and the pleasant poet Horace should laugh at sinne. Not one kinde of musike deliteth all passions: not one salve for all greuances."[41] He concluded his preface with commentary on the perversity of the day and the need for such admonitions to "holines" as Horace and Jeremiah together offer.

Drant's defense of his conflated edition illustrates that the aims and efforts of the ancient satirists and the biblical Prophets were seen as complementary in the English Renaissance. His view of the need for such efforts in times of "enormities" and his urging a combination of the "sharp" techniques of the Roman poets with the "wayling" wisdom of the Prophets sound quite similar, in fact, to the admonitions and pleas for zeal ("*anger* meddled with and mixed with *love*") that were preached from many sources. Moreover, his volume was not the only work that noted these similarities and delineated the zealous characteristics of the Prophets. The same view is present in the long commentary by Lambert Daneau *On the Twelve Small Prophets*, John Downame's *Spiritual physicke to cure the diseases of the soul*, Richard Greenham's 1597 defense of zeal, the anonymous *Glass of Mans Folly, and means to amendment of life*, the 1587 *Lamentations of Jeremiah in Meeter*, and Daniel Tossanus' introduction to his edition of the *Lamentations*.[42]

The view of the Prophets as Christian reformer-satirists did not originate, of course, with these late sixteenth-century commentators, scholars, and translators. The locus classicus for this conception, the sources noted by Tossanus and Daneau and referred to in the marginalia of the sermons, is the writings of the Church Fathers.[43] St. Augustine's discussion of the prophetic "laudable wrath" in *The City of God* (chap. 23) and *On Catechizing the Uninformed*, Gregory the Great's commentaries and *Moralia*, Thomas Aquinas' definitions of laudatory wrath in *Summa Theologica*, and Lactantius' *The Ire of God* offer the same view of the Prophets in their exegeses and admonitions to zeal. Lactantius' description is representative. Similar to the method which Donne's speaker evolves in *Satyre III*, in which the satirist concludes his meditation on the sources of his own "pitty [and] scorn" with a metaphoric description of the analogous "blessings [and] rage" of divine Power, Lactantius defended man's use of zeal by reference to the examples of God's wrath. God's message through the Prophets and Christ's actions in the Temple confirm, he urged, that "just anger," springing from an impersonal concern for public rectitude, "in order that discipline be preserved, morals corrected, and license suppressed," is natural to the good man. Just as we punish those in our power, so God punishes the sins of the world; and so far as anger checks sin, then it is useful and necessary to both God and man: "It cannot be removed from the one, nor ought to be removed from the other."[44]

The Church Fathers defended what the alarmed Elizabethans later called zeal on the basis of its power of reformation, its sanctification by biblical example, and its moral necessity. They agreed that such wrath, if initiated by a just cause, used out of love of goodness and hatred of sin, directed at sins rather than sinners, and aimed at moral reformation rather than personal vengeance, was "righteous" and "necessary."

The English poet, who in the apocalyptic climate at the end of the century, turned to verse satire, then, had a thoroughly Christian principle of satirical decorum on which to style his speaker. Patristic, homiletic, scholarly, and critical opinion—in addition to the example of the Prophets themselves—offered a "zealous" muse as well as a "cankered" muse to whom he could appeal. Donne's satirist speaks in the decorum of the former.

ii

The outstanding feature and in many ways the abiding concern of the speaker of Donne's *Satyres* is with zeal, with his "anger meddled with and mixed with love." In one sense, the five poems present varying attitudes of the satirist as he self-consciously searches for a correct and satisfying balance of these two extremes. Topically, as John Shawcross points out, "the five satires pillory five universal dilemmas besetting man,"[45] but the initial and final concern of all five is with the concomitant hatred and charity of the satirist himself. This is not to suggest that the *Satyres* are concerned only with the education of the satirist; such a private concern cannot be separated from his commitment to his fellow man. Satire, or the satirist's understanding of his own duty, is always viewed as a relationship: as a duty to himself, his countrymen, and his God. In the *Satyres*, examination and analysis of the virtues of the active and the contemplative lives (in *Satyre I*), the widespread abuse of language and the Word (in *Satyre II*), the need for continual *wise doubt* and the integrated use of the rational faculties required of "our Mistresse faire Religion" (in *Satyre III*), the dangers of thoughtless visits to a hellish court peopled with informers (in *Satyre IV*), the "Officers rage and Suitors wretchedness" which perpetuate perversions of the law (in *Satyre V*) are each evaluated from the perspective of the demands which they place on the satirist's own zeal. The originality of the *Satyres*, then, lies not just in their focus on the satirist as a self-conscious penitent concerned with his complementary duties as fallen man and moral critic,[46] but also in their application and elaboration of the decorum of the biblical satirists, the accommodation of a set of principles from biblical aesthetics to the moral and spiritual dilemmas of late sixteenth-century man.

Peter Medine points out that the superiority of the *Satyres* results in part from Donne's facility in yoking the major criteria of verse satire—to praise and to blame—into "a coherent poetic design" by offering a persona who embodies "viable alternatives to the viciousness" he satirizes.[47] The earliest (and crudest) attempt to fulfill this principle in the age was Drant's Englishing of Horace's satires, in which Drant appended a series of epigrams extolling virtuous examples to his rendition of the classical satirist's attacks on public vices. Similarly, in *Skialetheia* Everard Guilpin added praises of Lucretius and Epictetus to his attacks on perverse courtiers and vain women in order to fulfill this requirement. Even the most "cankered" satirist of the age, John Marston, integrated long praises of "reason," "Prudence," and "precepts of philosophy" into his otherwise pessimistic portraits of human viciousness and depravity to satisfy this tenet of satiric decorum.[48] It is Donne's *Satyres* that most brilliantly fulfill this principle. Indeed, the constancy, charity, and self-knowledge of the contemplative scholar of *Satyre I* do offer a worthy contrast to the adulterous clothes, actions, and aims of the "fondling motley humorist" (1) who tempts him to walk through the fashionable streets of London. In the same way, in the second *Satyre*, the satirist's legal and moral concern about the effects of "Good workes" (110) and about his own capacity to bring about reformation through his own poem (111) proposes an exemplary regard for the civilizing force of language in contrast to the mechanical, materialistic manipulation of words by parasitic frauds such as the poet-lawyer Coscus. Again, the satirist's meditative exertion of "all [his] Soules devotion" (6)—the memory, understanding, and will of his rational soul—in the search for "true religion" (43) provides a dramatic alternative to the adventurous abuses of memory, the sectarian abuses of understanding, and the secular manipulations of will that are scorned in *Satyre III*. The awareness of his own precarious position in the providential scheme and of the duty he owes to his "Mistresse Truth" (163) displayed by the satirist in *Satyre IV* provides tacit condemnation of and a worthwhile option to the self-ignorance and disruptive libels he encounters in the Presence Chamber. Finally, the satirist's allegiance to "righteousnes" (31) and his aspiration "To know and weed out . . . sinne" (34) reveal a sense of moral responsibility in direct contrast to the officers' greed and the suitors' self-destructive capitulations to the present forms of legal injustice described in *Satyre V*.

The superiority of Donne's *Satyres* rests, however, not only on the successful integration of *laus et vituperatio* in each individual poem. As a five-act sequence—a "*book*" of *Satyres*,[49] to use Jonson's description of them—the poems disclose the satirist's growing awareness of the nature and uses of Christian zeal. Sequentially, the *Satyres* portray the speaker's moral character (*I*), aesthetic development (*II*), spiritual awareness (*III*), and efforts to implement the lessons of that self-knowledge (*IV* and *V*). The first satire, for instance, endorses the scholar's "zealous" mockery of the humorist's inconstancy at the same time that it discloses the satirist's naive idealism and lack of self-criticism. The second delineates his development of a moral satirical criterion, based on his recognition that some sins deserve pity and others only hatred. But, at the same time, both poems intimate the limitations of his active Christian awareness. In the first he mistakes satire to be only the contemplative assertion of ideals to inconstant fools and thinks that his following the mercurial fop from his own study in order to reform him might be a "sin . . . against [his] conscience" (66). Although the constant charity he shows for his "wild uncertaine" (12) companion is not called into question, the fact that the scholar too is finally "ravish'd" (108) by the "lechery" of the town (in a metaphoric sense, through the fop's betrayal-desertion of him) suggests that this virtue *alone* cannot sustain the satirist-reformer. In *Satyre II* he turns melancholically to sarcastic self-criticism because no discernible results are realized by his "Good workes." Having expressed his "hate [for] all this towne" (1–2) and especially for the "excellently best" (3) societal illness represented by fraudulent lawyers, he is able only partially to overcome his melancholy with the derisive and cynical retort that at least he will escape the "vast reach of th'huge statute lawes" (112) since he has spoken the mere truth. Although the speaker in both poems enacts viable alternatives to the foolishness and crimes he denounces, his own doubts about his satire outweigh his confidence in its therapeutic potential.

In the third *Satyre*, on the other hand, he realizes that the charity he offered the popinjay in *I* and the hatred he directed at Coscus in *II*—his own "Kinde pitty" and "brave scorn"—are justified. The "cure [for] these worne maladies" (4) that he as a satirist seeks is, he realizes, actually the dynamic action of a mind in search for Truth and in open opposition to falsehood. The results of his efforts are best and only measured by eternal standards. Central in position and importance, this poem—as meditation and satire simultaneously—dramatizes the satirist's self-confirmation of the religious basis of his satire. It depicts his realization that the Christian "Sentinell's" (31) vigilant hatred of man's foes and the pilgrim's dynamic love of "Truth" are essential to both "true religion" and "wise . . . railing" (3–4).

Satyre IV chronicles the continuation of the satirist's education, his acquisition of God-given knowledge, his fullest appraisal of his fallen inclinations and God's active wrath, and his attempts to implement that knowledge at the Elizabethan court. Having first visited the Presence Chamber out of mere curiosity (*absentia recti*) and suffered the punishment of God's "furious rod" (50) in the form of a libellous *Inglese italinato*, the satirist fell into "a trance / Like his, who dreamt he saw hell" (157–58). Enlightened by this trance and urged by his "precious soul" (156) to return to the chamber, he sees that the court is indeed a hell, that he should feel pity for the suitors who go there, and that he must not fear that "huffing braggart, puft Nobility" (164) if he is to fulfill his duty to his "Mistresse Truth." Having run from the court after his first visit for fear of "Becomming Traytor" (131), he returns there after his vision, he admits, as a "Spie" (237), therein initiating his obedience as a satirist.

That obedience is extended in the last *Satyre*, addressed to the wretched suitors who suffer from the injustice of the courts and to the lord keeper who has been commissioned to investigate their predicament. Similar to the first *Satyre* in situation, this final scene discloses the triumph of the satirist over his previous lack of knowledge about self and vocation. Now he is able to replace the recitation of abstract ideals with "accommodated" maxims that instruct a complaining suitor in the need for self-knowledge. Convinced of the validity of his satire, aware through his own experiences that the way to reformation lies through self-knowledge, the speaker of *Satyre V* dramatizes the active completion of his education in the *ethos* of prophetic "zeal" integral to the entire sequence. Now he is assured that he is "Authoriz'd . . . To know and weed out . . . sinne" (34)—authorized publicly through his "service" to the queen's official and privately through the testing of his own moral confidence. Bolder and more confident than in any of the first four poems, the satirist exerts his energies finally to the instruction (and ridicule) of another fallen human being and laudatory advice to the lord keeper without rationalizations about the inevitable limitations of his helpfulness and without dissipating his energies in self-doubts. The meditative and public voices have merged completely here—"all things be in all" (9)—to achieve a satisfying balance of "Kinde pitty" and "brave scorn."

The exemplary character of the satirist's zealous self-knowledge is suggested also by the mythic structure of the sequence. The dramatic portrait of his own journey from innocence (*I*), to darkness and despair (*II*), and finally to self-knowledge (*III*), suffering and God-given knowledge (*IV*), and obedience (*V*) duplicates the mythic or Christian structure of human history as it was delineated in such influential Christian humanist works as Erasmus' *Enchiridion*, the official *Book of Homilies*, and *The Book of Common Prayer*.[50] As such, the satirist's own self-examination and zealous attitude provide the "easie wayes and neare" (*III*, 14) worthy of all men's imitation. Illustrative of the progressive regeneration of the speaker as satirist and as man, the sequential arrangement suggests that this self-awareness and zeal are the method and "cure" for "these worne maladies" on which the five *Satyres* focus.

In the third *Satyre* Donne's satirist offers the fullest defense of his zeal. His meditation on the dynamic use of the three powers of the rational soul begins with lines that read like a paraphrase of Becon's definition of the zeal of the Prophets:

> Kinde pitty chokes my spleene; brave scorn forbids
> Those teares to issue which swell my eye-lids;
> I must not laugh, nor weepe sinnes, and be wise.   (1–3)

Nowhere, in fact, is the affinity between the spirit of Donne's speaker and the Old Testament Prophets more pronounced than in this central poem.

This poem, which has proved so pivotal to critics concerned with Donne's early poetics, is equally useful for an understanding of the *Satyres*. Only once here does the merciful God of the New Testament appear. By and large, the God of Truth, the "Mistresse . . . worthy'of all our Soules devotion" of *Satyre III* is the Old Testament jealous God whose judgment is to be feared. Nine times is reference made to the Day of Judgment and to the punishment awaiting those who fail in their devotion.[51] The certain fact that motivates the satirist here, demanding his "zealous" meditation on the need for "true religion" at the present time, is the surety of damnation for those who refuse "God himselfe to trust" (110). In "Kinde pitty" and "brave scorn" the speaker of *Satyre III* finally evokes a vision of the sure Justice of God on "the last day" (95) fully in the spirit and character of an Old Testament Prophet, and in line with contemporary homiletic warnings that such zeal is the moral antidote for the "worne maladies" of the day. Unlike the speaker in *Satyre I* who feared that his active satire might be a "sinne against [his] conscience" and the speaker in *Satyre II* who concluded that his satire was "bred" by the disregard of his own "Good workes," the speaker of *Satyre III*, in his final metaphoric description and vision of the Mercy *and* Justice of the "Power" of God (103–10), finds a divine analogue to sanctify his own "Kinde pitty" and "brave scorn."

In the same vein, the initial question posed in *Satyre III*—whether "railing" can "cure these worne maladies"—is also central to all the *Satyres*. The structure and strategies of the satirist's progress in self-knowledge throughout the five poems and his final achievement of a working, divinely qualified balance between his hatred and charity suggest that "railing" can, as a balance of "Kinde pitty" and "brave scorn," be itself an exemplary attitude for all men. His examination of his own nature and genre shows others whom he loves but whose sins he hates that the way to avoid damnation is through Christian zeal. Donne's *Satyres* thus provide a dramatization of his satirist's understanding of and conformity to the decorum of the earliest biblical reformers. If we dismiss the assumption that the internal debates about the nature of his speaker's utterances in these poems are symptomatic of Donne's own insecurity in this genre, it is possible to focus on these poems as a progressive examination and application of attitudes acceptable to the decorum of a Christian satirist. Such a reading does not deny that Donne's poems are classical imitations, but merely suggests that Donne has replaced the spokesman of Horace, Juvenal, and Persius with a speaker of Christian zeal. Transforming the forms and norms of Roman verse satire, the five *Satyres* provide a dramatic definition of what the age termed *zeal*—as the decorum of Christian satire and as integral to man's response to the grace of God. In accordance with the specific calls for reformation in a time of apocalyptic fervor and alarm, the *Satyres* portray a speaker whose meditative explanation of what "decencie demands" of him conforms to traditional and contemporary descriptions of the zeal of the Prophets.[52] How Donne accommodates the techniques of Roman satire to these prescriptions in each of the poems is the major concern of this study of the persona, imagery, and design of the *Satyres*.

CHAPTER ONE

The Satirist as Scholar

in circuitu impii ambulant

Psalms 12:8

The first *Satyre* has been largely neglected, except for contentions that it is a juvenalian experiment, a modification of Horace's *Satire I.ix* into a conventional body-soul *débat*, or an autobiographical poem which reflects Donne's experience at the Inns of Court.[1] Admittedly, the poem does not achieve the rich complexity and brilliance of the third and fourth *Satyres*, but as Donne's first work in the genre it is most instructive about his conception of the features, limitations, and duties of Christian satire. In some ways, in fact, the poem is a comic study in failure, a witty dramatization of the radical and seemingly irremedial gap between the intentions of the satirist and the obduracy of his *adversarius*. By the end of the poem Donne's scholastic speaker has himself been "ravish'd," metaphorically at least, by the inconstancy of the town. Satire as a process of moral reformation seems an impossible ideal; and the speaker must desert his attempts to reform the fop he had followed through the streets of fashionable London for the aloof superiority of a meditative stance. Only the poet's facility with puns seems capable of forcing constancy on the fop.

Nevertheless, the speaker's failure to reform his foolish companion does not mean that his own attitude and conduct in the company of the fop are themselves satirized in the poem. Rather, as in Horace's poem, Howard Erskine-Hill points out, "the superior wisdom of [Donne's] speaker is unchallenged, except implicitly in its failure to make any impact upon ebullient folly."[2] Rather than satirizing the inadequacy of the speaker, the poem dramatizes the introductory nature of his experiences, his initial realization of the necessity as well as the limitations of satire. In fact, a close look at a specific features of Donne's persona in the context of late sixteenth-century thought discloses his conception of satire as the dynamic and charitable actualization of man's Christian duty. In terms of the paradigm of satire-as-zeal, the poem explores the problematic character of active Christian charity, how it issues from man's contemplative awareness of his position in a providential universe and how this realization demands the *vir bonus* become Christian satirist.

The specific feature most troublesome to readers is the apparent inconsistency of Donne's speaker in *Satyre I*. A scholar, perhaps even an idealistic scholastic, touched somewhat by the melancholy of that vocation, he ridicules the ostentatious courtiers on the London streets through a portrait of the "fondling motley humorist" (1) who mincingly adores their every affectation. The basic plot is borrowed from Horace's comic account of his unfortunate entrapment by a Roman bore, but Donne's poem reduces the dialogue in order to emphasize the attitudes, reflections, and reactions of the speaker. His scholar is aware that the fop who invades his privacy to invite him to tour the streets will abandon him for the finely feathered courtiers, but he accompanies him nevertheless. Once they are in the street, the scholar is ignored and occasionally deserted in favor of more gaily attired company, but he remains with his fickle friend until finally abandoned for a much-admired whore. And he apparently is so foolish or naive that he offers the fop shelter and friendship when he returns to the scholar's study after having been beaten and thrown out of the whore's house by her other beaux. The severity and harshness of the speaker's attack on the fop and his companions are apparently incongruous, then, with his continued acceptance of this adamant fool as a person worthy of his concern. He himself must be either a fool, a naif, or a poorly constructed persona—a delineating character intended only to serve as a foil to the fop through his own displays of constancy.

In some ways, the latter is precisely the case: the scholar is presented as an exemplary contrast to the inconstancy and foolishness of the fop (*laus et vituperatio*). To focus exclusively on this feature of the poem, however, is to overlook the primary tension it develops—the tension within the speaker in his anxious search for a satiric stance that will satisfy both his private and public duties as Christian scholar. With this distinction in mind, it is important that the central feature of Donne's speaker in the poem is his foolishness. It is the same sort of foolishness that Erasmus paradoxically praises in *Moriae encomium*, the type of foolishness that makes a man more concerned with the soul of himself and others than with what many would term rational behavior, that makes a man suffer personal pain and self-effacement in order to convince another man of the error of his ways and the spiritual consequences of his actions.[3] The wisdom of such *folly* is obliquely endorsed by the *providential* punishment the fop suffered because of his worldly foolishness, but the theodicean pattern of action in the poem is iterated throughout, especially in the speaker's self-portrait. In terms of sixteenth-century Christian thought, his *foolishness* is precisely the duty of the Christian scholar. What *Satyre I* examines, then, is the relationship between Christian satire and Christian scholarship—through a dramatic portrait of a scholar who discovers both the problematic character and the moral synonymy of his private and public commitments of Christian charity.

"Certain goals," writes Erasmus in his *Enchiridion*, "are incomplete and indecisive; we should not rest in them." Knowledge and the pursuit of learning are among them, for

> knowledge is of greater use to the good life than beauty or bodily strength or money, and although all learning can be made irrelevant to Christ, one kind is more directly useful than another. You should measure the usefulness, or uselessness, of all these indecisive resources in terms of this end. You love learning; that's fine—if you love it for the sake of Christ. But if you love it only that you may have knowledge, then you are coming to rest in a place where you should have made a step forward. . . . It is better to know less and love more than to know a great deal and love not at all.[4]

Renaissance definitions of wisdom, Eugene Rice points out, characterize the pursuit of knowledge as a dedication to God that becomes an *exemplum*, a conscious moral pattern for men to follow: "wisdom . . . flows from a God whose central attribute is virtue, from a Scriptural Revelation described as a code of conduct, and from a Christ whose function was livingly to illustrate that code."[5] The cornerstones of that code, of course, are love of God and love of one's neighbors. One must be "God's scholar," Roger Hutchinson insists,[6] and this, according to Beza, involves "doing work, the effects of those actions onely, which in the regenerate by working of the Spirite of God through faith, are squared according unto the prescript rule of Gods love, that in them God might be glorified, and our neighbours helped."[7] Robert Crowley's "lesson" to the scholar is for him to "let thy workes shine in Me[n']s syght. . . . Thy lyfe must be put in venture / For Christes congregation," for God

> wylleth thee fyrst to apply
> Thy mynde to knowledge, and to take
> The great beame out of they owne eye,
> And thyne abuses to forsake.
>
> And then he wolde, that in no wyse
> Thou shouldst be slacke or negligente
> To picke the motes out of mens eyes,
> Teaching them how they should repent.[8]

It is within the context of these prescriptions that the situation of Donne's scholar evolves—to remain constant to his pursuit of knowledge while at the same time "livingly" illustrating or witnessing the faith gained through knowledge which God's grace has revealed to him.[9]

That Donne's scholar adheres to these ideals of Christian scholarship is exemplified by the facts that he offers about himself and the attitude he displays concerning his studies. His first love, he reveals, is to his pursuit of knowledge. "Leave mee," he tells his meddlesome intruder, "in this standing wooden chest, / Consorted with these few bookes" (2–3), for here are

> Gods conduits, grave Divines; and here
> Natures Secretary, the Philosopher;
> And jolly Statesmen, which teach how to tie
> The sinewes of a cities mistique bodie;
> Here gathering Chroniclers, and by them stand
> Giddie fantastique Poëts of each land.   (5–10)

His humanistic training, he shows, has familiarized him with both spiritual and frivolous forms of human behavior; but he is careful not to overstate his own degree of knowledge or the ultimate spiritual sufficiency of his literary "consort[s]."[10] His proffered booklist does not undercut the validity of his studies so much as it discloses his own lack of arrogant presumption. His knowledge comes from God's grace, after all—"*With God*, and with the Muses *I conferre*" (48, italics added).

It is not surprising that, so committed, he pictures the fop's invitation to follow him into the street as a possible "headlong" (12) temptation and that he ponders the significance of such a "fall" in language that confirms his understanding of the necessity of grace in the lives of men. "How shall I be pardoned my offence," he rhetorically asks, "That thus have sinn'd against my conscience?" (66). In a sense, this important question is not answered fully until the third and fourth *Satyres*, in which the satirist formulates and then tests a more expansive definition of satire. Here the issue of the scholar's uncertainty is subsumed by his enactment of the roles of the Christian scholar. *Satyre I* is not designed as a definition of satire, in other words, but as an exploration of the *character* of the Christian scholar. The issue at stake in this satire, in the overall development of the five poems, is limited and introductory, even preparatory. The poet's initial presentation, like that of any good rhetorician, is the trustworthy character of his speaker. In this sense, the scholar's momentary, limited understanding of the character of Christian satire is secondary to the dramatization of his moral integrity. Thus, the emphasis of his question about the conscience (on the means of forgiveness) and the fact that it follows his insistence that the fop "repent [his] vanities" (50–51) focus attention less on his doubts than on his understanding of his insufficiency as a man to give or receive ultimate sanctification without the intervention of divine grace. This view is reaffirmed later in the poem when, deserted by the fool despite his own remonstrations, the scholar cries, not entirely in rage, "Oh, God strengthen thee" (100).

Despite his doubts, the scholar consents to follow the fop, to attempt to ridicule and to exhort him out of his foolishness. This willingness reveals his understanding of the insufficiency of knowledge alone and the need for fulfillment of the laws of love through active witnessing outside the confines of his study, an attitude suggested early in the poem by his view of the study as a possible coffin ("woodden chest"). The characteristic of the scholar that has most troubled readers, then, is his most important feature. He views his following the fop as both a temptation and his duty towards a "lost sheep" (93). He recognizes this silly Elizabethan *garrulus* is a "monstrous, superstitious puritan, / Of refin'd manners" (27–28) who will most assuredly desert him for "more spruce companion" (16), but cannot forget that he is a man worthy of and in need of his counsel. This paradoxical attitude towards the fop's invitation, coupled with his constant forgiving of the fool for his errors—his steadfast hatred of his sins but love for the sinner—and his insistence on showing the fop the spiritual significances of his actions, reveal the scholar's commitment to the duties of Christian scholarship. This focus on the self-definition of the satirist is typical of Donne's strategy throughout the five poems. Rather than exploring the functions of Christian satire directly, in the manner of Marston or Jonson, he presents the speaker of his poems as scholar or student or lawyer or religious devotee or legal counselor initially and then shows that the fulfillment of the duties of that role forces one to become a satirist, or that the fulfillment of that role and that of the satirist are synonymous. It is in this sense that the persona Donne assumes in the poems is most significant; thus, the focus of the first poem is on the way the duty of the Christian scholar leads him to satire.

The speaker's fulfillment of this duty is exemplified further in the various roles he assumes in dealing with the "humorist." At one point he envisions their relationship as that of a marriage: "For better or worse take mee, or leave mee," he warns the fop, "To take, and leave mee is adultery" (25–26). Thus, the speaker "consorts" with the fool in the same earnestness with which he approached his studies, offering him a relationship based on love—and sanctified by Love—in place of the adulterous companionship of whores and faithless courtiers, a relationship correspondent to his own consorting with God. Later, he acts as priest to the humorist and "Charitably warn[s] him] of [his] sinnes" (50) so that the fop "dost repent / These vanities . . . like a contrite penitent" (49, 50–51). Finally, he acts as the faithful shepherd to his "lost sheep" and "stays" (93) faithful to him in spite of the fop's frequent desertions, even to the point of welcoming him back into his company after the fool has adulterously abandoned him for a whore. If we add to these roles those of preacher and prophet assumed in his discussions of the state of man's soul and body "At birth, and death," of "Mans first blest state," and of the condition of "our Soules [when they] be unapparrelled / Of bodies" (42–45), it is evident that the scholar assumes those roles assumed by Christ and advocated in His parables, the roles of Christian scholarship assumed also by the earliest Christian "scholars," the biblical prophets. So, the scholar as lover, priest, preacher, and satirical gadfly attempts literally to save the fool's soul—actions essential to his status as Christian scholar. And his ridicule of and constancy to the fool are the manner in which he fulfills his duty as one of God's scholars. His steadfast love of the fool (and hatred of his sins) epitomizes, in fact, his commitment to the search for truth to which he as a scholar is dedicated. As Augustine words it, "in the correct education of man, the hard work of doing what is right precedes the delight of understanding what is true. . . . Love it is that asks, love that seeks, love that knocks, love that reveals, and love, finally, that assures the permanence of what is revealed."[11]

The duty of the scholar is further identified by his reliance throughout on images of apparel, imprisonment, and adultery. The fool's misdirected love for temporal honors and satisfactions and, more often, for gaudy apparel is viewed as a type of adultery and an "improvident" imprisonment in sin, as contrasted with the scholar's own choice of "course attire,"[12] which men were granted when their "first blest state" (45) of nakedness was "lost" through the Fall. The clothing imagery of the poem should not be dismissed as "the old sumptuary theme." Composed at a time when, according to the most popular preacher of the day, Henry Smith, the "world [was] like a Pageant, where every man's apparel is better than himself," the poem works imaginative variations on a theme of significant issue in the age.[13]

Clothing is one of God's "good gifts" to man, as Becon phrases it, "made in Paradise" and "ordayned" of God for certain purposes: "not onely for necessities sake, but also for an honest comelinesse,"[14] "to cover our vile nakednesse, and to defend us from the violence of tempestes,"[15] to "cover our unseemly parts, . . . to defend us from the injurie of weather, . . . and for dignities sake both to distinguish man from beasts, and men of high degree from the lower."[16] It is also significant of the general condition of fallen man, not only as a sign of God's ordination of degree and an emblem of His continuing care, but also of anagogical meaning: "the signe of our sinne, the badge of our rebellion, the witnesse of oure shame, and it remembreth unto us that we should weepe continually to thinke what we have lost."[17] It should remind man that "God clothed the noble subject of the soule with a vile body to teach us that we should not deck our vile bodie with gorgeous apparell"; "fashionable attire" is "contrarie to nature, . . . the devils fashion," for "apparell sheweth what manner of person one is."[18]

Apparel is significant of man's duty, too, and therefore is a frequent topic in discussions of the pursuit of knowledge, the need for humility, and the nature of marriage. Typical is Robert Allen's exhortation in his sermon on the seventh Commandment: "for in somuch as GOD hath advanced us to especiall dignitie, above all brute beastes, and everie kinde of unreasonable creatures, it is meete that everie of us should possess our bodies in more holinesse than they do . . . avoiding all light and curious setting out of themselves in bravery of apparell."[19]

In "The Wedding Garment," the fullest and most popular treatment of the subject, Henry Smith offers the same warning. Annotating the text he says is "the summe of the Bible," "Put ye on the Lord Jesus Christ" (Romans 13:14), he urges that the sinfulness of England is most evident in its extravagant apparel: "If ye could see how pride would walke her selfe, if she did weare apparel, shee would even goe like many in the streets: for she could not go braver, nor looke stouter, nor mince finer, nor set on more laces, nor make larger cuts, nor carry more trappings about her, than our ruffians and wantons doe at this day. . . . If they could but see their apparell but with the glance of a spiritual eye," he insists, "how monstrous it makes them, . . . they would fling away their attire . . . and be ashamed of their clothes, as Adam was of his nakednesse." There are many fashions of apparel, he continues, but only one "meete for all seasons, fit for all persons: the Wedding Garment." Only the garment of marriage to God will cover our sores:

Therefore when we seem most brave to others, we seem most foule to GOD, because his eye is on oure sinnes, which lye naked when all the reste is covered. . . . Christs righteousness muste be our garment, or else we shall be ashamed when our righteousness doth not reach to cover our nakednesse; and he which leaveth his righteousness to live in wickednesse, . . . he who studies for fashion as a Lawyer does for delayes, and count that part naked which is not gawdy as the rest . . . forsakes his spouse to commit fornication, and is divorced from Christe himselfe.[20]

Extravagant clothing or attire ill suited for one's degree constitutes a presumptuous desire for the very sign of man's sinfulness, a wanton misuse of one of God's providential gifts to man, and a form of adultery.

Such interpretations of the significance of apparel are central to the comingling of images of clothing, adultery, imprisonment, and animals in *Satyre I*. The scholar's emblematic defense of his "course attire" is framed by a picture of the ubiquity of extreme apparel in all stations of Elizabethan society and by his metaphoric view of apparel as either an act of love or a form of imprisonment. He ridicules that fashionable "adultery" peculiar to the military, the court, and the bar and the inconstancy of family, state, and national fashions while warning the fool to "First sweare by thy best love in earnest / (If thou which lov'st all, canst love any best)," not to desert him for "more spruce companion," "Bright parcell gilt . . . Captaine," "briske perfum'd piert Courtier," or "Velvet Justice" (13–21). But before they leave his study, the scholar acknowledges that the fool cannot remain constant any more than

. . . a cheape whore, that hath beene
Worne by as many severall men in sinne,
As are black feathers, or musk-colour hose,
[Can] Name her childs right true father. (53–56)

"Sooner may one guesse," he quips, "who shall beare away / Th'Infant of London, Heire to'an India" (57–58), or

sooner may a gulling weather-Spie
By drawing forth heavens Scheame tell certainly
What fashion'd hats, or ruffes, or suits next yeare
Our subtile-witted antique youths will weare. (59–62)

This description of matters of considerable spiritual, even divine, significance—the naming of children and the unity of the family, the question of royal succession, and the "heavens Scheame"—in terms of clothing imagery, the realization that issues rightly reliant on divine guidance have become as superficial as fashions, shows the concern the scholar feels is appropriate towards the adulterous inconstancy typified by the "motley humorist."

This identification of the fool's changing "humours" with a chaotic, presumptive society of nameless bastards and with a nation as unpredictable as the weather that is ruled in all estates by fashions instead of God's law is contrasted to the scholar's exhortation to a life of simplicity, constancy, and reliance on divine guidance. His own conduct is justified, he explains, by the condition of man since the Fall; and he finds its directive neither by searching the skies for "heavens Scheame" nor by temporal fashions, but by "conferr[ing] With God, and with the Muses." His exhortation to his presumptive companion follows another picture of the vanity and clothing of the fool as a form of adultery. "Why shoulds't thou . . . Hate vertue, though shee be naked, and bare," the scholar asks, and yet love "The nakednesse and barenesse . . . Of thy plumpe muddy whore, or prostitute boy?" (37–41). Again, his exhortation is phrased in terms of the original, present, and final clothing of man:

At birth, and death, our bodies naked are;
And till our Soules be unapparrelled
Of bodies, they from blisse are banished.
Mans first blest state was naked, when by sinne
Hee lost that, yet hee'was cloath'd but in beasts skin,
And in this course attire, which I now weare. (42–47)

Donne's scholar envisions luxurious apparel, then, as a proud flaunting of the very sign of a man's sin and as an adulterous cupidity which disregards the divine order at work in the world, a view substantiated by his depiction of man's natural and unnatural imprisonments in the world. In the initial epigrammatic description of himself and his books, the scholar, for example, describes himself as in prison: "let me lye / In prison, and here be coffin'd, when I dye" (3–4). Milgate points out that the scholar's booklist corresponds to the humanist's view of the appropriate schooling of the reason, the imagination, and the fancy,[21] and suggests that the images of imprisonment aptly iterate the actual setting of confined quarters in which Donne himself would have studied at Lincoln's Inn. But the prison motif is so extensive in the poem—to the degree of assuming a metaphoric description of the speaker and, by extension, of mankind in general, and in contexts beyond the periphery of the autobiographical—that a broader interpretation of this image is warranted. The images of imprisonment, confinement, and banishment, in fact, convey the scholar's view of the human condition as an imprisonment in sin and banishment "from blisse" because of the Fall; he likewise explains man's vanities as means of further imprisonment and isolation from the source of ultimate spiritual freedom. Thus, the fool's preferences for gaudy clothing, earthly honors, and the company of whores are seen to be the ways he misuses his freedom and chooses to clothe and imprison himself further in sin.

When the scholar insists that he shall remain "in prison" and "from blisse [be] banished" until death, and wonders aloud how he shall be "pardon'd [his] offence," he is invoking the traditional Christian metaphor for man's condition since the Fall, or, to use Aquinas' term, the "natural" imprisonment of man's will.[22] As the authoritative *Certaine Sermon* on "The Miserie of Man" explains,

> In our selves (as of our selves) we find nothing, whereby we may be delivered from this miserable captivity, into the which we were cast, through the envie of the devil, by breaking of GODS commandement, in our first parent. . . . To GOD therefore must we flee, or else shall we never finde peace, rest and quietnes of conscience in our hearts. For he is the Father of mercies, and GOD of all consolation.[23]

Imprisoned in sin because of the Fall and incapable of any wholly righteous acts except through God's mercy, by conferring with God, then, the scholar relies on the source of his eventual liberation.[24]

The fool, on the other hand, acts as if unaware that "this world and life is," as Henry Bull phrases it, "an exile, a vale of misery, a wilderness, of itself being void of all virtues and necessaries"; he remains "first of all / Improvidently proud" (68) in his love of temporal honors and the gaudy dress of the "prison-house of his soul."[25] The full import of the fop's moral myopia is conveyed by the scholar's description of the fool's initial act once they are in the street.

> Now we are in the street; He first of all
> Improvidently proud, creepes to the wall,

> And so imprison'd, and hem'd in by mee
> Sells for a little state his libertie.   (67–70)

This union of all the major images of the poem confirms that the moral stupidity of the fool results from the misuse of his freedom. In exchanging his freedom of will for a temporary "place of honor, the wall side, given in politeness to one's superior,"[26] a further type of clothing in sin as the pun of "hem'd" connotes, the fool extends his imprisonment in sin. The scholar's interpretation of the actions of the fool as those of one "first of all / Improvidently proud" affirms his own view of the necessity of Providence in the actions of man and the fact that the fool in his pride for clothing is not cognizant of the role Providence plays in every man's life. The foolishness of the dandy, then, is not just that he misunderstands the legitimate ends of his use of freedom, but that he is unaware of its source. The scholar limits his temporal luxuries to "course attire," turns to God as the source of any goodness of which he may be capable, and assumes those roles in his appeals to the fool which God has revealed in the Bible to be meritorious attitudes; the fool, on the other hand, sells his freedom like a "cheape whore" in order to "wear" the semblance of social prestige and is proudly satisfied with this "little state."

The fool's subsequent actions in the street also violate the providential order of Creation, and are aptly characterized as "stoopings," "droopings," and a form of self-willed death. He "stoops . . . nigh'st the ground" (78) before the most "bravely" attired, "droopt" (87) in his unwillingness to follow the prudent advice of the scholar, and, finally, when "violently ravish'd to his lechery" (108), having spied his whore, he ran from the scholar "like light dew exhal'd" (107). That his actions are "falls" and moral suicide is substantiated by the scholar's comparison of the fop's gestures to specific animals. "To a grave man [the fool] doth move no more," the scholar explains,

> Then the wise politique horse would heretofore,
> Or thou O Elephant or Ape wilt doe,
> When any names the King of Spaine to you.   (80–82)

Topically, these allusions are to animals that actually performed in London in the early 1590s,[27] but in the context of the poem they show that the fool's "stoops" violate the orderly Chain of Being. One of the reasons clothing was granted to man, Hill points out, was "to distinguish man from beasts."[28] But instead of distinguishing him from the animals, by illustrating his intellectual superiority, the clothing of the fool and his attitude towards the clothing of others illustrate his inferiority to "the wise politique" animals to which he is compared.

Additionally, the specific animals to which the fool is compared suggest his exact faults. The scholar objects not to any faults latent in the animals themselves, but only to the fool's likeness or dissimilarity to creatures below his own ordained station. The point of the comparisons is that even the horse, the elephant, and the ape are more *sensible* than the fool. In his *Historie of Foure-Footed Beastes*, Edward Topsell points out that God has preserved the animals in the Ark "for that man might gaine out of them much diuine knowledge, such as is imprinted in them by nature."[29] The immensely popular "sermons" of Physiologus, with their parodies of natural history, agree that "God has devised the habits and attributes of all animated nature simply for our instruction in the essentials of dogma."[30] The equally popular emblem books of the age reiterate this interpretation of God's Book of Nature, by illustrating how animals embody certain vices or virtues that man should avoid or emulate. In *Satyre I*, the animals to which the scholar compares the fool identify the precise virtues that the fool lacks.

The elephant, for example, is pictured in emblem books as a reminder of the necessity of man's humility. Representative is Andrew Willet's explanation of his emblem of a spirited elephant:

> Of the beastes most great in might
> The elephant call by right
> Whose picture to thy sight is set forth here.
>
> . . . .
>
> The Lord his power to show
> Hath placed this beast below
> That we to God might bow, of so great strength.[31]

In the same vein, Topsell points out that "there is no creature among al the Beastes of the world which hath so great and ample demonstration of the power and wisdome of almighty God as the elephant."[32] A frequent subject in emblem books, the elephant is usually explained in such terms: as emblematic of the consequences of the Fall (based on the belief that once an elephant falls down he cannot right himself) or of the power and variety of God's Redemption of man and Creation of Nature. Physiologus describes the elephant as a figure of Christ and the Apostles, Adam and Eve, and the humility Christ exemplified in "taking the form of a servant that he might redeem all."[33] In Donne's poem, then, the contrast between the fool's constant bowing before "the most brave" and the elephant's refusal to bow upon hearing the name of the villainous "King of Spaine" emphasizes emblematically the fop's misplaced devotion. The humility and devotion he owes to his ruler and his God are paid to the temporal powers of fashion in the world.

Likewise, the horse is a symbol of loyal service, created by God, George Chapman says, "to express and teach . . . subjects / To serve as if they had the power to command."[34] Certainly, no quality is more evident in the fool than disloyalty—unless it is his propensity to ape the manners and dress of an affected courtier. Probably the most frequent subject from the animal world appearing in emblem books, the ape usually appears as a reminder of man's specific place in the divine design and man's ability to imitate the creativity of God through moral recreation of himself. Considered the most intelligent and the most like man himself, the ape is seen as emblematic of man's imaginative and creative powers, his propensity for imitation, his powers of creation that render him most God-like.[35] Physiologus points out that the ape instructs man "as often as thou fallest so often stand up again, and forthwith thou seest clearly the love of God and his mercy vouchsafed to us penitents."[36] On the one hand, then, the contrasts between the fool's bowing before the gaudily attired and the refusal of these animals to bow to any name but that of their sovereign castigate the fool for stooping below the level of even an animal; but, at the same time, these analogies stress the spiritual dimension of the scholar's portrait by ironic allusion to the qualities of humility, loyalty, and creative imitation of the good—the very qualities that the fool lacks.

The major images of the poem, then, the scholar's concatenation of the imagery of clothing, imprisonment, and adultery, supported by images of animals and stooping, reiterate the human condition as envisioned in Christian thought. In this sense, the scholar's imprisonment in his study and the fool's imprisonment in various forms of worldly pursuit—the first conferring with God, the latter selling his liberty for the appearance of social prestige— are indicative of the choices available to man in his fallen state: to rely on God's grace in the hope of meriting eternal bliss or to continue in the type of folly that caused man's present bondage. This vision is reinforced by the central structuring device of the poem, the manipulation of time.

The first half of the poem, which takes place in the scholar's study, is told in the present tense. As we have seen, the scholar manages to cover the broad spectrum of time present, past, and future in order to understand his present duty towards the fool. His identification of his own mortality ("coffin'd") and bondage in sin, the adulterous clothing of the fool, and the necessity of his own contemplative isolation are viewed from the advantage of a Christian interpretation of time:

> At *birth*, and *death*, our bodies naked are;
> And *till* our Soules be unapparrelled
> Of bodies, they from blisse are banished.
> *Mans first blest state* was naked, *when* by sinne
> Hee lost that, yet hee'was cloath'd but in beasts skin,
> And in this course attire, which I *now* weare,
> With God, and with the Muses I conferre.   (42–48: my italics)

His concern, he shows, is with the efficacy of his present conduct in light of the spiritual significance of man's past and future. The scholar's actions are based on his understanding of man's original state of bliss, his loss of that through the Fall, and his duration in sin until the Judgment. Generally, he endorses Augustine's contention in the *Confessions* that time is merely a distention of the soul, that all time is present when considered from the vantage of man's soul, and that the past and future are only in reference to the present. Indeed, the traditional Christian ideas of the circularity of time and the simultaneity of all moments under the aspect of eternity underlie the scholar's examination of his own virtue and the folly of the fop.

The second half of the poem, however, which takes place in the street, is fraught with rapid and unexpected shifts in time. As Hughes points out, "time sequences overlap one another in dizzying succession" as the fop is viewed first in the present tense, then in the past tense, and then in the future, before being telescoped into a simultaneous consideration from multiple points of temporal view (104–12). In the last nine lines "past, present, and future are telescoped together . . . , capping the excursion into the complexities of time. What is real past, or where is real present, what persists and what evanesces is the issue which commands; and the relativism of time becomes an emblem for the conflict of roles within the poem."[37] Ignorant of, or indifferent to, the providential patterning of human time, the fop creates his own context of chaos, emblematic of his own sinfulness purposelessness. Throughout these shifts, the scholar is always described as being in the present, while the fool is, in a sense, manipulated by time or is at its mercy. These rapid shifts in time mirror, of course, the faddish inconstancy of the fop and his townsmen in their fervent shifts of attention, fashion, and desire: "Sooner can" the much "worn" whore name the true father of her child than the fool "show / Wither, why, when, or with whom [he] wouldst go" (63–64). Indifferent to the benefits of Time-the-revealer, they suffer the consequences of Time-the-destroyer, legacy of the Fall.[38]

The contrast in the scholar's uses of time in these two sections of the poem enforces his Christian perspective. The relatively stable first half takes place in the sanctity of his study, which he images as a cell for meditation where he constantly confers with God; and his defense of this meditative stance is based on his understanding of his position within providential time. The shuttling, shifting second half of the poem takes place in the streets, and the shifts in time are as frequent as the shifts in motive and attention by the courtiers seen there. Only the scholar's insistences that the fool realize the spiritual consequences of his actions remain in the present tense throughout. The contrast between the two scenes and the two characters enforces the scholar's praise of the eternal and condemnation of the temporal. In a sense, the scholar controls time in the poem while the fop and his townsmen are controlled by it. The scholar's control comes from his understanding of his position and duty as a fallen man in need of Grace who must earn bliss through good works sanctified by God. The fool and his acquaintances are controlled by time because of their moral stupidity, their constant reenactment of the first event in human history. The scholar may seem idealistic in his insistence that they adopt the "course attire" of man's early state; but surely his understanding of the human error that divested man of his glorious raiment in Eden is preferable to their nugatory repetitions of the mistake that resulted in man's exposure to the "ravish[es]" of time and mortality. They may refuse to "consort" with Him and with the source of their true liberation, but their "motley" immorality only reiterates their imprisonment in the "coffin" of mortality.

The circular movement of the poem, then—it begins and ends in the scholar's study—is emblematic at once of the circle of eternity and the eternal design of human history, and of the moral shape of the scholar's and the fop's conduct. A formal image of the simultaneity of the present within the perfectness of eternity, it traces the moral design of the scholar's aim to end up where he began, both at the start of time and at the start of the poem—in communion with God. At the same time, it figures the circle of moral stupidity endemic to the life and opinions of the fop; ironically, his actions have had the same result as those of the scholar, but with different connotations. At the end of the poem, he finally discovers the type of bliss for which he has been searching, which he finds most satisfying, when he "At last his Love . . . in a windowe spies" (106). Upon entering the whore's house, however, he finds that "Many were there, he could command no more; / He quarrell'd, fought, bled," and was finally "turn'd out of dore" (109–10). His actions ironically result in his expulsion from the place he considers most blissful. Prepared for by the picture of the fop's stooping lower and lower, by the description of his behavior as a form of death in the dew simile preceding it, and by the confusing, even chaotic, collision of tenses, the fop's expulsion is fittingly presented as a reenactment of man's original fall from grace into the mortal pains of temporality. If there is no moment but the present, and the future and past are merely distentions of the present, then each man reenacts the Fall in his every sin. Comically, but justly, the fop ends up where he began—a "fondling," homeless victim of his own humors, a "motley" fool subject to the divinity that shapes our ends.

The justice (and Justice) of the beating and expulsion he received is inherent in the scholar's wry castigations. This incident, which illustrates, however comically, a Justice operative in the world, confirms, in fact, the scholar's insistence that there is intercession of divine Justice in the life of man. That the fop is a fallen creature in need of God's mercy the scholar has insisted repeatedly, in his demands that the fop repent his vanities and in his hope that God will mercifully "strengthen" him. But the fop has relentlessly ignored these warnings and ends up, ironically, hoist with his own petard. "The irony of pride," Henry Smith preached, "is that that which the proud man taketh to win love, getteth hate," that the "golden chains" of fashion he imprudently pursues are the means of his own moral suicide: he is "hanged by them."[39]

"Violently ravish'd to his lechery," the fop pursued the whore to her house but found that there he "could command no more." The beating he received there, depicted in terms appropriate to a sexual act, is a result of circumstances, of his being unable to control his situation. But there are no accidental circumstances in a providential world.[40] The other *beaux* of the whore were the means of the fop's receiving the retribution he so richly deserved. So the fop ends up where he began, literally at the mercy of the scholar, seeking his friendship and help, but, more important, as much in need of grace as before. The final line of the poem, showing that, ironically, the inconstant fop "constantly a while must keepe his bed" (112), confirms the scholar's insinuations throughout the poem about the active role of Providence in the world. The manipulation of tenses within the poem, then, exemplifies the scholar's theodicean appraisal of man's condition and duty.

Besides reinforcing the satirist's providential view of the world, this final line also firmly establishes his attitude of Christian charity towards the fool. Having constantly been ignored, repulsed, and deserted by the morally ignorant fop, the scholar's final decision to welcome him back into his study, to offer him shelter, help, and friendship, exemplifies his adherence to the principles of Christian charity. He earlier referred to his wandering friend as "my lost sheep," and now the scholar enacts the moral of Christ's parable from which that phrase is taken. In Christian charity, he offers protection and understanding to the fop, reaffirming his constant opinion of the fool as a man with a soul worthy of redemption and needful of charity. It is in this final action that the scholar also exemplifies those characteristics of Christian zeal so insisted upon by Donne's contemporaries. At no time has he displayed anything but anger at the sins of the fool, yet in his final action of the poem he reveals that his anger is "meddled with and mixed with love."

At the same time, to offer the speaker as a viable alternative to the foolishness attacked in the poem is not to suggest that he is ideal; such a discrepancy, in fact, produces the tension that underlies and animates the first *Satyre*, and is a central problem that Donne's character confronts in this poem. The scholar is certainly exemplary by comparison to his London *adversarius*; but he too is a victim of the lechery of the fop, at least in the sense that he has been rejected by the fop just as the fop was rejected by the whore. Even as a satirist, his nearly exclusive reliance on the recitation of scholastic ideals in his attempt to reform the fop shows that he is not yet Donne's most effective or mature satiric spokesman. He does come close to fulfilling the ideals of Christian behavior he cites as models for the fool to pursue and emulate, and his growing understanding of his own functions as a scholar and critic do instruct him in his own condition as a fallen man in a providential world. But his idealism and flawed methodology intimate the limitations of his position as a satirist and as a man.

Satyre I, then, does endorse Horace's comic view of the satirist as idealist caught in the obdurately myopic society of man. In one sense, like Horace's poem, *Satyre I* is a comic study in failure that delineates the radical and seemingly irreconcilable distance between the good intentions of the satirist as *vir bonus* and the *adversarius* as obdurate fool. The speaker's recitation of Christian ideals serves finally only to place him in a precarious position where he, too, is victimized by the self-destructive adultery of the town. Reformation by satire is left at the end of the poem as seemingly an impossible ideal. The *dramatic* view of the fop's providential punishment, after all, is balanced by the pun on "constant" in the final line. In one sense, he has received his due; but, at the same time, we realize that the *poet*, not the scholar, has imprisoned the fop in constancy. Thus, in a sense, the poem merely presents the problematic character of the Christian scholar in the world of adamant fallen nature. The poem discloses, then, not the best method of zealous satire so much as the initiation of the *vir bonus* into the rigors of active Christian satire. As an initiation piece it presents the scholar's adventures as a fortunate fall which shows that the problem of the scholar is that he must venture from the secure confines of his private study into the hopelessly sinful world. But it also establishes firmly the exemplary character of Donne's speaker by illustrating satire to be the duty of the Christian scholar. Here we see the scholar as satirist, the scholar's education or initiation into the necessity of satire. From the rhetorical point of view, the moral bases of the scholar-satirist's perspective are established: his character as spokesman for a Christian satire is reviewed and defended. That he is not successful in his "course" attempt at reformation cannot detract from the praiseworthy character of his motives. In these senses, then, the poem offers an introductory study of the moral superiority and problematic conditions of Christian charity in the fallen world.

CHAPTER TWO

The Satirist as Apologist

Behold, ye trust in deceptive words to no avail.

Jeremiah 7:8

Lawyers, more than others, have ever been Tyrants over words.

Essays in Divinity, p. 27

Satyre II addresses the nature and potential of the satirist's medium—language. Made aware in the first *Satyre* that the Christian scholar cannot escape the adulterous follies of the fallen world even in the sanctity of his own seclusion (because they are also his own follies, the later poems will detail), and threatened now by the deformation of his own medium, the speaker assaults rather than merely reacts to the abuses that confront him and his civilization. He never goes so far as to endorse Juvenal's view that man's irrationality has reached a degree that makes reformation impossible; total degradation is yet only a threat. Still, he does assume a stance much closer to the *saeva indignatio* of Juvenal than the Horatian ridicule of *Satyre I*. The charity and stewardship of the first poem are replaced here by the satirist's hatred: "Sir," he begins, "(I thanke God for it) I do hate / Perfectly all this towne" (1–2). In terms of the paradigm of satire-as-zeal, this poem dramatically isolates the anger or "brave scorn" of the prophetic dialectic, in order to evaluate its applicability in a moral climate that threatens the viability of satire itself.

Despite his vituperative tone, the satirist does not assume the role of *satyr*-satirist raging at the shapes of evil surrounding him, however. He carefully distinguishes degrees of sinfulness that demand differing responses by the man of moral sensitivity; the comic veniality of "poore" poets deserves pity, for instance, whereas the tragic immorality of fraudulent lawyers and landlords merits hatred. One of his major concerns remains the search for a satisfying balance of these contrasting reactions. In this case, rather than making one last charitable effort to instigate reform, he distances himself from his satirical adversaries by way of irony and sarcasm, retreating melancholically to a sort of wry wit to distinguish his own poems from the corruptions he has attacked. Once again, the speaker dramatizes an alternative to these vices, his own creative attitude towards the formative potential of language providing a moral contrast to the pernicious abuse of words he sees throughout his country; but the problem of satire in the larger arena of social-moral man, the place of the zealous satirist in society, is still unsettled. Here the ability of the satirist to shape the protean potential of words into a persuasive vehicle of man's moral reformation—the use of words to return man to the Word—is viewed *via negativa*, through a portrait of the demonic power of words to deform man and nation. The moral legitimacy of satire (as a "Good worke" [110] and an image of the Word) is ironically established by the satirist, but its therapeutic character in a land "compasse[d]" (77) by habitual linguistic abuse remains an implicit rather than explicit contention. The "course attire" of the satiric word is still viewed as less than totally effective in a land where law, love, and literature are fashioned to satisfy only appetite.

Satyre II also provides the first view of Donne's speaker *qua* satirist. The first poem by and large concerned a humanist scholar forced to accept the responsibilities of satirist and teacher. Here is no such initiation. From the opening lines the emphasis and characterization of the speaker focus attention on his role at satirist. The first *Satyre* delineated the problems confronting the *vir bonus* who is forced to resort to satire because of the encroaching folly of the times; appropriately his assumption of the formal role of the satirist in *Satyre II* is presented as a traditional satirical apologia. In fact, the major difficulties critics have had with this poem are removed when it is seen as an ironic satirical apologia that is unified by the speaker's concern with public and private perversions of language and presumptive abuses of the Word.[1] Even the most puzzling concession by the satirist—his apparent admission of his own ineffectiveness—is central to his vision of England as a "country of profanation"[2] in which the foundations of civilization are threatened by the widespread disregard and abuse of meaningful, truthful expression.

On one level, as suggested by the name of the satirist's central target (Coscus),[3] the poem is a conventional attack on corrupt lawyers, a common type in verse satire from as early as Horace's fifth satire of Book II and Juvenal's tenth satire. In Donne's poem the dissembling lawyer, who is also a "scarce Pöet" (44), is identified as a sort of Uncreating Word that is both the perpetuator and product of a mechanical, materialistic prostitution of the words of man, nature, and God. The poem thus engages a problem that speaks to the essence of the satirist's own use of words—the problem with the protean nature of words.[4] Here the focus of attention is how words can disfigure both their user and his society when their energy is exerted solely in the service of appetite. Each of the examples of Coscus's insolence (39) anatomized by the satirist is identified and defined as an abuse of language that threatens to transform English civilization into a tautological analogue to the greedy lawyer's moral vacuity. And the numerous transgressions to which his linguistic entropy are compared (the supposed "ingenious similes" of the poem)[5] disclose the range of such abuses throughout the Elizabethan world and their significance as abuses of the Word that man's words should image.

Cast into the role of advisor (or scourge) to a world of decaying communication, then, a world in which words have become mere substance and matter, their civilizing powers transmuted by sexual and mercenary acquisitiveness, the satirist turns ironist, like the ancient satirists, and offers both the apparent ineffectiveness of his own words and the venial abuses of "poore, disarm'd" poets (10) as symptoms of the spiritual sickness that threatens to "compasse all our land" (77). Like Montaigne's paradoxist, who likens his *Apology* to the final desperate foil of a fencer who disarms himself in order to defeat his opponent,[6] he admits that "Poëtry indeed [is] a sinne" (5) and that his own attempts to stir reformation are "out of fashion now" (110) in order to confirm the sinister implications of the verbal prestidigitation he attacks. "Witchcrafts charmes" may not "Bring now their old feares" (17–18), but abuses of the miraculous powers of words can still bring great "harmes"; a satirist may not evoke the "old feares" (18) of the ancient rhymers,[7] but his genre should be recognized as a "Good worke" (110). Thus, the disregard that satire currently suffers is another sign of the nation's capitulation to the destructive, perverse logomachy of men such as Coscus. The ironic satirist even goes so far as to endorse (seemingly) the outrageous claims of the *misomusoi*. However, his hyperbolic mimicry of their attacks actually reiterates that poets are not the present enemies of the state but only victims of the disease by which the Coscuses of the world thrive (76). By emphasizing the disregard of his own satire, then, Donne's ironist validates his claim that the current abuse of word and Word which "breeds [his] just offence" (40) is the ultimate enemy of English morality and civilization. *Satyre II* thus goes beyond assault against the Horatian personal follies mocked in the first poem to a vituperative exposure of the Juvenalian crimes that threaten the well-being of the nation as well as the creative potentialities of its own genre.

i

The appraisal of the condition of a man, a nation, or a race by the quality of its language is a central concern of the Renaissance, from the earliest

Battle of Books in the age between the Humanists and the Scholastics to Pope's attack on the "progress" of the Smithfield Muses in *The Dunciad*.[8] In fact, the belief that humanity achieves its fullest development through "eloquent wisdom" has been "a continuous force in European law, letters, and politics from the time of the Greek Sophists."[9] Supported by a body of precepts and principles concerning the value of man's "gift of utteraunce"[10] in classical, biblical, and medieval commentary, the Renaissance reiterated that words are the means and sustenance of civilization, the artifex of order, and the mirror of an individual's degree of sanity: "We are what we are depending upon how we shape ourselves with words."[11] The cautionary warnings of Cicero and Quintilian about the powers of oratory, the epigrammatic attacks on plagiarists and bad poets by Martial, and the stern admonitions of the Church Fathers provided influential examples of this important precept for the Renaissance author. But the classical expressions most relevant to Donne's poem are the satirical apologiae of the Roman verse satirists, those programmatic defenses by Horace (*Satire II.i*), Juvenal (*Satire I*), and Persius (*Satire I*) that judge Roman civilization by the caliber of its law and letters while relying on a traditional scheme and strategy.[12] This same philosophical attitude towards language and structure of argument are central to *Satyre II*; in fact, the satirist's concluding evaluation of the legal status of his own poem echoes in word and theme the concluding appraisal of satire as "bona carmina" in Horace's apologia.

The formulaic strategy of the Roman apologia involves a tripartite argument. It begins with the satirist's expression of misgivings and essential, personal imperatives about writing satire; proceeds to an examination of the literary or legal practices of the day (which is, in effect, "an attack upon the prevailing corruption of which these tendencies are the efflorescenes");[13] and concludes either with concessions about future satire, with the affectation of differing forms of ironic modesty, or with a final ambiguous disparagement of the poet's own works. Donne's satirist follows this same strategy. Opening with a description of his own mixed emotions of pity and hatred, their causes and degrees, he first ridicules the failures of contemporary poetry, then denounces the legal corruptions typified by Coscus, and concludes with an ironic appraisal of the status of his own poems. He relies more heavily on mimicry and parody than the classicial apologists, but he directs attention to the same problem they confronted. The result in *Satyre II* is an even stronger defense of satire than found in the Latin poems, a defense that gains aesthetic authority by its glances at and specific echoes of the Roman satiric triumvirate and moral authority by the speaker's demonstration of the vatic character of his genre.

A major difference between *Satyre II* and the classical apologiae is Donne's accommodation of their argument to Christian principles. In this vein, Thomas Wilson's representative view of the entire pattern of human history in terms of words and the Word is instructive. God's original gift of reason was so damaged by the Fall, Wilson explains, that "none did anything by reason, but most did what they could by manhood"; but during this interval of violence God "stirred up his faithful and elect to persuade all men to society [and] granted them the gift of utteraunce, that they might with ease win folke at their will, and frame them by reason to all good order."[14] Through this gift, man's moral regeneration was initiated and the bases of social order were constituted. Like the premise of Sidney and Puttenham, that language "was th'originall cause and occasion . . . of ciuil society among men,"[15] Wilson's thesis is that words are potent instruments of force and truth capable of restoring society from the effects of the Fall, and are therefore indicative of an individual's or a nation's character. "For he that is among the reasonable of all most reasonable, and among the wittie, of all most wittie, and among the eloquent of all most eloquent: him I thinke amonge all men, not onely to be taken for a singuler man, but rather to be counted for half a God."[16]

But if man can become "half a God" through the creative use of words, their protean nature also makes them capable of enormous destruction: "danger is in words."[17] Quintilian especially elaborates such a possibility in the last book of his *Institutio*, and Sidney's defense of poetry reiterates the warning that such a vessel "beeing abused . . . can doe more hurt then any other Armie of words."[18] For Sidney the tremendous destructive power inherent in words only strengthens his faith in their power to reshape the human community beneficially: "yet shall it be so far from concluding that the abuse should giue reproch to the abused, that contrariwise it is a good reason, that whatsoeuer, being abused, dooth most harme, beeing rightly vsed . . . doth most good."[19] In fact, even the harshest attacks on poetry in the late Renaissance are based on a view of the creative potentialities of language. Stephen Gosson's assaults on the theater, for example, obtain from his belief that current drama is an "abuse" of the major weapon with which "God hath armed every creature agaynst his enemie." "The right use" of language by "whetstones of wit," he argues, establishes a standard of morality, virtue, and order against which current failures can and should be judged.[20] The age's attention to the dangers of linguistic abuse is epitomized by Donne's classmate, John Hoskyns, in a paraphrase from the influential *French Academie*. "The shame of speaking unskillfully were small if the tongue were only disgraced by it," he writes, "but as the image of the king in a seal of wax, ill represented, is not so much a blemish to the wax of the signet as to the king whom it resembleth, so disordered speech is not so much injury to the lips that gave it forth or the thoughts which put it forth as to the right proportion of things in themselves, so wrongfully expressed."[21]

The king analogy is most significant, for it suggests the cardinal principle of the Renaissance view of language—that, even fallen, words retain the potency of the Word from whence they derive and which they should image. Just as the Word created, formed, and reformed the shape of human history, so man's creative or destructive uses of words "fashion" (7, 110) his personal, national, and racial character. Hoskyns's "direction" captures, in fact, the precise spirit and perspective of Donne's second *Satyre*, in which the satirist expands his attack on the misuse of words by bathetic poets and mendacious lawyers (who "lye in every thing, / Like a Kings favorite, yea like a King" [69–70]) into a picture of the chaos and sterility the land of England suffers because of such insolence. The associations throughout the poem of abuses of words with abuses of God's Book of Scripture and Book of Nature, and the final vision of the abuse of the satirist's own "Good workes," enforce the conviction that the quality of human speech and the use to which man puts God's "gift of utteraunce" are significant indicators of the moral health of the individual and the nation. Relying on the structure of the classical poets' attacks on abuses of words and deprecations of satire, *Satyre II* presents a tightly organized argument that accords with the Christian accommodation of ancient writings about the nature and potential of language, spoken by a poet whose own concern with the efficacy of words as vehicles of truth and instruments of persuasive "Good workes" provides a standard against which the abuses he attacks can be judged.

ii

Like the Latin defenses, Donne's apologia begins with an analysis of the character of his satire, its moral bases and restrictions, fully in the bold spirit of Juvenal's "difficile est saturam non scribere":

> Sir; though (I thanke God for it) I do hate
> Perfectly all this towne, yet there's one state
> In all ill things so excellently best,
> That hate, towards them, breeds pitty towards the rest. (1–4)

The pose of the misanthrope is standard to verse satire, and the distinction between objects of "pitty" and objects of "hate" sounds almost like a comparison of the *fools* Horace mocks and the *knaves* Juvenal scourges.[22] Indeed, throughout the poem the pitiful poets are treated with the comic ridicule perfected by Horace while the crimes of Coscus and the lawyers are treated with the impassioned, harsher satire characteristic of Juvenal. But the most surprising note here (and that which has most disturbed modern readers) is the parenthetical comment by the satirist. It is not meant as a parody of Christian teaching but, in accordance with the distinction between venial and mortal sins, conforms to Christian teaching about the correct and necessary uses of hatred and anger;[23] hatred of sins is natural and creative, "bred" by man's God-like ability to discern the "best . . . In all . . . things."[24] In the larger strategies of the poem, it serves to establish from the outset the satirist's moral stance as an imitation and a gift of God ("Perfectly"). It also affirms, and the conclusion of the poem confirms, that even the assent to folly and crime by "all this towne" cannot obviate the need for and the value of the satirist's moral perspective. The careful detailing of the moral uses of language by the satirist in his opening self-endorsement establishes, in other words, an exemplary alternative to the foolishness and "insolence" that stir his "just offence." In this sense, his distinction between the pitiful character of the poets' offences and the menacing enormity of the lawyers' is central to his argument. The poets, he discloses, are not so much the major culprits of linguistic abuse as its victims, victims of both the punishment that results from abandonment of their vatic function and the town's acceptance of the ethos of the lawyers. Not that his pity for these poetasters is unqualified; the complexity of his attitude towards them is gradually uncovered in his ironic assessment of their current abuses. There is, after all, a difference between unwilling and willing victims (as the satirist's own case reveals); and although he can pity the poets for their degrading predicament, he still sharply castigates their ambitious motives and ready submission to such a condition. The poets are, then, as much the product as the source of that "one state," that attitude towards words exemplified and perpetuated by the toleration of Coscus' abuses.

In this vein, the ridicule of the "poore" poets is richly humorous, resilient in hyperbole and parody that undercut the claims of those like the *misomusoi* who call poets the major enemies of the state. The estimate of contemporary poetry begins, for instance, with the seemingly self-effacing acknowledgment of the Platonic-Puritan warnings about poetry:

> Though Poëtry indeed be such a sinne
> As I thinke that brings dearths, and Spaniards in,
> Though like the Pestilence and old fashion'd love,
> Ridlingly it catch men. . . .   (5–8)

The ineffectiveness of the satirist's own poetry is evidently deserved, then, if poets are the economic, military, medical, and ethical enemies of the nation. But the ironic hyperbole here undermines the clause's literal meaning. The speaker does not even bother to answer directly his detractors' best argument, but merely states it baldly to reveal the foolishness of its extravagant claims and reasoning. In fact, this claim does contain truth: poetry does work "Ridlingly"; poetry is motivated by "old fashion'd love"; and, the ensuing description of the current plague of poets implies, as it is "in-deed" practiced, poetry does perpetuate the nation's moral "dearth." But by granting the *misomusoi* their most severe criticism the satirist shows that, even if it were true literally, the poets would still not be the greatest threat. Although this association of poetry with recent calamities in England does acknowledge the current failure of poetry to realize its civilizing and moral capabilities, it is in the main an ironic strategy that discloses the ultimate harm the insolence of Coscus portends. In fact, a view of the satirist as minister and scourge is ironically suggested by the associations of poetry with calamities that the authoritative *Book of Homilies*, the medical authorities of the day, and the weekly sermons taught were brought in because of God's anger with the community[25]—and supports the satirist's initial view of himself as an agent or benefice of God's ire. Satire *can* be associated with dearths, famines, the Spaniards, and the plague since it too arises from God's anger or that of God's agent. Thus, as far as the techniques of an apologia are concerned, Donne has merely allowed his persona to voice sarcastically the objections to poetry that Horace's legalistic Trebatius, Juvenal's pragmatic interlocutor, and Persius's effeminate monitor supplied in the Latin defenses.

Rather than responding directly to these criticisms, Donne's satirist continues in an ironic vein by pointing out that the poets constitute a harmless threat because "their state / Is poore, disarm'd, like Papists, not worth hate" (9–10). This line alludes to the specific statute that had recently led to the arrest and suspicious death of Donne's younger brother (for harboring a Jesuit priest).[26] It also intimates that the sharp attack on legal procedures that propels the poem probably had specific biographical origins, and that the impetus for the poem was not, as has been assumed, the group of anonymous sonnets, *Zepheria*, which appeared in 1592. The relatively light treatment of the foolish poets compared with the bitter attack on the lawyers, the intimation that Coscus gains lands in part by preying on recusants and suspected Catholics, and the final pejorative denotation of the statutes as "huge" and "vast" certainly support such a contention. But regardless of the autobiographical origins of Donne's reactions, in the overall argument of the poem, this allusion reinforces the opening contention that the major dangers to the nation do not originate with the pitiable poets but have internal causes within the fearful machinery of the state and the abuse of its authority by mendicants such as Coscus.

The satirist's ironic denigration of poetry continues with the allusion to the old Irish belief that the "riddles" of satire have magical powers of life and death over its victims. This power is no longer believed in, he reveals: "witchcrafts charmes / Bring not now their old feares, nor their old harmes." Whether the satirist would support such a theory about satire is not clear, but the syntax of his admission, with its superbly ironic rhyme, reveals that he views this change in the opinion of satire as another instance of the general loss suffered by his countrymen. He does undercut the validity of this lore by suggesting that the "harmes" resulting from such "charmes" must have been merely psychological, but even the admission emphasizes that this change is another instance of the loss of faith in the powers of language, and hence a decrease in the satirist's effectiveness with the people.

Even the specific examples he offers to confirm supposedly that poets are national enemies insist that they are not the country's true foes, for each of these examples shows only how the poetasters bring "harme" not to the nation but to themselves. Apparently, the power of satire to curse and wound the guilty has been ironically retained in the power of "poore" poetry to bring misery on its perpetrators. The playwright who "gives ideot actors meanes / . . . to live by'his labor'd sceanes," for example, succeeds only in propagating personal misery, "Starving himselfe" (pp. 13–14). The poet who "would move Love by rimes" proves equally impotent; he can cause no real "harme . . . or feare" because he relies on the wrong weapons in his wars of love: "Rammes, and slings now are seely battery, / Pistolets are the best Artillerie" (pp. 17–20). Like the thrust of the ancient apologiae, then, the attack upon the practices of the contemporary poets actually points to the moral failures of society. After all, when compared to "Pistolets," the "rimes" of the lyricists are as pitiable in the wars of love as archaic martial weapons would be in the wars of nations. It is only gold, as the pun on "Pistolets" (a *Spanish* coin) affirms, that has any power today. Thus, it is not any innate "sinfulness" in poetry that dooms poets to ineffectiveness but the moral depravity of the times. The Spanish "Artillerie" that poses the greatest threat to English civilization has already been brought in, not by the silly poets but through the invasion of naked appetite and aggressive materialism which now advance through the land. Even the poets who "write to Lords, rewards to get" and who "write, because all write" only harm themselves by becoming "singers at doores for meat" (21–23). The punishments of fruitless labor, constant starvation, and general wretchedness they experience are the joint products of their own moral stupidity[27] and the insensitivity and pride of the men whom they solicit. Even the worst of the contemporary poets, the poet who

> doth chaw
> Others wits fruits, and in his ravenous maw
> Rankly digested, doth those things out-spue,
> As his owne things,

is punished by the fact that the ultimate result of his plagiarism is "excrement" (25–30). Therefore, the four major threats to the nation that poetry supposedly poses—the invasions of dearths, Spaniards, plagues, and "old fashion'd love"—are actually suffered by the poetasters themselves in their starvation, their ineffectiveness in comparison to "Spaniards" coins, their "ill" writing, and their reliance on out-moded, "old-fashion'd" forms of persuasion.

"These do mee no harme" (31), the satirist concludes, and by "mee" he intimates that these poets cannot after all efface the power of his own "Good workes as good." They are signs and victims of national decay as much as perpetuators of any unhealthy attitude towards language. They are not even as dangerous as those more numerous counterparts to their activities in contemporary society, those who are accustomed

> To out-doe Dildoes, and out-usure Jewes;
> To'out-drinke the sea, to'out-sweare the Letanie;
> Who with sinnes all kindes as familiar bee
> As Confessors. (32–35)

If one scans English conduct, he can find habits that "out-doe" the threats from dearth, pestilence, blasphemy, and Catholic invaders supposedly brought in by the poets. So, the satirist's attack on the poets begins with hyperbolic mimicry of their detractors and concludes with a catalogue of worse malefactors who exhibit even more severe perversions of the sacred, creative gestures of exchange and community. But, begun by observations that focus on the immoral conditions in which "poore" poets abound and concluded by comparisons with corruptions less "worthy" of pity, even the harshest words for the poets are tempered by the satirist's contention that it is not they who deserve immediate legal punishment.

Therefore, the paradoxical role of the speaker in his opening criticisms is central to his ethical strategies and therapeutic aims in *Satyre II*. His condemnation of all poetry and his association of his own poetry with disease, defenseless soldiers, and materialistic beggars invert the traditional roles of satirist as doctor, moral soldier, and disinterested commentator on mankind's follies and crimes. This pose, as well as his avowal that he will attack only those who "harme" him, actually exposes the error of those who blame national disasters on the poets. By suggesting that society's moral depravity produces and victimizes poets and by refusing to defend himself overtly, he allows—even forces—the reader to discover the terrible truths about society for himself, thus initiating that recovery of communication whose loss he bemoans. Forced to rely on irony because of the plight he shares with disregarded poets, he dislocates the reader from accepted standards and forces him to see the truth.[28] In fact, by forcing the reader to struggle with the harshness, obscurity, and parodic techniques of his poem, the satirist initiates in the reader an awareness of the potentials of language ("ridling" as it is) for the communication of truth as well as for the gratification of material appetite to which it is presently restricted in his society. The first step towards recovery of language is begun, therefore, in the reading of the poem.

The ironic poses of the satirist also enforce an implicit ethic. By portraying poetry as a weakened vessel, he seems a fool for continuing to write. His harshness towards mercenary poets reveals that he continues to write not for military, medical, or political reasons, but only for moral reasons: his is a "just offence" and a natural reaction of the moral man, bred by his "pitty" for the "disarm'd" victims of the nation's spiritual enemies. Other poets prove reprehensible because their motives are material and personal; they become "Puppits" of the whimsical "Lords" of this world. disgracing themselves and their art. But the ironic military imagery of the poem underscores the satirist's contention that he is not concerned with material gain but with identifying and castigating those true enemies of the realm. Thus, if his foolishness is "out of fashion," the fault lies not with his motives or manner, or even with the present ineffectiveness of his craft, but somewhere else. That "one state . . . excellently best" that threatens the civilizing powers of language is the subject of the second part of his apologia.

iii

Like his ironic defense of the poets, the satirist's attack against Coscus proceeds by degrees, moving from ridicule of the pitiable "mad[ness]" of Coscus as a "scarce" poet to denunciation of his legal abuses and the general abuse of the English woodlands which his greed precipitates. Initiated by a dramatization of the poet-lawyer's bathetic attempt to reestablish an adulterous affair first launched in 1588 (50) and concluded by a picture of the sterility, dearth, and disease of Christian charity that Coscus' "prostitution" of words brings to England, the satirist's attack on Coscus reveals that it is his perversions of words that deserve the epithets of the *misomusoi* and the sectarian polemicists. Like his treatment of the poets, the satirist's dramatization of the lawyer's absurd attempts at poetry mimics the insufficiency of those precepts to account for the dangerous effects and criminal extravagances engendered by such practices. Both views of Coscus—as poet and as lawyer—retain the focus of the classical apologiae on the abuse of words. The portrait of Coscus when he was "sicke with Poëtrie, 'and possest with muse" (61) discloses how his poetry foreshadowed in motive and method his ill repute (63) as a parasitic lawyer; and the descriptions of his legal maneuvering, which are motivated by the same appetites as his sexual solicitations, reveal them to be abuses of language. The large number of similes enforces the idea, in fact, that his conduct as poet and as lawyer amounts to the perversion not only of God's "gift of utteraunce" but to abuse of the Word itself. Rather than an abrupt transition in subject, then, the picture of Coscus as poet provides a clear progress from the satirist's mockery of current poetic failures to his "offence" against legal swindles and abuses of the Words of God by lawyers such as Coscus.

The initial picture of Coscus as a "scarce Poët" who habitually wooes "ever wench" by "throwe[ing] / Like nets, or lime-twigs . . . / His title 'of Barrister" (45–47) evokes the commonplace bird-lime image of man's sinfulness.[29] This interpretation is reinforced by the pejorative description of the poet-barrister's title as the product of "plodding"[30] mortality, the advanced form of a disease, and basically animalistic. He was made a lawyer only by

44

> time (which rots all, and makes botches poxe,
> And plodding on, must make a calfe an oxe).   (41–42)

As a reminder of the mortality of man (time "rots *all*": *tempus edax rerum*), this parenthesis supports the satirist's earlier remarks about the eventual punishment for all malefactors; but, in addition, by identifying the thoroughly temporal manner and motive of Coscus' activities, the interpolated clause offers a microcosmic simile for his growth from a sinful but essentially foolish poetaster into a national enemy. Coscus-the-poet was like a calf and a blister, harmless in themselves, still manageable; but as a lawyer he has become a cumbersome, dangerous animal and a social disease because of the size of his hunger and the extent of his contagiousness. The "dearth" of sense in his "scarce" poetry indicated the disease of meaning and order of which he would be capable once his mercenary pestilence invaded the law. The satirist can even forgive him for his foolish poetry, since as a silly versifier he must have been "mad" (62) to render himself so ridiculous. This reliance on another dictum of the *misomusoi* (poetry equals madness) allows him to treat Coscus' ludicrous verses with the same wit he used on the "poore" poets. Even the depiction of Coscus' poetry as a form of prostitution does not "breed" his hatred (prostitutes, after all, can infect only those who come to them for their services). The suggestion, once again, is that, *even mad*, poets have not effected as much moral corruption as meretricious lawyers; both mad poets and prostitutes can be seen as the sterile victims of a national sickness, not its major cause.

The motives Coscus exhibited in his solicitation of the adulteress—his regard for her as a piece of property to be gained by clever manipulation of legal language[31]—were immoral, but not as dangerous to the national health as the proclivities of "men which chuse / Law practice for meere gaine" and thereafter "repute / Worse then imbrothel'd strumpets prostitute" (62–64). The description of Coscus' poetry, therefore, discloses the dangerous temporal motives, sexual appetite, and gross size which remain his characteristics as lawyer. Now, however, they are worthy "onely [of] hatred" because they threaten

> Shortly ('as the sea) . . . [to] compasse all our land;
> From Scots, to Wight; from Mount, to Dover strand.   (77–78)

It is the conquest of England by the moral dearth he personifies that threatens the health of the nation, just as it is Spanish pistolets that corrupt the English exchange.

That Coscus' legal activities are illegitimate extensions of the sexual appetite motivating his seductions is made clear by the satirist's repeated insistence that the lawyer always "lyes" and by the comparisons of his activities to those who thrive on "Bastardy . . . Symonie'and Sodomy" (74–75). Coscus' words are all "lyes": "to'every suitor [he] lye[s] in every thing, / Like a Kings favorite, yea like a King" (69–70). He presses forward into the crowded courtroom only so that he may "lye, to the grave Judge" (73). His lies are merely an expansion of the sexual appetite he exhibited as a poet, as suggested by the homosexual implications of the comparison of the "Sodomy" by which he thrives to that which "abounds . . . in Churchmens lives" (74–75), by the comparison of his lies to the male prostitution used to gain royal preferment, and by the insistence that his bearing in the courtroom is "more shameless farre / Then [that of] carted whores" (72–73). These metaphors, then, equate Coscus' mendacity with violations of the major vessels of social stability: sex and generation, money and coining, health and religion. Thus, the satirist's amplification of the precepts of the *misomusoi* and the antipapist controversialists, the application of their severest charge against their enemies (that they promulgate lies) not to the poets but to Coscus, identifies the corrupt lawyers as the liars who parody and threaten the creative order of the realm.[32]

Likewise, the temporality and corporeality—the sheer verbose magnitude—characteristic of Coscus' "poetry" are shown to be even more destructive once he has become a lawyer. His love poetry was mere volume:

> *words, words,* which would teare
> The tender labyrinth of a soft maids eare,
> *More, more,* then ten Sclavonians scolding, *more*
> Then when winds in our ruin'd Abbeyes *rore.* (57–60, italics added)

A violent rape of sense and decorum, it was a destructive barbarism[33] even more voluminous than the winds that now haunt the monasteries, the desertion of which recalls again the nation's abandonment of the spiritual in pursuit of the material. In the hands of the hungry lawyer, however, this aptitude for voluminous lies could become a means of gradually possessing all of England, for his major strategy of attaining land "Peecemeale" (85), of satisfying his hunger for others' lands,[34] is through the shrewd and fraudulent manipulation of the size of his writings:

> In parchments then, *large as his fields,* hee drawes
> Assurances, *bigge,* as gloss'd civill lawes,
> So *huge,* that men (in our times forwardnesse)
> Are Fathers of the Church for writing lesse. (87–90, italics added)

Even the sheer bulk of his writing, here derided through puns as a perverse form of phallic hyperbole and corrupt procreation, is of little concern to Coscus, however, for he does not have to copy them nor pay to have them copied.

> These hee writes not; nor for these written payes,
> Therefore spares no length; as in those first dayes

> When Luther was profest, he did desire
> Short *Pater nosters*, saying as a Fryer
> Each day his beads, but having left those lawes,
> Addes to Christs prayer, the Power and glory clause.   (91–96)

Verbosity is not an obstacle to Coscus because he has left the law in his unscrupulous dealings. Brutally legalistic when it will benefit him personally, he is anxious to abandon the law just as readily when he can gain by leaving those laws. The "Power and glory" phrase is highly ironic, of course; and although its saucy use here may accuse Luther of a "personal laziness,"[35] its major effect is to render the charge against Coscus doubly damning by the contrast between the power and glory the lawyer seeks through defrauding clients and the power and glory Luther demanded to be paid to God in daily prayer. Actually, the simile is quite precise in its reiteration of Coscus' "Shrewd" manipulations of legal words as analogous to perversion of the Word: Luther at prayer altered a document of the Law, omitting from the *Pater noster* acknowledgment of the eternality of the Father's justice and mercy (*for ever and ever*); Coscus in private ("unwatch'd") alters documents of the law, omitting from testaments the phrase ("*ses heires*") that enforces the father's undying love for his children. Once again Coscus' uncreating words pervert an exchange of love into a sterilized gratification of his own economic will.

This analogy also strengthens the original description of Coscus' illicit conduct once he became a lawyer:

> now he must talke
> Idly, like prisoners, which whole months will sweare
> The onely suretiship hath brought them there.   (66–68)

He arrives at the court talking idly, claiming that only the debts of others have brought him there, posing as a helper of the poor, when he actually seeks only personal profits. Both similes emphasize that from the time he enters the courtroom, "like an owelike watchman, . . . / His hand still at a bill" (66), rapacious for money, until he joyfully sights those "heires melting with luxurie" (79) whose "sinnes" make them easy victims, Coscus' motives and methods are purely material. Feeding his insatiable appetite for land and money by piling volumes of legal jargon on his clients in order to hoodwink them, he is "like a wedge in a blocke" (71), wedging in between his clients and their money, between word and meaning. And the wedge he uses to "wring" their titles is his discordant, voluminous "rore" of words. Since the words of the law are mere legalistic objects to Coscus, just as susceptible to reduction as expansion, he omits "*ses heires*" when changing the titles of lands so that the land will not devolve upon heirs but default to him as executor of the property. Just as he claimed to the adulteress that his "letters should take

[the] place / Of affidavits" (56–57), so now his own manipulations of the letters of his clients take the place of legal writs. Imaged as sexual abuses that pervert the generative and hereditary order of the realm, his "farre worse" abuses of legal language are aptly compared, then, to the desecration of God's Word for personal increase by sly "Commenter[s]" (99) and clever "controverters" who misrepresent and alter "vouch'd Texts" (101) in order to gain prestige and power. Coscus-the-poet is pitiable; his ridiculous poetic distortions, like those of the other poetasters, are a disgrace to that profession and to himself, a misuse of personal talent that may warrant damnation— but hardly the threat to the soul of the nation, its foundation on justice, covenant, and creative exercise of the "gift of utteraunce" that his legal dealings constitute.

The final example of Coscus' legal fraudulence denounced by the satirist evinces the essence of the lawyer's threat to the nation. Up to this point he has been imaged as the embodiment of expanding corporeality, a purely physical presence that has invaded and now threatens to overwhelm English civilization completely. Motivated only by material appetite, his formless character is mirrored by the perverse shapes of his words, which seem to expand or contract according to the dictates of his appetite and which transform or deform the spirit of the law (and love) into a disfigured mass of things. His final legal maneuveurs—he "writes *not*" (91), "spares *no* length" (92), and "leave[s] out" (101)—figure the essence of him and his words: they are absence, negation, privation, "sinne . . . in-deed," or, in Augustine's words, *"Dictum, factum, concupitum, contra legem . . . ; Forma peccati, deformitas."*[36] The gradual unfolding of Coscus as Uncreating Word aptly concludes with this focus on the verbose lawyer as essential negation.[37]

Then, in a marvelous transition from cause to effects, conveyed by the internal rime of "words . . . words . . . woods," the satirist shifts attention from the grasping forgery of Coscus to the stripped English woodlands. "Where," he complains,

> are those spred woods which cloth'd heretofore
> Those bought lands? not built, nor burnt within dore.
> Where's th'old landlords troops, and almes?   (103–5)

"Bought" or fraudulently stolen and left to rot (like diseased prostitutes) by lawyers such as Coscus, the woodlands clearly reflect the extension of the sterile Uncreating Word into the Book of Nature. This spread of Coscus' disease, his corruption of love, law, and labor (the tasks of Adam), is complete: his perversions of the Books of Man (as adulterer), Law (as lawyer), and Nature (as landlord) threaten now to remake the Books of God in his own image. Caring as little for the land as they do for the law, men such as Coscus treat it as a mere object to be possessed, the more the better. These new landlords have let the woods rot, have disbanded the attendants and servants maintained by the old landlords, and have abandoned the "old fashion'd" giving of alms.[38] The creative, charitable obligations of property have been replaced by the desire for titles, just as the mere "title'of Barrister" became Coscus' proudest possession. Their typical representative, Coscus was "made a Lawyer" through the process of a slow rot, the satirist pointed out, and his type threatens "now [to] rot" all of England through the abundant possession and careless disregard of the land. Words and the law are like the land: if not cared for dutifully and used carefully their creative potentialities can be lost. Thus, this transition by the satirist from Coscus-as-lawyer to Coscus-as-landlord discloses the awful power over words and with words that man possesses. Significantly, this thematic shift is reflected by the shift of attention from Coscus-as-lawyer to Coscus-as-negation: once he "leaves out, *ses heires*" he literally disappears from the poem.

This image of the "spred woods" as the last word uncreated by Coscus' insolence has been anticipated by the numerous similes describing his activities. The satirist's persistent comparisons of literary corruptions and legal transgressions with perversions of ecclesiastical functions and sacred words insist on identification of the abuse of language with the abuse of the Word.[39] Coscus' arrogance about his "title'of Barrister," for example, parallels the vanity of "new benefic'd ministers" who are prouder of their new titles than they are responsive to their duties as vessels of the Word. His inflated legal jargon is like the "rore" of winds in the ruined abbeys and the barbaric babble of "Sclavonians scolding." Similarly, the analogies drawn between Coscus' quantities of words and the voluminous writing by which some become "Fathers of the Church," between his omissions of essential legal terms and Luther's lengthening and shortening of the *Pater noster* and commentators' "sly" omissions of phrases from the Word that might disprove their exegeses, and between his legal swindles and the "Symonie'and Sodomy in Churchmens lives" urge the same conclusion. These comparisons—the supposed "ingenious similes" of the poem—depict, then, the abuse of word and Word which Coscus' insolence typifies and perpetuates. Through them the abuse of language is identified as the hallmark of an age of decayed sensibility, a world of moral chaos in which understanding and action, word and spirit, have been sundered by lust, pride, greed, and acquisitiveness. Thus, Coscus is both the prime example and embodiment of the Uncreating Word that reigns in a world where the civilizing and sacred power of the words of God and man have been perverted into instruments of personal, material gain. The barren woodlands merely mirror the uncreating words of Coscus, which have been stripped of their proper spirit of justice and charity. And "Time," which "hath made a Lawyer" of Coscus, now threatens to make a sterile wasteland of the nation because of the uncharitable, fraudulent, irresponsible actions of such Englishmen. The rottenness of the woods reflects not just the effects of the enclosure movement but the permeation of the nation by the spiritual blight manifested in the infectious abuse of word and Word typified by the mendacious lawyer-landlord.

This same analogy informs the satirist's final exasperated plea to his country:

> in great hals
> Carthusian fasts, and fulsome Bachanalls
> Equally'I hate; meanes blesse; in rich mens homes
> I bid kill some beasts, but no Hecatombs,
> None starve, none surfet so.   (105–9)

Words are food, too, and can be images of the spiritual food of the Word. Coscus' bacchanalian verbosity, on the other hand, is finally and merely a "Carthusian fast" spiritually. Only physical and spiritual starvation result from the spread of his verbal antifeasts of words. Perhaps he is the "beast" that signals the destruction of English civilization. In fact, the vision of Revelation hovers at the edges of *Satyre II* throughout. The allusion to the year 1588 alone would have reminded Donne's readers of the dire forecasts about it as the year of Antichrist.[40] Whether or not the satirist's imperative is intended to elicit such an association, this final exhortation does evoke a significant image of the satirist. His plea, literally, is for a community feast, a ceremony, if you wish, of charity and brotherhood. What he urges, then, is the reestablishment of the Christian spirit of community, a national participation in or celebration of the Feast of Love to counter the antifeast of Coscus' deformed words. This vision, the Renaissance urged, was especially the responsibility of the poet, the poet as the moderator or, in Augustine's term for the Word, the *mediator*. The "beast" of Coscus' Uncreating Word can be vanquished, after all, by the country's return to meaningful, charitable communion. The unreality of Coscus' words can be displaced by the reestablishment of a sense of community that images the example of the Word and His loving sacrifice: "Blessed are those who are invited to the marriage feast of the Lamb" (Rev. 19:9).

The final example of the effects of linguistic abuses offered by the satirist returns to his own situation. The disregard of his own "Good workes," works "bred" by an "old fashion'd love" of truth and hatred of criminal rapes of justice, shows that the "Pestilence" presently ravaging English words, woods, and works was brought in not by the poets but by the verbal pollution of men like Coscus. After his exhortation, the satirist admits saucily and sarcastically that

> (Oh) we'allow
> Good workes as good, but out of fashion now,
>   Like old rich wardrops; but my words none drawes
>   Within the vast reach of th'hugh statute lawes.   (109–12)

As an endorsement of his earlier statement that "Poëtry indeed be such a sinne" and his avowed determination to attack only those who "do mee harme," these lines might seem to argue a philosophy of despair or at least to substantiate the view that *Satyre II* reveals Donne's aversion to print, a "paradoxical aversion to poetry . . . strongly expressed."[41] Ignoring the irony of these concluding lines could support the view that the poem discloses Donne's dissatisfaction with the genre altogether and his squeamish inability to convert it into an adequate expression of his supposed skepticism.[42] Such views overlook the rich ambiguity of the satirist's conclusion, however, and its function in the larger strategy of his apologia. Like the classicial apologists in their final ironic self-disparagements, Donne's satirist must be granted a full measure of his irony. His admission that he uses the wrong "Artillerie," since he comes armed solely with the truth, only strengthens his anatomy of the nation's fashionable capitulation to a gross materialism that amounts to a sort of linguistic sterility. His concession that his own words lack the physical effectiveness of those of lawyers who clothe their illicit, rapacious appetites in volumes of legal jargon does not invalidate his efforts. Rather, his ironic acknowledgments affirm once more that he, as a representative poet, is not the true enemy of the state. Not he, nor any poet, can create the havoc Coscus threatens. The satirist's words, after all, *are* "rich wardrops," the appropriate dress for the values and spiritual self-knowledge that the nation has discarded. As "Good workes," his own words are an image of the Word that mediates in man's behalf.

The authority of his concluding remarks is strengthened, in fact, by their reiteration and accommodation of Horace's ironic defense of his art in *Satire II.i.* In the Roman poem, an account of the classical satirist's consultation with the famous jurist C. Testa Trebatius about the reception he can expect for his satires, Trebatius advises Horace to disregard objections to his satires ("Quiescas"), to give up verse altogether, or to turn to panegyric or epic. When Horace responds with an explanation of the *laws of satire*—pointing out that he is instinctively provoked to satire by the ubiquitous foolishness of the Roman citizenry and appealing finally to the precedent example of Lucilius ("Sequor hunc, . . . nostrum melioris utroque"), his *adversarius* reminds him that there are laws against libel: "si mala condiderit in quem quis carmina, ius est / iudiciumque." This warning provokes the final exchange of the poem:

> [Horace] . . . sed bona si quis
> iudice condiderit laudatus Caesare? si quis
> opprobriis dignum latraverit, integer ipse?
> [Trebatius] Solventur risu tabulae, tu missus abibis.

If he writes "good verse" (*bona carmina*—that is, verse that does not violate the ancient prescription against the evil use of powerful incantations or the

Lex Cornelia strictures against libellous songs),[43] the poet is assured, then he need not fear any legal prosecutions. This concluding exchange between the jurist and the satirist about the legal status of satire is incorporated into the concluding lines of *Satyre II*. Although the addition of the pejoratives "vast" and "huge" presents a more fearful and anxious attitude towards the law than in Horace's poem, the intimation that his satire is a "Good worke" repeats Horace's *bona carmina*. And although the Latin satirist does hint that it is merely matters of scansion that keep him awake at night, both poets insist that the legality of satire must be determined by the truthfulness of its vision. The issue at stake in both poems is the legal status of satire, and both suggest that neither the ancient *Tabulae* nor the "huge statute lawes" are violated by them. The ambiguous reference to "none" in *Satyre II* (as a reference to the satirist as well as to those malefactors who go unpunished in spite of his revelation of their crimes) recalls Trebatius' admission that the satirist frees himself from legal culpability if his verse is *bona carmina*. Thus, the echo of the Latin poem, like Horace's reference to Lucilius, elicits ancient authority from the canon of satire to support the claims of Donne's satirist about his mission.[44]

As typical in Donne's poems, the Elizabethan satirist also adds a religious dimension to his self-appraisal not found in the Latin original. He finds religious sanction for his efforts, playing on the doctrinal controversy over the efficacy of good works by suggesting that the Anglican society, having discarded this doctrine from its salvation theology, disregards the meritorious character of such acts as well. But Donne's imitation retains more than merely verbal echoes and structural parallels with Horace's poem. As commentators have pointed out, part of the wit of the classical dialogue lies in the discrepancies in meaning that the satirist and jurist ascribe to certain central words.[45] Foremost in this sense are the Latin speakers' different interpretations of *legum* and of phrases such as *mala* (or *bona*) *carmina*. The cynical Trebatius reacts to the satirist's situation legalistically and lectures him on the strict legal ramifications of his verse in terms of Roman laws of libel. The Roman satirist, on the other hand, is more concerned with the laws of satire and its moral bases. Thus, the agreement that the two reach is richly humorous: the jurist is satisfied that the poet does not violate the rules of libel, the satirist that the law does not ultimately prohibit or infringe upon the laws of satire. Donne's satirist evokes the same rich complexity in his ambiguous and wry conclusion. He adds the melancholic and ironic observation that while his satire is ineffective—in failing to bring about the prosecution of parasitic lawyers such as Coscus—neither can he be prosecuted simply because he has told the truth about present conditions. His own effort to initiate moral reformation must be accepted as a "Good worke," if for no other reason than its truthfulness. That it results in no moral reformation or legal prosecution reflects poorly solely on the perverse character of national morality and law. Donne's satirist does indeed recall Horace's authoritative conclusion that poetically meritorious satire is legal both as poetry and as social criticism. Yet at the same time he admits to ineffectiveness in order to reinforce his ongoing argument: that the widespread abuse of language and law has drastically reduced the civilizing force of the words of poetry and law. His own situation is the final symptom he anatomizes in order to prove his case, to verify that England suffers from the abuse and disregard of the truthful potential of language.

Horatian echoes also add ancient authority to the satirist's implicit equation of the nation's response to satiric language and its moral health. The comparisons to Horace's situation legitimize the harsher tenor of Donne's poem. Absent in the caustic sarcasm of Donne's conclusion are Horace's calm urbanity and civilized temperament, his ability to intensify, while maintaining lightness and moderation, the irresolvable differences between the jurist's expedient ethic and the satirist's idealistic aesthetic.[46] Like Horace, the Elizabethan also counsels moderation: "meanes blesse" (107). Even here, however, there is a wry modification of the Horatian dictum, conveyed in this case by the pun on "mean" as "lowly" and "immoral" and by the suggestion that only the meanest of actions finds the blessing of his materialistic society. The witty reliance on puns is fully in the spirit of Horatian ridicule, but alien to it are the harsher irony and more melancholic tone.

Thus, besides tacitly explaining his view of the "poore" poets as victims of powerful and influential men such as Coscus, the satirist's admission to ineffectiveness remains the best proof of the moral depravity of a country more interested in the letter than the spirit of law and letters. By offering himself and the disregard of his own works as final symptom of the abuse of word and Word he attacks throughout the poem he is not engaging in that "pessimism" of which many Renaissance commentators charge Juvenal. Every satirist might be accused of skepticism and a tendency towards despair; the nature of the genre demands focus on the failures rather than the successes of mankind. In fact, Donne's satirist has turned the "dark mood" of satire into a challenge to his opponents, for his pose of ineffectiveness thrusts yet once more: his inability to elicit any response from a corrupt legal authority can be disproved only if his words *do* effect the changes he deems imperative.

iv

In many ways, then, the satirist's concluding irony expands the appraisal of the role of satire in *Satyre I*. His own condition, as in the former poem, is still presented as a symptom rather than a cure for the conditions he attacked even though the ethos of his stance provides an exemplary alternative for the abuses criticized in each poem. His satire is now "rich wardrops" rather than "course attire." Yet, the reversion to a sort of defiant sarcasm at the end of this poem suggests that the satirist has not resolved those doubts about his role as satirist. The first two *Satyres* do establish his criteria as a Christian satirist by their display of his charity for sinners and his hatred for their sins as well as his possession of the two essentials of successful oratory—good character and eloquence. His own realization of the function of satire as a form of Christian devotion and as the balanced integration of the qualities he displays in these first two poems is the major concern of the next *Satyre*.

Before turning to that poem it is worth noting, since *Satyre II* has been the object of so much critical dispraise, how the poem affirms many of the attitudes of Donne's more popular works. *Satyre II* might be read, in fact, as an initial apologia not only for satire but for the central concerns of many of Donne's later works. The satirist's vision of the abuses of communication corresponds to the dismay with cramped, superficial, and abusive attitudes towards love and the language of love voiced throughout the *Songs and Sonets*, *Metempsychosis*, *Conclave Ignati*, and the *Anniversaries*. The vision in *The First Anniversary* of the "nightmare landscape of the fallen world,"[47] in which "art is lost, and correspondence too,"[48] is first sketched in *Satyre II*; and the prophetic satirist who "invokes" that vision also appears in this early apologia. Likewise, the satirist's ironic attacks upon self-serving desecrations of word and Word establish a basis for the satirical portraits in his later poems of formalistic Petrarchists (in "The Computation," "The Expiration," and "The Paradox"), superficial Platonists (in "The Undertaking" and "The Relique"), evasive Neoplatonists (in "The Dissolution," "Farewell to Love," and, perhaps, "The Exstasie"), and dangerous "innovators" (in *Conclave Ignati*). Even the "serious" love lyrics explore the perspectives on language manifested in this early poem; poems such as "The Sunne Rising" and "The Good Morrow," for example, explore the applicability of scientific designs and language to the experience of love, forcing the reader to discover the emotional and spiritual truths about love as the center of man's universe. The language of love and man's loving response to the Word, after all, are the major subjects of all Donne's poetry. In this sense, the poems following *Satyre II*, even the *Holy Sonnets* in their urgent search for communication with the Word, elaborate the concern with the creative potential of "Good . . . words" and the dangers engendered by abuses of language and communication. "All cohaerence" is indeed "gone," this early apologia explains, when man's "gift of utteraunce" is so abused as to isolate him from his civilization, his fellow man, and his God.

CHAPTER THREE

Satire as Religion

he whose soul is not upright in him shall fail.

Habakkuk 2:4

There is no Vertue, but Religion.

To Mr. Rowland Woodward

In his notes to Pope's "versification" of Donne's second and fourth *Satyres*, William Warburton regrets that the Augustan poet did not offer a "Paraphrase" of "the noblest Work of not only This but perhaps any satiric Poet," the third *Satyre*.[1] His praise echoes the opinion Donne's contemporaries held of *Satyre III* and foreshadows its esteem by modern readers. Despite their consensus about its excellence, however, recent critics have reached little agreement about its central meanings and strategies. Debate has focused particularly on the poem's structure and its attitude towards satire's reformative capabilities.[2] When seen in the context of the first two *Satyres*, these questions seem answerable. By the end of *Satyre II*, we have a satirist who has anatomized dramatically his own foolishness (*I*) and his own ineffectiveness (*II*)—far from the *Lucilius ardens* of the classical satiric stance. What, then, is he to do? That is the subject of *Satyre III*: "Can railing then cure these worne maladies?" (4). The poem dramatizes the satirist's initial discovery of the *devotional* character of his satire, and deliberates the nature of satire as much as the nature of "true religion" (43). It is here, in fact, that the satirist finds a satisfactory balance between the charity he offered the fop in *I* and the hatred that overruled it in *II*, through his meditation on the dynamic use of the three powers of the rational soul. Relying on the patristic interpretation of the rational faculties—the "enumeration [of] St. Bernard," Donne later called it in one of his sermons[3]—*Satyre III* examines the correct use of the satirist's own mental faculties as exemplary alternative to the failures of devotion that the poem ridicules.

In one of his baptismal sermons, Dean Donne later explained that God has afforded man three "Trinities" for his "Testimony" to his Creator. After elucidating the divine Trinity of the Godhead and the trinity of "witnesses" provided for man in the Church, he delineated a "third Trinity *in our selves.*" Applying the Christian psychology of St. Augustine and St. Bernard to explicate the *imago dei* in man, he insisted that even the "naturall man" can effectively be a witness for God's love through the correct use of his rational faculties.[4] The ensuing charge to his congregation accorded with his affirmation in an earlier sermon that although the rational faculties "be not naturally instruments of grace, yet they are susceptible of grace." The memory, understanding, and will "have much in their nature, that by grace they may be made instruments of grace: which no faculty to any creature, but man, may be." Thus, he warned, "doe not thinke that because a naturall man cannot doe all, therefore he hath nothing to doe for himselfe."[5] This view of man as a creature of both dignity and degradation is typical of Donne's paradoxical salvation theology, as is the idea that man must "tune the Instrument"[6] of his rational soul in order to respond to and prepare for the grace of God. Just as familiar is this application of theological distinctions to the interior life and the reliance on patristic learning to describe the psychology of spiritual effort.[7] These same concepts are central to the analysis of religious ascent and satirical decorum in *Satyre III*.

In the baptismal sermon, Donne's major concern was that man's rational faculties had "fallen into a third Trinity": "The *memory* [has fallen] into a weaknesse, that that comprehends not *God*, it glorifies him not for benefits received; The *reason* to a blindnesse, that that discernes not what is *true*; and the *will* to a perversnesse, that that wishes not what's *good*."[8] This is identical to the condition of Elizabethan devotion portrayed by the satirist in the third *Satyre*. The "worne maladies" that he ridicules and hopes to cure are the popular abuses by Elizabethans of the memory, understanding, and will. The brave adventurers, for example, those warriors who imprudently trek to the heights and depths of the physical world in pursuit of "gaine" (26), are characterized as men limited to expressions of their bodies only because of their failures to use the memory adequately. The sectarian lovers of religion, whose denominational choices are based on irrational and illogical prejudices, are portrayed as men who subvert the reason by determining what is "true" according to the dictates of only their emotions. And the officers and suitors of the court are viewed as men who maliciously manipulate the wills of others or allow their own wills to be manipulated unjustly. The three satirical portraits of the poem disclose how man's faculties have "fallen into [that] third Trinity" about which Dean Donne later complained.

At the same time, the satirist's own realizations about his duty as a Christian "Sentinell" (31), which he achieves in the process of his meditation, portray an exemplary exercise of man's "naturall faculties." The exhortations that follow his considerations of current abuses provide the fullest defense so far of the central principle of verse satire—*laus et vituperatio*. By exemplifying the exercise of "all our Soules devotion" (6), the use of all the faculties of the soul of which all men are capable, the satirist provides an option to the mental failures he anatomizes. His own satire becomes, then, a form of Christian "devotion" as well. The paradoxical combination of "Kinde pitty" for sinners and "brave scorn" for sins (1), the "zeal" he announces to be his emotional condition and impetus to satire, is evinced both by the charity shown to fallen men in counseling them how to recover spiritual sanity and by the hatred displayed for their habitual failures. His poem provides, in this way, a dramatic interpretation of "true religion" as the exertion of all man's faculties in the pursuit of Truth while exemplifying the methodology ("Kinde pitty" and "brave scorn") on which one can rely to actualize such "devotion."

Like the first two poems, *Satyre III* exhibits significant similarities to Roman verse satire. The major satiric strategy of the poem—the alternation of "pitty" and "scorn" towards pathetic and ignoble examples of misdevotion—is similar to Juvenal's attack on the vanity of human prayers in *Satire X*. Like Donne's attack on failures in personal devotion, the Roman satire castigates the spiritual myopia of Rome: "pauci dinoscere possunt / vera bona atque illis multum diversa." It, too, begins with a consideration of the appropriate satiric manner, debating whether Heraclitean tears or Democritean laughter is wiser: "de sapientibus alter / ridebat, quotiens de limine moverat unum / protuleratque pedem, flebat contrarius auctor."[9] Anderson points out that Juvenal finally settles on the latter mode, recommending a Senecan withdrawal from the irrationality of human society.[10] However, this Stoic resolution is confirmed only in the last verses; throughout the body of the satire, Juvenal's satirist dismisses neither stance but relies on both alternatively, respectively laughing and weeping over examples of human conduct. The downfall of Sejanus, for example, is treated as both tragic and ridiculous, depicted as the result of both the consul's achievement (58–62) and his inconsequentiality (63–71).[11] Discovering cause for both tragic irony and comic mockery in the *exempla* of figures such as Cicero, Demosthenes, Marius, Pompey, Silius, and Messalina, the satirist denounces and ridicules the self-destructiveness and comic vanity of human prayers for wealth, civil power, eloquence, military glory, longevity, and physical beauty.[12] Prayers for such ephemereal satisfactions lead men not to the discovery of "true *bona*," but to the tragicomic realization that "their engagement with inferior goals has been suicidal and plunged them inevitably towards misery and death."[13] It is best that they cease this presumptuous pursuit of worldly efflorescences and let the gods decide what they deserve:

Nil ergo optabunt homines? si consilium vis,
permittes ipsis expendere numinibus quid
conveniat nobis rebusque sit utile nostris.

If man should pray for anything, it is for virtue:

monstro quod ipse tibi possis dare; semita certe
tranquillae per virtutem patet unica vitae.

The same alternation and blending of the philosophical stances of these ancient "wise" men distinguish the manner of Donne's satirist in *Satyre III*. His "Kinde pitty" and "brave scorn" for the tragic folly of popular commitments to gold, honor, temporal satisfaction, and power by representative English types reaffirms Juvenal's censure of the quixotic bases of human desires. Laughing at his countrymen's comic ambitions and scorning their tragic misdevotion while exhorting them to realize "worthy" (6) moral alternatives, Donne's satirist provides in his own meditation a model of devotional *virtus*. Just as the Roman satirist concluded with a metaphoric *exemplum imitandum* (the Stoic Heracles)[14] that intimates how man can move beyond the tragedy and mockery of this world, so Donne's speaker concludes with a metaphoric plea for humble devotion that suggests how man can escape the spiritual suicide of those who "more chuse mens unjust / Power from God claym'd, then God himself to trust" (109–10). Juvenal's exhortation for man to trust in the divine and to seek the virtue of a sound mind is reiterated metaphorically and dramatically in *Satyre III*. And just as Juvenal's speaker, alternating between scorn and laughter, finally achieves and recommends a Senecan detachment from the outrages he describes, dramatizing in his own *rational* observations a tranquil distancing quite different from the emotional engagement of his earlier satires, so Donne's speaker, exhibiting the same alternating stances, provides an exemplary contrast to the examples of misdevotion he attacks through the meditative ordering of his own mental faculties. Both satirists actualize the *mens sana*, the humility and right reason, prerequisite for devotion, in their demonstrations of the imminent and perpetual destructiveness of human misdevotion. The similarities between *Juvenal X* and *Satyre III* suggest, then, that Donne's satire on "true religion" might well be an attempt to convert the Latin satire on the vanity of ambitious human prayers into a vehicle of Christian meditation: the obvious similarity of their opening presentations of the appropriate satiric stance is reinforced by their similarity of theme, argument, and conclusion.

Thus, as a satirical meditation on "true religion," as satire and devotion simultaneously, rather than leaving moot the question of satire's moral purpose, *Satyre III* dramatizes the "easie wayes and neare" (14) by which the satirist and mankind can "cure these worne maladies." As the *active* pursuit of Truth and assault against sin and the *contemplative* realization of the necessity and justice of such activities, the poem allows no separation of its satirical and devotional aims. It is the integration of the faculties of the rational soul and their zealous exercise both privately and publicly, moreover, that the poem illustrates to be the moral responsibility of man—the means by which he "tune[s] the Instrument" of his soul in order to prepare for God's grace.

i

Satyre III opens with the "Question" of a typical meditation—a consideration of "What [he] thinkes and should thinke"[15]—which also announces his satirical ethos and methodology:

> Kinde pitty chokes my spleene; brave scorn forbids
> Those teares to issue which swell my eye-lids;
> I must not laugh, nor weepe sinnes, and be wise,
> Can railing then cure these worne maladies?   (1–4)

The thrust of his announcement is that he must not laugh *only* at the habitual sins of his countrymen nor weep *only* for their failures. Rather, because these maladies are "worne," that is, habitual and therefore not easily displaced, he must both illustrate the moral idiocy of such practices (through ridicule—"brave scorn") and explain the need for and acceptability of healthy alternatives (through charitable exhortation—"Kinde pitty") in order to "be wise." In this sense, his oxymoronic urgings do not render him impotent as a satirist but dictate the form and method his railing must assume. In such a context "railing" takes on several connotations.[16] As the angry ridicule of ancient satire, it is a pejorative term here; but if "railing" means the combination of *laus et vituperatio* prescribed by Renaissance verse satire and, in this case, zealous charity for sinners and hatred for their sins, then it can posit a cure for the present age. Precisely such a form of railing—borrowed from Juvenal but accommodated to Christian principles—is employed by the satirist throughout the poem, as he follows each satirical portrait of a current mental failure with charitable instruction for overcoming that limitation.

The meditative *modus recolligendi* is extended by the satirist's consideration of the worth of what he and all men "should thinke":

> Is not our Mistresse faire Religion,
> As worthy'of all our Soules devotion,
> As vertue was to the first blinded age?
> Are not heavens joyes as valiant to asswage
> Lusts, as earths honour was to them?   (5–9)

The delineation of the present as the second blinded age and the contrast between the eternal rewards of devotion and the temporal insufficiency of virtue are native to Christian satire (with perhaps a glance back at Juvenal's defense of *virtus*); but the most significant phrase here is "all our Soules devotion." It denotes, on one hand, the satirist's concern with the soul of every man and, on the other, his concern that devotion entails the exercise of "all" of each man's soul, that is, all his rational faculties: memory, understanding, and will. His own exercise of the first of these faculties has already been initiated in his recollection of the "vertue" of the ancients, and continues in his recalling the imputation of Christ's love and the eventual judgment of man, which have been revealed by Scripture. The concomitant functions of his poem as both a meditation on religion and a satire on misdevotion are thus begun in the opening lines of the poem. And the general procedure followed in these lines—the satirist's reliance on one of the faculties of the rational soul in order to illustrate the value and necessity of "devotion" and to confirm the dangers of present practices—is followed throughout the remainder of the poem as the satirist ridicules a group of men for their mental abuses before describing a correct exercise of that faculty.

This modification of meditation into satire continues in the description of the Elizabethan adventures (13–42), which, in terms of the meditative scheme, is an ironic "Excussion: A repelling of what [he] should not thinke" (13–32), followed by a "Choice, or Election of what [is] most necessarie" (33–42). Both responses, the "brave scorn" he heaps on the "courage of straw" (28) of the adventurers and the "Kinde pitty" he offers to them by pointing out their true "foes" (30), emphasize the correct use of the memory. The meditator's "Preparation" is completed, in other words, by ridicule of abuses of the memory, issuing from the satirist's own exemplary use of his memory. The self-deceptive cowardice of the first group of fools in the poem, then, those worldly adventurers whose "valour[ous]" (16) searches for earthly "gaine" only "seeme bold" (29), contrasts directly with the speaker's exercise of his memory to discover the worth of devotion to God's glory.

Recalling the "vertue" of the ancients that merits them God's saving Grace and "heavens joyes," the imputation of Christ's love to those who have been able to "asswage / Lusts," and the value of fearing for one's salvation "in the end" (11), the satirist directs his assault at the imprudence of the valiant adventurers. The commitment of all their energies to merely physical action, he shows, results in and from their failure to use their memory correctly, in accordance with the claims of Cicero, Aquinas, Augustine, and Bernard that the healthy exercise of this faculty is essential to achieving prudence.[17] Obviously, such a view of the memory extends beyond the definition of it as mere recall. St. Bernard defines it, rather, as "all which wee know, although we thinke not of it."[18] The memory includes knowledge not only of what has happened to one in the past but of what the future portends, as revealed by

God's Revelation and the Books of Nature and Scripture.[19] Thus, the satirist's warning that the fathers of those who have failed in devotion shall "Meete blinde Philosophers in heaven . . . and heare / [Those sons] damn'd" (12–15) recalls knowledge of eternal Justice that the Book of Scripture provides. Since the memory "knows" our beginning and our end, our heavenly origins, divine image, and sinful inclinations, and the terms of our eventual salvation or damnation, man can refuse to apply this knowledge to his own condition and can choose not to remember what Providence has revealed to him, but no man can plead ignorance. As Donne said in one of his sermons on the Psalms, "*Plato* plac'd *all learning* in the memory; wee may place *all Religion* in the memory too. . . . All instruction, which we can give you to day, is but a remembring you of the mercies of God."[20] To continue, like the adventurers, to pursue only "earths honour" and to exhaust one's energies in the performance of social codes, "forbidden warres" of "gaine," and suicidal feats of physical daring, as if one's duty of devotion to God were not clear, amounts to imprudence. Such imprudence results from failure to "remember . . . the mercies [and justice] of God."

Therefore, the warriors who only "dare" the perils of the world "leave th'appointed field" of God's service by eschewing, in St. Bernard's words, "that which we knowe." They fail to use their memory. The description of their treks to regions of extreme heat and cold recalls, in fact, the warnings of Renaissance rhetoricians and psychologists that such extremes were harmful especially to the memory. They are the "two principal causes which hurte the memorie," writes Gratarolus. "Corruption [of this faculty] . . . commeth of over muche heat and drynes." "Forgetfulness," concurs Paulus Aegineta, "is the doughter of coldenes."[21] Spurred on merely by their desires, the adventurers' "courage of straw" is fittingly described, then, in merely physical terms. They dare to "*ayd* mutinous Dutch" (17), to "*lay* . . . in woodden Sepulchers" (17–18), to "*dive* seas, and dungeons of the earth" (20). They dare the "frozen North" (22) and "beare" the greatest physical extremity— all for temporal "gaine" and all without knowing or exploring their true role in God's "garrison" (31). Sister Geraldine points out that they exhibit a "lack of awareness [that] lead[s] to imprudent and improvident behavior,"[22] but their fullest significance, as contrasts to the satirist's own mental progress, is their failure to *know* and confront their true spiritual foes. The satirist's pleading exhortation to them ridicules both their failure to distinguish appearance from reality and also their improvident separation of God's will from their own; they fail to remember "who made thee" and for what purpose:

> O desperate coward, wilt thou *seeme* bolde, and
> To thy foes and his (who made thee to stand

Sentinell in his worlds garrison) thus yeeld,
And for forbidden warres, leave th'appointed field?

(29–32; italics added)

That Elizabethans did accomplish all these heroic deeds might, from one
context of values, suggest a paean to their tremendous daring and accom-
plishment.[23] But the ambiguity of that repeated verb "dar'st" (meaning "how
can you dare" as well as "have you dared")[24] and the imagery of death and
suicide that dominates these lines support the satirist's exasperated conclusion that such acts of physical prowess are actually "courage of straw," rash-
ness that amounts to physical and, more important, spiritual suicide.[25]

This attempt to stir the failed memory of the adventurers is supported
by the tone, allusions, and word choices of the satirist's derisive portrait.
The *memento mori* tone focuses on the mortality of man: his ships are mere
"Sepulchers," his body cannot withstand long the assault of the elements, his
own words are "poysonous," and his physical existence is the constant "prey
/ To leaders rage, to stormes, to shot, to dearth" (19). His "daring" adventures in the tropics in search of "gaine" are ironically compared to the example of Shadrack, Meshach, and Abednego, the "divine Children" who
survived through the grace of God the fires of the furnace into which Ne-
buchadnezzar cast them for their refusal to worship the golden image.[26] All
his actions, in fact, are described as descents and as evocative of his helplessness or precariousness ("dive," "lay," "cryes," "beare," "yeeld") in the "dungeons," "fires," and "ovens" of the fallen world—images which recollect the
individual insufficiency of man and the fires of hell promised the unregener-
ated soul. The satirist's mock encomium counsels, in other words, the recollection of central revealed facts about the human condition.

The truly brave man, he urges, is the Christian "Sentinell," the man who
recalls his origin in God and his eventual judgment by Him and therefore
weds his purpose to God's and remains steadfast to His "garrison." "The first
step towards devotion," St. Bernard points out, "is reached when a man,
with the fear of God before his eyes, *does not allow himself to forget*, but is ever
mindful of all God's precepts, *remembering* that such as contemn God fall into
hell for their sins and that life eternal awaits such as fear him."[27] "This feare,"
Donne's satirist advises, "great courage, and high valour is" (16). The adventurers are unable to achieve it because their memory has "fallen into a weakness . . . that comprehends not God, glorifies him not for benefits received."

Contrasted to the adventurers' weakness and misdevotion is the satirist's
own realization of man's true foes—the world, the flesh, and the devil. His
instructive "Know thy foes" (33), offered as a remedy for the adventurers'
plight, might appear to be an appeal to the understanding; but in terms of
Christian psychology, which views the memory as "all that we knowe," it is

actually a function of memory. As St. Bonaventure explains, "the function of the memory is to retain and re-present not only things present both corporeal and temporal but also things subject to succession whether simple or eternal. . . . This actual retention on the part of memory [is] of time, past, present and future."²⁸ In this sense, it is significant that the foes identified by the satirist are the old foes of man, the same three temptors identified in Christian apologetics as man's eternal enemies. His description is not a revelation that comes to him in his meditation on the basis of rational analysis, but is properly a personal application-explication of what is known already through God's Books. His metaphoric description is an application (a "Post-dating") of what he knows through memory.²⁹

The application of his recall continues the opening fair mistress metaphor of his meditation. The "foule Devill" is one who "for hate, not love, would allow / Thee faine, his whole Realme to be quit" (33–35). The world is "thy other lov'd foe" (37) and "a wither'd and worne strumpet" (39); and the flesh is actually given "joyes" only by "thy faire goodly soule" (41). Again, the emphasis is on what man should remember about his origin and end: the realm of hell that awaits the devil's lovers, the eventual end of a world of which "all parts wither away and passe" (36), and the immortal source of "joyes" for all men, the soul. The recollection of these crucial facts about man's condition in the spectrum of eternal time provides, then, an exhortative directive and viable alternative to the adventurers' imprudent, spiritual amnesia. And in the process of his exhortations, in the very act of exhorting the imprudent fools, the satirist displays that "Kinde pitty" for them as sinners and "brave scorn" for their sins—that charity for "our Mistresse faire Religion" and hatred for man's "foes"—which are the concomitant ingredients of true devotion.

ii

The second target of the speaker's satire is introduced in response to his meditative "Commemoration" ("An actuall thinking upon the matter elected")—"Seeke true religion" (43). Having used his memory to "know" the proper emotions for his poem and to establish the "worth" of his considerations, his understanding is evoked by his decision to search for the sources of "true" devotion. In accordance with St. Bernard's declaration that "wee attribute to the *Understanding*, all which we finde to bee true in thinking,"³⁰ the satirist describes the five lovers of religion (44–69) as suffering from that fall of "the *reason* to a blindnesse . . . that discerns not what's *true*." Their failure to seek the "hard knowledge" of the "mindes indeavours" (86–87) and to evaluate objectively the modern claimants of Truth amounts to the abuse of their understanding. Their "blindnesse," he quips, "too much light breeds" (68–69) and merits his ridicule not because of the practices of their specific sects but because of the lack of understanding underlying their individual choices. All five seem to have progressed beyond the moral cowardice of the adventurers—their having adopted religious stances connotes their awareness of the "worth" (or, in this case, the practical, political necessity) of religious devotion; but the fact that they rest smugly in the particular interpretation of devotion that they find most satisfying personally, most suitable to their emotions and "humors" (53), reveals that their aims are temporal "gaine" also. The satirist's meditative "Explanation" ("A clearing of the thing considered by similitudes"), then, concerns typical abuses of the understanding by his contemporaries, relying on ironic comparisons between the choice of a wife and the selection of a sectarian "Mistresse."

That these religious amorists suffer from failures or abuse of the understanding in their reliance on their sensitive souls alone is suggested, again, by the satirist's diction. Mirreus, "*Thinking* [true religion] unhous'd here . . . / Seekes her at Rome . . . because hee doth *know* / That shee was there" (43–46); Crants "loves her onely, who'at Geneva's *call'd* / Religion" (50–51); Graius "stayes still" on the basis of what "vile ambitious bauds" and recent laws "*bid him thinke*" (55–57); and "Carelesse" Phrygius and Graccus have both ceased the search for true religion because of extreme and fallacious generalizations and liberal opinions. Their "errours in the understanding," which Donne identified in his sermons as the cause of religious errors,[31] correspond to that abuse of reason Augustine called *scientia*, knowledge only of this world, in contrast to *sapientia*, knowledge of the next world as well.[32] Trying to recognize the Bride of Christ by her clothes,[33] temporary housings, friends, or appearances, these amatory sectarians fail to use their understanding, strive to satisfy only their own emotional needs, and conclude the search for Truth by adoring or hating mere signs.

Mirreus, for example, worships authority more than Truth and looks to Rome "because hee doth know / That shee was there a thousand yeares agoe" (45–46). Satisifed with this tropological view of tradition, this partial, temporal truth, he ends up loving "her ragges so, as wee here obey / The statecloth where the Prince sate yesterday" (47–48). Crants is equally illogical, depicted as comparable to a masochist who is "inthrall'd" (49) by only the ugliest of women, "judg[ing] / No wenches wholsome, but course country drudges" (53–54). Graius, on the other hand, chooses practically by embracing "such [a wife] as [his] Guardians offer" in order to avoid "Pay[ing] valewes" (61–62). His "values" do, of course, "pay" because of his mental sloth, for, like the other religious amorists, he values only what he can see, realize, or compute easily. Enthralled by the temporal world and its partial, momentary truths, each of the figures in the satirist's wry anatomy is unwilling (or unable) to see the ultimate insufficiency of the single dictum which he embraces. Directed by their humors, satisfied with sensual perceptions of the world, they are unable to distinguish what is temporary from what is sacred and eternal.

The grotesque irony of their failures is that each of them seems to realize one aspect of the complex dialectic of "devotion."[34] Mirreus seems to understand the value of tradition ("aske thy father which is shee, / Let him aske his" [71–72]), but rests in superstition through his failure to inquire beyond this one verity. Crants seems to realize that "mysteries / Are . . . plaine to'all eyes" (87–88) in his preference for a religion that is "plaine," but misapplies his criterion absurdly. Graius seems to understand the need to search for her who is "onely perfect" (58), but relents too easily to the appeal of "fashions" (57). Phrygius is full of doubt, but does not "doubt wisely" (77); his decision to "stand inquiring right" (78) results only in a denial of the existence of "right." Likewise, Graccus, who seems to understand the value of religious tolerance ("to'adore, or scorn . . . / May all be bad"), fails to understand that "unmoved thou / Of force must one, and forc'd but one allow" (69–70).

In contrast to the emotional scientism of these five whimsically uncritical lovers is the satirist's declaration of the difficult nature of the search for Truth. In his meditative "Tractation" he realizes that a vigilant understanding is essential to such a task: "To stand inquiring right, is not to stray; / To sleepe, or runne wrong, is" (78–79). And such uncompromising inquiry makes "doubt" necessary, as elaborated by the "Dijudication" and "Causation"[35] of his meditation—the famous metaphor of the hill of Truth:

> On a huge hill,
> Cragged, and steep, Truth stands, and hee that will
> Reach her, about must, and about must goe;
> And what th'hills suddennes resists, winne so;
> Yet strive so, that before age, deaths twilight,
> Thy Soule rest, for none can worke in that night. (79–84)

Although the attainment of Truth may appear awesomely impossible ("Cragged, and steep"), she can be reached, the satirist exhorts. More important, whether certain of her attainment or not, one must aspire to possess her by a continuous mental quest ("winne so; / Yet strive")—by the effort of an unrelenting understanding. Unlike the myopic lovers who require immediate, tangible benefits in the search for Truth, the satirist is able to maintain apparent contradictions in his mind and to distinguish the "worth" of eternal truths from the measure of temporal and spatial circumstances. The worth and necessity of this mental pilgrimage is confirmed by the seventh of his nine references in the poem to man's eventual end,[36] echoing this time the admonition of St. John that man "must work the works of him that sent me, while it is day: the night cometh, when no man can work" (John 9:4). Under the aegis of eternity, the satirist accepts both the limitation and potential of his rational powers as the legacy of fallen man, and views the perplexities of mortal insecurity as an impetus to his struggling understanding of an object worthy of his love.

Several humanist sources have been suggested for the "huge hill [of] Truth" metaphor here, most of which had become commonplaces by Donne's time.[37] What has not been discussed, however, is the manner in which this image depicts the mental movement of the pilgrim of Truth as well as the shape of the hill. In this sense, the most significant aspect of Donne's figure is the spiral motion of the pilgrim up and around the hill, which is enforced by both the diction and syntax of Donne's image. The alternation of short phrases ("on a huge hill"—"Cragged, and steep"—"and hee that will") around the strong spondee "Truth stands" connotes the circular path of the seeker. These are reinforced by the explicit description in the following line, which repeats that struggling, uneven alternation of rhythms ("Reach her"—"about must"—"and about must goe"). This vivid metrical presentation of the circularity of the eternal hill and, more important, the circling of it by the rational soul in pursuit of Truth is combined with a view of the mind's progress horizontally and rectilinearly in the next line, in which the long clause describing the height of the hill—"And what th'hills suddennes resist"—is offset by the short, imperative "winne so." It is the combination of these two lines that produces the most significant effect and meaning of the image. The circular progress up the hill in combination with the gradual rectilinear ascent by the pilgrim images that spiral motion which ancient, medieval, and Renaissance philosophy alike delineated as the movement peculiar to the rational soul of man.[38]

In the dramatic context of the poem, this description of the spiral motion of the rational quest for Truth strengthens the contrast between the love of the speaker and the brute instinct of the figures he has ridiculed. The adventurers, for example, go to the North, to the South, and all across the flat map of the world in their "forbidden warres." But their activities are only serpentine rectilinear movements, the simplest and lowest form of movement, germane on a universal scale to the realm of matter alone. Likewise, the amorists attempt no ascent. Their emotional flights to Rome, Geneva, London, nowhere and anywhere, duplicate the rectilinear motions of the adventurers. The speaker's recommendation of a gradual, spiraling ascent towards the circle of eternal Truth provides a direct contrast, then, with the fugacious motions or inactivity of these men. That the ultimate and eternal success of such an endeavor does involve the participation of God's grace is suggested by the location of Truth on a high hill, traditionally "the scenes of theophanies, where God reveals Himself to man."[39] But the emphasis of the image is on what man's rational soul can do to earn and to prepare for such enlightenment. "Hard knowledge too / The mindes indeavours reach," the satirist concludes, "and mysteries / Are like the Sunne, dazling, yet plaine to'all eyes" (86–88).[40] In accordance with ancient and Christian descriptions of the rational soul's motion as the harmony of man's body and soul, the emblem of his perfection as a creature of rectilinear duration and the circle of eternity, the satirist's description of the movement up the "huge hill [of] Truth" as spiral motion focuses on what man's reason can and must do to achieve "true religion." The hill can be won and man one with God through His Son, the satirist confirms.

Once again, then, Donne's satirist integrates *laus et vituperatio*, here in the implicit contrast of the lovers' abuse of understanding with his own exercise of reason. His mental journey beyond the limited conclusions of the sectarian amorists to the establishment, recognition, and amorous quest of timeless values dramatizes the ability of reason to initiate the reconstruction of an eternal union with God. His clearsighted vision of the type of action germane to man's paradoxical condition exposes the culpable sloth of doctrinal controversy, sectarian intolerance, and all myopic failures of understanding. The use of his reason to discover the values and aims of reason, in addition to bespeaking that timeless union with the Creator of his understanding, provides a laudable alternative to the dissonant quibbles and blind illogicality of the rationally asleep sectarians.

iii

One of the features of the satirist's exhortations throughout *Satyre III* is their simultaneous function as critiques of popular religious practices. Donne's life-long contempt for religious controversy (and, at this time, his recusant sensibility) is noticeable even in this early poem in his wry derision of the *political* motivations of human devotion.[41] At one point, for example, Donne's speaker counsels that the pilgrim of Truth "unmoved . . . / Of force must one [religion], and forc'd but one allow." In one sense, his words prescribe the necessity of choosing "the right" religion, that one is obliged to find, or to quest lovingly and absolutely after, the one absolute Truth. At the same time, his advice ridicules contemporary religious intolerance by which one is "forc'd [to] allow" the wisdom of a particular sect whether one is "mov'd," stirred, or convinced by its doctrine or not. The same type of rich ambiguity and multiple evocation dominates the third section of the poem, especially in the evaluation of the nature, effects, and sources of human and divine power.

This concluding section, concerned with the abuses and functions of the will, does not follow the elaborate seven-stage procedure through the affections prescribed by Mauburnus-Hall as closely as does the meditative scheme in the earlier sections of the poem. Instead, the speaker, in accord with his satiric methods, provides a portrait of the abuses of will by his contemporaries (89–99) and follows it with an exhortation to their wills and his own (100–110). His final appeal does conform to the features of a conventional colloquy, framed in this case not as a prayer to God but as a metaphoric description of the dangers of failing to seek and to submit to (and therein not participating in the gracious beneficence of) His infinite will. An affective metaphor of the nature of temporal and eternal Power, the concluding image of the poem does aim "with the freedom of our will [to] draw forth sundry Affections, or vertuous Actes, conformable to that which the Understanding hath meditated . . . [such as] resignation of our selves to the Will of God."[42] Thus, this final "act of self-immolation" fulfills the simultaneous meditative and satiric stance of the speaker, providing an imaginative contrast between "idolat[rous]" (102) submission to the "tyrannous" (106), unjust forces of power in the world and the humility required of Christian devotion. The satirist clarifies his strategy for concluding with this metaphoric colloquy by his disclosure of the fall of "the *will* to a perverseness, that that wishes not what's *good*."

His consideration of the function of the will in the present state of misdevotion focuses on the current state of justice in England. Justice, after all, is both external and internal. As Aristotle points out,

> Metaphorically and in virtue of a certain resemblance there is a justice, not indeed between a man and himself, but between certain parts of him; yet not every kind of justice but that of master and servant or that of husband and wife. For these are the ratios in which the part of the soul that has a rational principle stand to the irrational part; and it is with a view to these parts that people also think a man can be unjust to himself, viz. because these parts are liable to suffer something contrary to their respective desires; there is therefore thought to be a mutual justice between them as between ruler and ruled.[43]

St. Thomas' elaboration supports this view of justice as internal order:

> Justice, by its nature, implies a cetain rectitude of order. . . . First, inasmuch as it implies a right order in man's act, . . . thus justice is placed among the virtues. . . . Secondly, justice is so called inasmuch as it implies a certain rectitude of order in the interior disposition of a man, in so far as what is highest in man is subject to God, and the inferior parts of the soul are subject to the superior, i.e., to the reason.[44]

Justice is the inner rule of the reason of the soul, the ordination of the will by the dictates of the reason. Thus, the satirist's evaluation of the current habits of men in the realm of justice, of the willful manipulation or willing submission of their wills to "mens unjust / Power" (109–10), provides a rational and practical guide for men to avoid those subversions of the will that amount to spiritual self-betrayal. The final cure for such "idolatrie" that he realizes—"God himselfe . . . trust" (110)—announces that reasonable and just conclusion by which man can achieve both justice in the world and justice in his soul. And, again, the internal and external, the private and public actions of man are seen to be inevitably yoked: to act justly to achieve devotion in the world, one must attain and maintain an internal justice among the rational faculties. This is the imperative to the will that begins and concludes the "*gradus processorii, voluntaris*" of his meditation: "Keepe the truth which thou'hast found" (89)—"trust . . . God himselfe."

To achieve this order within oneself and to employ one's will correctly, the satirist counsels, one must distinguish the origin and end of all human power. "Men do not stand / In so'ill case here," he explains, "that God hath with his hand / Sign'd Kings blanck-charters to kill whom they hate" (89–91). The application of Psalm 82[45] and the legal terms here recall the eternal charter or covenant that man has with God, but the emphasis of the lines is that the covenant God "hath with his hand" made with man is one of love—love of Him and of one's neighbors. Men of power, then, may be God's vicars, but even so are only "hangmen to Fate" (92) who violate their charge when they administer in hatred instead of love. It is not men's opinions that rule the world finally, after all, but God's Providence; and he who considers his "Soule [to] be ty'd / To mans lawes, by which she shall not be try'd / At the last day" is a "Foole and wretch" (93–95). God is not only the original source of all power in the world but also the final power man must face. Those who allow their souls to be manipulated by the hangmen of the world misdirect their devotion.

The satirist's emphasis on the direction of the will by eternal standards is continued in his final rhetorical question, in which he strips King Philip, Pope Gregory, King Henry VIII, and Martin Luther of their temporal authority in order to view them as they shall be examined on "the last day":

> Will it then boot thee
> To say a Philip, or a Gregory,
> A Harry, or a Martin taught thee this?
> Is not this excuse for mere contraries,
> Equally strong? cannot both sides say so? (95–99)

Kings, popes, and reformers, Protestant and Catholic alike, are only men in God's eyes. To appraise Truth only by their standards or to trust solely in their apparent power is no excuse for willfully failing to defend the truth that has been revealed to or achieved by one. Committing oneself exclusively to sectarian and international struggles amounts to the assignment of one's will to "mere contraries," to struggles that are mere temporal battles and contrary to the interest of one's soul: "That thou may'st rightly'obey power, her bounds know" (100).

Praise and blame, exhortation and ridicule of correct and incorrect acts of the will are also combined in the concluding metaphoric description of "Soules" as "blest flowers." A directive to see the desperate foolishness of men who "chuse mens unjust / Power from God claym'd, then God himselfe to trust," the satirist's metaphor counsels humility. Established in his earlier definition of "idolatrie" as being humble to limited forms of power and temporal agents of Power, the perversions of will attacked here are contrasted to the humility dramatized by the satirist himself. His concluding effort to stir the will of his reader (and himself) to accept the correct attitude towards Power provides a final instance of his exemplary use of his mental faculties to "cure these worne maladies." This metaphor of souls as flowers, a colloquy to himself and his audience, urges recognition of the foolishness of men who resign their wills to the imperial and ecclesiastical tyrants of this world:

> As streames are, Power is; those blest flowers that dwell
> At the rough streames calme head, thrive and prove well,
> But having left their roots, and themselves given
> To the streames tyrannous rage, alas, are driven
> Through mills, and rockes, and woods,'and at last, almost
> Consum'd in going, in the sea are lost:
>> So perish Soules, which more chuse mens unjust
>> Power from God claym'd, then God himselfe to trust. (103–10)

Part of the complexity of this passage resides in its function both as a laudatory description of the attributes of divine Power and as a satirical warning about the practices of temporal power. On one level, it explains how power functions in the world, how temporal power, issuing from and condoned by divine Power, can benefit those who dwell within its boundaries—an amplification of the commonplace Renaissance defense of "right order."[46] Kings are God's vicars and are to be obeyed. Man must keep the "truth which [he] hast found" but must understand his limitations, the bounds of his condition, and should not allow himself to be led improvidently into rebellion against His agents. They who obey them are "blest" and do "thrive and do well." But, at the same time, the analogy warns those who claim that their "unjust / Power" is ordained by God; He did not give them power so that they could "kill whom they hate." Thus, men who worship "unjust / Power" that claims God's ordination are committing "idolatrie." Man must not only know that all temporal power eventually comes from God, but also that "unjust / Power" is not of God's ordination and should not be called power but tyranny; her bounds "past, her nature, and name is changed." Such men, however, have no power here, in issues of the soul.

In addition to suggesting that those who obey just forms of power will be "blest" and will "thrive and do well," these terms, as descriptions of mere temporal honors and temporal wealth, connote the speaker's awareness of the nepotism and favoritism that often exist in courts. In this sense, the analogy is satirical (and perhaps quasi-autobiographical). It ridicules the manner in which power is too often used to benefit only favorites in one's own household or coterie; those in power often reward, protect, and allow to thrive only those who dwell or agree with them (especially as in the persecution and prosecution of recusants). As a description of the power of this world and its bounds, its limitations, and its failures, then, the metaphor defends the God-ordained order of the world, criticizes the unjust use of power and its abuse for the benefit of one's friends and supporters, and denounces any form of secular or religious tyranny.

At the same time, this concluding analogy details the attributes of the power of God. In this sense, it strengthens the satirist's appreciation that true devotion rests on understanding man's relationship to God and that individual destructive inconstancy comes from failure to submit one's will to God. The appellation of "blest" to the flowers that dwell there, like Christian "Sentinells," recalls the joys experienced through the adoration of one's own soul (which amounts to love of God) and the "heavens joyes" of those with the "great courage, and high valour" to fear damnation and trust in "God himselfe." In fact, the observation that souls dwelling in continual trust in God do "thrive and do well" suggests that such trust may lead to the "cure for these worne maladies" for which the speaker has been searching.

Nonetheless, the satirist's concentration is less on the heavenly joys of those who reside with God than on the tribulations and eventual destruction awaiting those who refuse "God himselfe to trust." The view of the same stream able to bless man's soul and capable also of destructive rage suggests both the wrath of God (already exhibited in one "rage" of water, the Flood) and the tribulations to which the "idolatrous" soul submits itself in humbling before temporal powers. As Donne declared, in one of his sermons on the Psalms, "the Holy Ghost . . . abounds in no Metaphor more, then in calling Tribulations, *Waters*. . . . Neither doth he onely intimate temporall, but spirituall afflictions too, in the name of *Waters*" (IX, 328–29). The course of the erring flowers "Through mills, and rockes, and woods" intimates that the world offers only tribulations and destruction for those who misplace their trust. The purpose of the water imagery here is to effect that willful trust in the Justice of Him who is the source of all power and all life in the world. If the water in which foolish souls are "almost / Consum'd in going" is the world of tribulations where fallen man struggles, the grace of God that can save him from that "streame" is intimated by the words "blest" and "well." More concerned with the "rootless flowers" of the world (those that "dwell / At the rough streames calme head" do not need to be "cured"), the satirist stresses that the exercise of Power is "rough" and that men's souls "perish" and "are lost" by failing to "know" the bounds of Power. His view of Power as a stream that can either bless or destroy man, according to where he places his trust and toward whom he submits his will, evokes once more, then, the Christian view of God's providential Mercy and Justice.

The speaker's affective reading of God's Book of Nature to learn the bounds of his own and all men's power, coupled with his observations on the natural chain of being—especially the human link—significantly concludes his rational search to understand his power as satirist and man. The final image shows God's Mercy and Justice as well as the satirist's own zeal. Yet, at the same time, his own progress through the "naturall faculties" that led to this revelation seems to answer the opening question, "Can railing then cure these worne maladies?" The cure, his poem suggests, is exercise of the mental attitude that is religion. That involves the just and healthy integration of one's rational faculties, entailing hatred of one's eternal enemies, love of man's eternal soul, and trust in the ultimate Power of all time. ("Wit [must not] / Be colleague to religion," Donne later told the Countess of Bedford, "but be it.") Having pressed beyond the doubts about satire as a "sinne against [his] conscience" and its ineffectiveness even as a "Good worke," the satirist has found a divine analogue to sanctify his zeal. Satire, then, is a form of religious devotion for the satirist of "Kinde pitty" and "brave scorn." He ridicules those people ignorant of the worth of devotion, stupid concerning what such devotion entails, or malicious in abusing such devotion or in manipulating others so that they cannot realize it. This ridicule provides a dramatic example of the "easie wayes and neare" by which they may cure themselves. Satirically, the poem attacks that "third trinity" into which man has fallen because of the abuse of his "Soules devotion." At the same time, the satirist's beneficial use of those faculties of his soul provides not only a methodology for religious regeneration but an illustration of the devotional exercise of "all our Soules" faculties.

Therefore, to restrict one's reading of *Satyre III* to either the devotional or the rhetorical aspects of the satirist's voice is to overlook its most significant characteristic—its union of private and public discourse, its concomitant meditative and satirical stance. As a meditation on "true religion," the poem dramatizes the internal process on which man's active life must be based. As a satire spoken to a general Elizabethan audience, its ridicule of fallacious and inadequate mental efforts is the dynamic actualization of the speaker's private conclusions. The speaker's own successful integration of his mental faculties and of his contemplative and active lives exemplifies that healthy integrity that is the cure for both private and public failures in devotion to "our Mistresse faire Religion."

In one of his verse letters roughly contemporaneous to his *Satyres*,[47] Donne, after referring to his "Satyrique thornes" (5), which may have accompanied the letter, advised Mr. Rowland Woodward that "There is no Vertue, but Religion" (16):

Seeke wee then our selves in our selves;

. . . .

So wee, if wee into our selves will turne,
Blowing our sparkes of vertue, may outburne
The straw, which doth about our hearts sojourne.

. . . .

Wee are but farmers of our selves, yet may
If we can stocke our selves, and thrive, uplay
Much, much deare treasure for the great rent day.

(19, 21–24, 31–33)

The imagery of this *nosce teipsum* counsel is remarkably similar to that of the third *Satyre*: true religion is equated with dynamic self-knowledge. And the cultivation of the self that the speaker of *Satyre III* undergoes and advises for all men wishing to thrive both now and on "the great rent day" of Judgment dramatizes the process and content of that "Vertue" Donne advised his friend to achieve. For Donne's satirist, the cure for which he searches is one with the mode of discovery itself. The exertion of all the "mindes indeavours" in the pursuit of Truth demands both hatred of the failure that results from inactivity ("brave scorn" for sins) and devotion to the pursuit itself ("Kinde pitty" for one's soul and the souls of others). Such exertion is the central character and method of satire and religion. Each of these demands recognition not only of one's fallen state in the providential universe but also of the need to hate sins and love sinners; each demands the regeneration of the mind that is the only cure for misdevotion. Satire *is* religion in *Satyre III*. Thus, the poem dramatizes the satirist's realization of the artistic and moral rectitude of the zeal recommended for Donne's age. The testing of this personal stance in the dangerous arena of Elizabethan politics and religion is the subject of the next *Satyre*, but in this poem Donne's' satirist has at least achieved a private realization of the devotional character of his public role as satirist.

CHAPTER FOUR

The Satirist as Traitor

I am the man that hath seen affliction by the rod of his wrath.

Lamentations 3:1

The superiority of Donne's third *Satyre* to his first two and to other contemporary English verse satire cannot be denied. Nor can the timelessness of its portrait of man's unending struggle for truth. The description of *wise doubt* in that poem might well serve, in fact, not just as an emblem of "the mindes indeavours" central to all Donne's poetry, but also as a speaking picture of the quest for truth and beauty fundamental to all poetic experience. Nevertheless, the nearly exclusive critical attention paid to *Satyre III* has had one regrettable effect—neglect of the excellence of *Satyre IV*. Several readers have noted recently that *Satyre IV* does merit fuller attention: K. W. Gransden, for example, calls it "the longest and most powerful of Donne's Satires"; Bald says it is "the most brilliant of them all, . . . a brilliant display of wit and high spirits"; and Ejner Jensen describes it as Renaissance satire "at its brilliant best."[1] However, except for Erskine-Hill's discussion of its elements of Horatian imitation and Geraldine's perceptive comments on its anagogical perspective, *Satyre IV* has received only scant critical attention, mostly in unflattering comparisons with Pope's "versification."[2]

Actually, *Satyre IV* provides a fuller view of Donne's opinion of the genre than *Satyre III*. A dramatic meditation on the satirist's fearful experiences at the Elizabethan Presence Chamber, it tests and expands the view of satire-as-religion in the previous poem, concluding that satire is not only a form of Christian devotion but, more important, a perilous, even dangerous, celebration of and participation in the unfolding of the Word. On one level, the poem recounts the satirist's responses to the "wretchednesse" (156) he "spyed" (237) during two visits to the court. His retrospective dramatization shows how those experiences clarified for him both his precarious position as a fallen man in the theatre of God's judgments and his fearful duty as a Christian satirist who is obliged to confront and expose the extremities of "puft Nobility" (164) even if it means risking the charge of treason. At the same time, the meditative satirist's typological interpretations of his adventures at court signify the spiritual as well as the literal dimensions of his situation. The court, he reveals, is a hellish prefiguration of the *poeni damni* awaiting those who fail their obligation to God; an ironic reminder of man's bondage to death *aera sub lege*, its daily routine realizes the spiritual vacuity and moral sickness that prefigure and exist in hell. Described as a corporealized travesty of religious rites and emblems, it is the "destinie" (11) of those fallen men who, like the satirist during his first visit, act as if ignorant of their role in a providential universe. Fortunately, however, the satirist's experiences have also revealed the spiritual significances of his satiric role. His own potentially traitorous fulfillment of his duty to his "Mistresse Truth" (163) is presented as a type of *effectus passionis*, as a daring (238) response to the unfolding of the Word in the world, and as an exemplary fulfillment of man's duty *aera sub gratia*.[3] Thus, the poem explains, the satirist's own fortunate fall into the hellish "jaw" (132) of the court has served as a "Purgatorie" (3) for him; the "hand-writing" of God in his adventures has revealed the continuing imputation of God's grace to His fallen Creation and the manner in which satire can be a "Canonicall" (244) witness to this redemptive power of the Word in man's life. In *Satyre IV*, then, the largely *private* stance of the previous poem is expanded into an examination of the problematic *public* role of the satirist *sub specie aeternitatis*.

The poem also offers Donne's boldest commentary on his own situation in the 1590s through its equivocal but consistent glances at the predicament of the Catholic in Elizabethan England. Like Sidney's delightfully "rich" sonnets of *Astrophel and Stella*, in which the poet displays "fact as fiction [and] uses fact to explore the nature of love,"[4] in the fourth *Satyre* Donne subtly weaves controversial and dangerous aspects of his own recusancy into the fabric of his examination of the rhetorical and moral bases of Christian satire. Conveyed largely through incriminatory comparisons of Anglican hypocrisy and Catholic devotion, this subject never becomes the major thesis of the poem. Nevertheless, the result is a much stronger critique of the Elizabethan Establishment than the cryptic derision of the Anglican doctrine of justification and severity toward papists in the second *Satyre*, and a bolder stance than the implicit plea for religious tolerance in the third *Satyre*. Here Donne applies the central contention of the recusant apologists—that they were being persecuted for religion and not for treason—to his evaluation of the satirist's dangerous obligations to Truth. In recounting the satirist's confrontation with pursuivant trickery and self-serving debasements of religious gestures in the court,[5] he identifies the satirist's own imitation of Christian types and antetypes as an exemplary contrast to the pernicious forms of imitation that dominate the Presence Chamber. The satirist's own conduct, he admits, may be termed treasonous, just as the recusant was termed "Traytor" (131) and "Spie" (237) by the legal machinery and "Giant Statutes" (132) of Elizabethan England. But such a threat, he urges, cannot intimidate him into abandoning his much more awesome commitment to his "Mistresse Truth." Thus, in *Satyre IV*, the personal situation of the poet as political and religious outsider is recast in terms of the central dictum of Christian humanism—*imitatio christi*; and the role of the satirist is evaluated in terms of his role in the divine cosmic drama. Like the recusant, the satirist might be accused of treason against the state; he might even end up on Tyburn Hill. But such a menacing possibility cannot detract him from his dedication to the imitation of Christ's passion and sacrifice. In addition to being his fullest exploration of the duties and dangers of satire, then, the fourth *Satyre* also offers a provocative appraisal of Donne's own situation as heir to that "suppressed and afflicted Religion"[6] of his famous forefathers. How the poet was able to respond artistically to that situation, transforming the particulars of his own situation into a dramatic anatomy of satire, is part of the brilliant achievement of the poem.

Abundant in that "aggressive vitality," "radical play of mind," and "purposeful mental resource"[7] that have gained praise for Donne's most famous poems, *Satyre IV* deserves equal acclaim for its structural and imagistic design. The witty portraits and penetrating ridicule of courtly vice common to verse satire are here at their best, especially in the transformation of the ubiquitous bore of Horatian satire into a Renaissance malcontent traveler, sinister spy, and agent provocateur who embodies the court's disregard for meaningful gesture and expression. But the major achievement of the poem is the manner in which it satisfies both the rhetorical requirements of verse satire and the moral injunctions of Christian ethics by embodying the moral and aesthetic principles it defends. As such, it shows Donne's fullest and most audacious transformation of the ancient satirical techniques into zealous Christian satire.

i

Satyre IV is the longest, the most complex, the most comprehensive of the five poems, its narrative complicated by the conflation of horizontal and vertical levels of discourse, its unity complicated by diverse strands of imagery. It is important to clarify the narrative complexity of the poem first. Framed as a traditional *meditatio mortis*, the poem falls into five sections: an introduction (1–4) and conclusion (237–44) spoken from the dramatic present moment, and three central sections of retrospective analysis, which recount and evaluate the satirist's adventures prior to the time of the poem. After the opening four lines, the satirist composes a dramatic critique of his first visit to the court (5–154), an adaptation/modification of Horace's *Satire I.ix*. This is followed by an analysis (155–74) of the Dantean trance (157) into which he fell when he ran from court to the "wholesome solitarinesse" (155) of his home, which in turn is followed by a description of his second visit to court (175–237), and by the closing eight lines, the fullest estimate of his experiences and what they taught him about his role as a satirist.

The first two recollected events, then, reveal how the satirist's action (first visit) led to meditation (the trance). Such was the pattern of the first three *Satyres*, which are meditative evaluations of his encounters with fops, lawyers, and religious fakes. In *Satyre IV*, however, that pattern is expanded. The satirist's return to the court "the second / Time" (177–78) illustrates how, in this case, meditation led to renewed action. The significance of this pattern is explicated by the opening and closing sections. In the opening *nunc dimittis* passage he explains that these experiences have purged him of the idle curiosity and moral cowardice he exhibited during the first visit to court. The final colloquy expands this personal perspective by suggesting, on the one hand, that while his satire is only an attempt "To washe the staines away" (241) of his former errors, it is, at the same time, comparable to the "Wit and Arts" of "Preachers" (237–38) and ought to be "esteeme[d] Canonicall" (244). The structure of the poem, then, presents satire as a form of meditative action: the satirist's meditation is a verbal extension and enactment of his role as a devotee to his "Mistresse Truth" and participates in some important manner in the divine immanence. To appreciate the foundations of such an *exquisitia scrutatio*, we need to look closely at the terms in which it is unfolded in each section of the poem.

As suggested above, the first third of the poem returns (like *Satyre I*) to the plot of Horace's humorous account of entrapment by a sycophantic *garrulus* on the *Sacra via*. Donne's speaker "went to Court" and was "forc'd" by his "destinie" to "suffer" the unwanted companionship of a nebulous "Makeron" who knows no language except "complement." There are more verbal echoes of the Latin satire here, especially in the broad military imagery, which was replaced by the marriage analogy in the first *Satyre*; but the comic tone of Horace's mock epic[8] *sermo* disappears almost altogether in Donne's tense dramatization of the satirist's perilous misadventures with this salacious Elizabethan courtier. In the Latin poem the bore was attracted by the satirist's friendship with the powerful Maecenas, and finally was fortuitously dispatched by the arrival of the bore's adversary in a law suit: "sic me servavit Apollo," Horace's satirist facetiously concluded. The English bore, on the other hand, presents a real threat to the physical well-being of the satirist, assumes much more than a merely circumstantial relationship to him, and can be dispersed only by a bribe: his "needy want" is satisfied by "the prerogative of my Crowne" (149–50), the English satirist sarcastically concludes. Also, whereas Horace's "unwilling warrior" was able to disarm the "meaningless verbosity" of the bore with satiric ridicule,[9] Donne's satirist discovers that his seemingly innocent verbal duel with this Elizabethan popinjay could have cost him his life.[10] If the bore is, as the poem intimates, a "priviledg'd spie" (119) or agent provocateur, then the satirist could have been named "Traytor" (131) as a result of this trial.

Thus, on one level, the English satirist's description of his encounter with this absurd but menacing comic type offers a tacit criticism of the conversational method of the Horatian satiric stance. In this case, the satirist's adoption of the ironic urbanity and witty repartee of the classical satirist only prolonged and accentuated his discomfort and susceptibility to more severe harm. In *Satyre I* the application of this approach led to nothing worse than comic betrayal by the fop's inconstancy; but it proves totally inadequate and potentially dangerous to the satirist in the malicious atmosphere of the Presence Chamber. The initial concern of the satirist's recollections raises formally, then, one of the overriding issues of the entire poem—satire as an act of imitation. Horace proves a precarious model for the Christian satirist at court. The reasons for and ramifications of the satirist's implicit rejection of this ancient type of satiric discourse are clarified by the changes Donne makes in the *adversarius* borrowed from his classical model.

One more note about the design of Donne's poem is necessary first, however. The Horatian model is followed only in the first third of the poem. As the opening reference to the Four Last Things signals,[11] *Satyre IV* is cast as a *meditatio mortis*, in which the satirist's encounter with the court bore is framed as a composition of place. Thus, the satirist's description of that experience is complicated by the confluence of horizontal and vertical levels of discourse. Both his original, limited responses to the bore and his present, clearsighted understanding of its significance are presented simultaneously. In order to measure the relative value of his experience and his meditation on that experience one must distinguish between the satirist's original and his present reactions to the court bore. The former shows the pitiful condition of fallen man without God's intervening grace, the latter his fortunate situation as the benefice of His eternal grace. Such a distinction also clarifies the satirist's final claim that his satire is "Canonicall"—by showing how and why his meditative account of his re-creation (8) as a satirist by God's grace was both personal and apocalyptic, both an individual type of the Passion and a providential exemplification of the *effectus passionis* that imputes salvation to men. In this sense, his account of his first visit to the court exposes the satirist's initial, limited understanding of his entrapment by the punishing sycophant. Not only did he misunderstand the motives of the bore, he also failed to appreciate the providential design of that experience. The bore, as an embodiment and probably even a legal agent of the court, figured forth the bondage of man *aera sub lege* and the suffering of Christ that liberated man from that bondage. The meditative satirist's corrected response to that painful entrapment, his typological interpretation of it in the poem, on the other hand, exemplifies how the hand of God in that visit served to "re-create" or save the satirist by revealing his own mortal condition as man and as satirist. Thus, the dual perspective of this section of the poem presents the paradoxical condition of man as the subject of both nature and grace. The horizontal perspective—his past reactions—shows the natural condition of fallen man under the law/Law; the corrected view—his typological inter-pretations—shows his right relationship to God in the vertical perspective of heaven and hell.

During the first visit the satirist recognized the "Monster" (22) who pun-ished him with his unavoidable company to be more than the archetypal court popinjay. He identified him immediately as an instrument of divine wrath, but did not at that time understand the significance of that punish-ment; "God!" he exclaimed, "How have I sinn'd that thy wraths furious rod, / This fellow chuseth me?" (49–51). He admits that his own visit was some sort of "sin of going" (12) and recognizes now that the bore was indeed his "fellow" morally and spiritually, but at the time of their encounter acted as if the suffering the bore entailed could have been avoided. Originally, he reacted to this trial (109) with clever deflections, hatred, and revulsion, thinking that he could gain release through ridicule, "Sullennesse," and other verbal "Crossing[s]" (91), even feigning sickness in order to escape. The bore was unresponsive to his pointed sarcasm, however, and the satirist's witty repar-tee only increased his own suffering:

> I belch, spue, spit,
> Looke pale, and sickly, like a Patient; Yet
> He thrusts me more. . . .   (109–11)

The bore "nam'd" him (57), "squeakt . . . like to'a high stretcht lute string" (73), then changed "to another key, his stile" (92), and "thrust [him] more" (111), constantly altering the form of his discordant loquacity and increasing the severity of the satirist's "torturing" (142). Even more than "Glaze," who was fined for attending an illegal Mass, the satirist was tortured like an out-law recusant for his sin of going to court.

When this linguistic Circe (129) turned from idle conversation (51–60), self-flattery (61–67), gossip (95–108), and the affectation of foreign manners to lies, "Libells," and scandal-mongering (120–28), the satirist's wit and Hor-atian ridicule failed him altogether. Further efforts to mock the bore resulted in more abrasive attempts to capture the satirist's attention, only increasing his discomfort, until he finally realized that this effusive "thing" (20) was more than the pathetic fool he seemed. Just as Glaze, "catch'd, was faine to [suffer] the Statutes curse" (9–10), so, the satirist realized, he might be implicated for complicity in the bore's treasonous slime (18):

> I more amas'd then Circes prisoners, when
> They felt themselves turne beast, felte my selfe then
> Becomming Traytor, and mee thought I saw
> One of our Giant Statutes ope his jaw
> To sucke me in; for hearing him,
> . . . I might growe
> Guilty, and he free.   (129–33, 135–36)

He finally gained release by paying a bribe (just as Glaze had to "disburse / The hundred markes" [9–10]), for whatever might be the political sympathies of the bore, they were overcome by the prerogative of the satirist's crown (150). And the satirist fled the court in fear, as "one / who feares more actions, doth make from prison" (153–54). Thus, the conduct of the satirist during his first visit was composed mainly of ignorance, naiveté, and, as his present evaluation suggests, moral cowardice. Like a recusant accused of a penal crime, he was glad simply to pay his fine and get away alive.[12]

The satirist's description of his first visit to court is framed by the Glaze analogy. Glaze attended an illegal Mass "in jeste" and had to suffer the curse of the Statutes; the satirist visited the court for no apparent reason and was forced to suffer the punishment of the bore and was threatened with the charge of treason. This simile is strengthened and expanded, its typological significances clarified, by the imagery of disease, privation, monsters, and spiritual treason that punctuate this section of the poem. "The justice of God is subtile," Dean Donne later pointed out, so that God "oftentimes punishes sins of Omission, with other sins, Actuall sins, and makes their lazinesse, who are slack in doing what they should, an occasion of doing what they should not." Such ironic workings of God, he explained, are actually acts of divine love by which God stirs an "Act of Recognition" in the sinner (*Sermons*, V, 316). This is precisely what happened to the satirist. His punishment at the hands of the "strange" bore led to recognition not only of the temporal but the eternal justice of such punishment: it was actually "an act of particular grace and mercy, a purging [and] rectifying" through which he was able to "conform [his] will to the will of God" (*Sermons*, V, 316–17).

That the satirist's visit was a sin of omission is established immediately. His reason for the visit is left purposively unclear:

> I had no suit there, nor new suite to shew,
> Yet went to Court.   (7–8)

His action was without purpose, absent of rectitude, or, as Pope says in his versification, "'twas no form'd Design of serving God."[13] So, it is fitting that the satirist's punishment assumed the form of a morally ignorant fool of ephemeral allegiances who is characterized mainly in terms of negatives. "Guilty'of [his] sin of going" to court for no reason, the satirist was forced to suffer the psychological pains, the sickness and disease, of the sinful, for he and the bore were, in fact, "fellow" sinners whose actions denote "no reason." Thus, in line with the traditional Christian definition of sin as "absolutely nothing, . . . onely *Absentia recti*, . . . an obliquity, a privation [or] action deprived of that rectitude, which it should have" (*Sermons*, V, 80), the satirist was scourged by a sort of *Angelus Satanae*,[14] whose every gesture intimated his moral vacuity. Dressed suspiciously in worn-out clothes (indicating either the devious pretense of Jesuit priesthood by an agent provocateur or an emblem of his satanic character),[15] this mendacious libeller embodies the privation of the satirist's idle visit. The bore "speakes all tongues" (35) but "no language" (38),[16] supposedly has traveled widely but has never "travaile[d]" (61). He "knowes who loves; . . . who'hath sold his land, . . . Who loves Whores, who boyes, and who goats" but actually "knows" nothing but "triviall houshold trash" (101, 103, 128, 98). Donne is having great fun with the court's xenophobia, its mistrust of "strangers," "papist atheists," and foreign intriguers,[17] by intimating that the most preposterous enactments of Ascham's proverbial "Inglese italianato è diabolo incarnato" occur within the court (and probably with the court's support). But these ironic applications of the popular epithet only support the portrait of the bore as an emblem and scourge of the satirist's own moral failure. "Sins . . . which are but the Children of indifferent actions," preached Donne, "become the Parents of great sins" (*Sermons*, V, 301); the satirist's curious sin of going entailed its own punishment, its own curse.

At the same time, the bore is identified as even more than a verification of the homiletic commonplace. The bore, who caused the satirist to sweat like Adam (Gen. 3:19), figures forth also the satirist's own generic sinfulness as fallen man. At one point during the visit, for instance, the satirist became sick; at another he felt himself "turne beaste"—traditional images of man's sinfulness.[18] And throughout the visit, he was forced by his "destinie"[19] to think himself

> As prone to'all ill, and of good as forget-
> full, as proud, as lustful, and as much in debt,
> As vain, as witlesse, and as false as they
> Which dwell at Court. . . .   (13–16)

The punishment by this unnatural "thing, which would have pos'd Adam to name" (20)—since Adam was ignorant of sin when he spontaneously correlated word and thing in the Garden—was the satirist's personal curse for repetition of his "forefathers sinne" (138). No man and no court, he now realizes, can be separated from God's governance; and his own reenactment of Adam's sin, like every sin, was justly punished—just as his forefathers were after the Fall (29), in the Flood (9), and at the Tower of Babel (35–36). "Vex[ed], . . . amas'd," and finally made aware that he must pay (138) for his sinfulness "To the last farthing" (139)—further descriptions traditionally applied to man's relation to divine immanence[20]—the satirist now knows that man's mortal sickness and God's eternal Justice cannot be avoided, regardless of the forms in which either they or consciousness of them arrives. Thus, the commonplace encounter with a court popinjay is presented in the poem as a *figura* of man's fallen condition and need of grace; the literal experience of the satirist was a *figura* for his heritage as a fallen man who repeated Adam's sin in going to court *absentia recti*.

The problem, of course, is that man himself cannot pay for his sinfulness "To the last farthing" because of his fallen inclination "to'all ill." But in order to respond to the atonement already made for him on Calvary, he must understand the terms of his precarious condition. "Grace could not worke upon man to Salvation," Donne preached, "if man had not a faculty of will to worke upon. . . . God saves no man without, or against his will" (*Sermons*, V, 317). In this sense, the monstrous (22) fop forced the satirist to experience the *poeni sensi* that he naturally merits. Monsters, after all, as Pierre Boaistuau's representative statement explains, are sent by God to monitor and reprimand man's sinful behavior: "they do for the most part descover unto us the secret judgment and scourge of the ire of God, which maketh us to feele his marvellous iustice so sharpe, that we be constrained to enter into oure selves, to knocke with the hammer of our conscience, to examin our offences, and haue in horrour our misdeeds."[21]

The satirist deserved such a reprimand because he had, in fact, become a "Traytor" during that first visit, joining the Old Testament types alluded to in the poem. He was not, of course, a traitor to the state, but was a traitor to his "Mistresse Truth" for going to court *absentia recti*. So he was justly forced by the "strange . . . priest" of the court to "bear," "tast," and "suffer" the infernal pains awaiting the unregenerate. His own experience was a personal reincarnation (a "recreation") of the experiences of those fallen types like Job and Jeremiah who "hath seen affliction by the rod of his wrath." As Dean Donne explained in his sermon on Jeremiah as type,

Every sin [is] a Treason, yea a wound to God, . . . a Treason *against Jesus Christ* [that] lies an obligation upon us all, to fulfill his sufferings. . . . The afflictions and tribulations of this life . . . (*Omnis caro corruperat*) . . . force us to practice the death of Christ. . . . His death is delivered to us, as a writing, but not onely in the nature of a peece of *Evidence*, to plead our inheritance by, but a writing in the nature of a Copy, to learn by; It is not onely given us to reade, but to write over, and practise, . . . to *fulfill his suffering in our bodies*, by bearing cheerfully the afflictions and tribulations of this world. (*Sermons, X,* 195–96)

Before looking at the manner in which the poem associates the satirist's sin with man's wounding of Christ, it is helpful to note one additional aspect of the bore that reiterates the significance of the satirist's sin as treason.

As glosses on *Satyre IV* in the seventeenth century indicate, the bore was also the satirist's Antichrist,[22] and provided just punishment for the speaker's abnegation of his satiric responsibility. As a man supposedly devoted to the charitable use of language for God's glory, it is not surprising that the satirist was most repulsed by the bore's malicious and self-serving abuses of language:

> If strange meats displease,
> Art can deceive, or hunger force my tast,
> But Pedants motley tongue, souldiers bumbast,
> Mountebankes drugtongue, nor the termes of law
> Are strong enough preparatives, to draw
> Me to beare this, . . . his tongue.   (38–44)

The allusions to food, art, soldiers, and medicine—traditional figures for the therapeutic power of satire[23]—reiterate that he had to be content (43) with the bore's satanic tongue because it was, in a sense, the verbal equivalent of his own abuse of his role as a satirist. The bore's encomium of the pleasures of the court does ironically disclose, in fact, its moral chaos. But his pictures of the court's depravity (at least those that are not lies or attempts to get the satirist to commit an indiscreet remark) are more *laus* than *vituperatio*; "you would love court," he tells the satirist. Nevertheless, it is fitting that the satirist's own betrayal of his satiric vocation was punished by a figure who transforms the "termes" of satire into libellous trash. A parodic doppelgänger of the satirist, this "Interpreter / To Babels bricklayers" (64–65) embodied the satirist's own spiritual enemy, that particular manifestation of the Uncreating Word that assaulted him, and, more important, that he himself had spiritually become by his vacuous visit. Thus, the emblematic or typological identifications of the satirist's composition of place disclose his present understanding of his relation to the "subtile" workings of God's grace. The bore is described as Sin, Satan, the Father of Lies, Antichrist, the Uncreating Word, Nimrod, and divine scourge—as the fallen instruments of the natural world that God uses to punish and instruct the sons of Adam. And the satirist is related to Adam, Jeremiah, fallen man, spiritual traitor, and traveler in hell—as the types that bespeak man's need for grace. The satirist's ability now to establish these identifications intimates not only his own capacity to respond to God's instruction but also shows how His "furious rod" was an agent of divine Love through which He initiated the speaker's re-creation as a satirist. In this sense, the meditative speaker's composition of place presents not only a symbolic description of his mortal condition but also an illustration of how God's grace initiates moral regeneration in those who naturally merit infernal punishment.[24]

The fullest spiritual significance of the satirist's sin of going is conveyed by an imaginative variation on the most popular subject of Christian medi-tation: the Passion of Christ. Throughout this section of the poem the de-scriptions of the satirist as like a suffering "Patient" bearing torture associate his predicament with the traditional iconography of the Cross.[25] This image is accentuated in the recollection of his escape from the punishing grasp of the bore. Unable to dissuade or evade that torture by either mockery or ridicule, his pain and helplessness increasing until he saw the hellish jaw of the Statutes "ope" to accuse him of treason, the satirist found that "Crossing hurt mee" (91). In one sense, this image conveys the inability of man's words, in this case the satirist's Horatian ridicule, to save him from pain, death, or hell. He was finally forced to "beare this crosse" until "the houre / Of mercy . . . was come" (140–41); his release from the infernal "torturing" (141) of the bore was achieved only by a "Ransome" (145)—by "the prerogative of my Crowne" (150). On one level, these puns reinforce the satirist's portrait of the venality that dominates the Presence Chamber, and perhaps provide another derisive comment on the mercenary intentions of the government's enforcement of the recusant penal laws. If his visit to court was like attend-ance at an illegal Mass, then all the torture he suffered, like that threatened English Catholics, was actually intended only to encourage his contributing to the court's treasury. But, once again, such a topical referent is subsumed by the typological symbolism of this image cluster.

Reinforced by his recognition that he would gain his freedom only by paying the debt of his "forefathers sinne / To the last farthing," the satirist's ironic (but not facetious) allusions to the *gloria passionis* disclose his present understanding of the nature of his sin of going and of his relationship to the wrath and mercy of God. In the first case, this motif reiterates that his visit was a reenactment of the action for which Christ had to ransom man's soul in order for him to escape the suffering of eternal damnation;[26] this torturing was a re-creation of the suffering Christ was "content [to] bear" in order to release man from the grasp of the Uncreating Word. "You cannot escape.it," says St. Thomas à Kempis of the Cross, "whithersoever you run. For where-soever you go you carry yourself with you, and shall always find yourself; . . . everywhere you shall find the Cross."[27] It is, affirms Erasmus, the "one remedy to any and all temptations . . . the example for those who fall, the refuge for those who toil, and the weapon for those in the fray. . . . There is no temptation or vice for which Christ did not furnish a remedy on the Cross."[28] In recapitulating the sin of the Old Adam, the satirist justly suffered the misery of the New Adam: "[E]very sin is a Crucifying of Christ" (*Sermons*, I, 196).

This imagery also intimates the satirist's renewed understanding of man's place in the scheme of salvation history. He, after all, is not Christ, and his release from the satanic bore was achieved by money. That he ran from the court in fear of more actions (154) suggests the thoroughly temporal nature of his "Ransome." He is yet a weak, fallen creature in need of God's grace. But the crucifixion imagery conveys his recognition that his mortal culpability has already been atoned for by Christ's Passion. The association of his suffering with that of Christ, then, recognizes both his debt to the Old Covenant and his fulfillment through the New Covenant. By applying the suffering of Christ to himself, the meditative satirist accepts his responsibility for the Crucifixion and acknowledges the benefits of that "Ransome."

Thus, the satirist's composition of place expands Horace's comic account of his confrontation with a silly, talkative bore into an exploration of the fatal possibilities, mortally and spiritually, of thoughtless activity in a providential universe, possibilities that in this case led to his fuller understanding of his moral condition and his personal role in the theatre of God's judgments. Like Dante's poet during his pilgrimage through Purgatory, Donne's satirist discovers that he cannot escape his position "as a man seeking salvation and an artist seeking definition"[29] simultaneously. The ramifications of this discovery for Donne's satirist are clarified by the analysis and colloquy of *Satyre IV*, in which the *puanteur* of his sin begins to respond to and emulate the *douceur* of Christ's love.[30] This opening composition of his own place in the scheme of grace is clarified by his analysis of its relevance to his role as satirist and his rectified fulfillment of that duty.

ii

The last two events retrospectively evaluated by the satirist elaborate and specify the typological symbolism established in the first section. The second event dramatizes how the satirist's fortunate fall at the court led to a renewed understanding of his duty as satiric truthteller, making explicit his recognition that satire is a moral duty that demands he brave the dangers of the court in order to avoid spiritual treason. The third event, an account of his return to the court as "Spie," more fully characterizes the court as a dramatic enactment of the conditions of hell, specifically, as a theater of blasphemy that prefigures the *poeni damni* of those who fail to respond to the "handwriting" of grace. The satirist's return fulfills, thus, his own response to the *effectus passionis*, as he returns as a satirist to harrow the hellish court. Aware now of the apocalyptic as well as the personal dimensions of his situation as a fallen man redeemed by grace, he responds to Christ's sacrifice by daring legal treason in order to fulfill his spiritual duty to his "Mistresse Truth."

The analysis section of the poem recounts the satirist's Dantean trance that followed his thoughtless first visit to court. It clarifies that the literal charge of treason against the state that terrified him during that visit actually signified the spiritual treason obtained from his desertion of his satiric function. Once again, this moral clarification is described as a prompting by the hand of God:

> At home in wholesome solitarinesse
> My precious soule began, the wretchednesse
> Of suiters at court to mourne, and a trance
> Like his, who dreamt he saw hell, did advance
> It selfe on mee. . . .   (155–59)

Whether this trance is a vision from God or the product of his rectified conscience is not made perfectly clear. Devotional tradition argues that trances are one of the benefits of consideration of the Passion.[31] But whether or not this tradition informs Donne's poem, clearly the amendment of the satirist's foolishness resulted from his meditative realization of the significance of his position in the providential world and that the workings of Providence remain finally mysterious to fallen man. Most important in this case is the order of occurrences here. Having fled from what he interpreted as the embodiment of divine wrath that he encountered in the court, he responded to the conditions he saw there with charity. As Augustine points out, it is what one makes of the Cross that determines one's worth; the Cross "shows the way from fruitless works to charity."[32] The trance occurred only after the satirist's "precious soule" (one manuscript reads "piteous soule")[33] responded charitably to the sinners of the court. Once his brave scorn for their sins (and his own) was augmented by his kind pity for sinners, in other words, the satirist was either granted the trance or was able to respond positively to the intervention of grace. The paradigm of zeal as satire (and true religion) outlined in the former poem as the satirist's private model and as an exemplary pattern for the cure of man's "worne maladies" is reiterated and expanded here. In *Satyre III* this exemplary conduct was endorsed by a metaphoric, imaginative view of the divine attributes as analogue to his *laus et vituperatio*. Here the view of satire as an image of the Word is presented empirically—the satirist's renewed understanding of his genre as an image of the Word is energized by the mysterious workings of the Word. It was only after his scorn for the court, fear for his own life, and naiveté about his moral situation were overcome by charity that he was capable of understanding the obligations of his satiric charge. "Low feare," he realized then,

> Becomes the guiltie, not th'accuser; Then
> Shall I, nones slave, of high borne, or rais'd men

> Feare frownes? And, my Mistresse Truth, betray thee
> To th'huffing braggart, puft Nobility?
> No, no. . . .   (161–65)

This acknowledgment led to the even more fearful realization that he must once again desert the "wholesome solitarinesse" of his home. Kind pity in and of itself is not sufficient either. To re-create his role as satirist, he had to return to court, and that requires both pity and brave scorn. Thus, reformed in understanding through analysis of the deforming spiritual effects of abnegation of his satiric responsibility, he returned "the second / Time" to the court, fully aware this time of the mortal and immortal consequences of his success as a satirist. The analysis section of the poem, therefore, recounts the satirist's acceptance, with the aid of grace, of the zealous paradigm: the "furious rod" of wrath instilled charity (he began to mourn); mercy (the trance) instilled scorn; and he went back to court prepared to castigate the sins of the sinners he is bound to pity. Zealous satire is figured once again as a response to and fulfillment of the grace of God, and is more fully examined than in the previous poems. In *Satyre II*, he concluded that the satirist could not be legally prosecuted; in *Satyre III*, he engaged the moral laws of satire as devotion. Here the limitations of both those approaches are confronted: both legalism and contemplation solely are shown to be inadequate responses to the mysterious "Crossings" of the eternal into human time.

The third event recounted in the satirist's meditation describes his return to the arena of fallen man, as signalled by the mention of the specific time, "'Tis ten a clock and past" (175).[34] What he witnessed during that visit confirmed for him the importance of fulfilling his role as satirist, specifically, that the terms of man's salvation or damnation are the moral validity of the roles he chooses to play in the world. A warning to those who might be tempted to visit the court idly as he once did, the satirist's rectified appraisal of the daily routine of the court shows it to be a manifestation of the infernal frustration awaiting those who abnegate their spiritual responsibility. Having suffered the pains of the Cross during his first visit and been enlightened by a Dantean trance afterwards, he now returns to harrow that hellish chamber of blasphemies. "All are players" there (185), he explains; but the play they perform is a perverse black Mass, a "Masse in jeste" characterized by travesty of the gestures and rites that should serve as reminders of man's need for grace. What he witnessed during that second visit was abuse of the *effectus passionis*, ironically but fittingly dominated by an absurd figure named Glorius and distinguished by the abuse of those ceremonies that were created as vehicles for man's response to and participation in the eternal "Presence" of God's unfolding Word.

This section of the poem is controlled by variations on the play motif, that most popular of Renaissance commonplaces—the world as play, the world as God's theatre, religious ceremony as play, human history as the unfolding of God's drama, and, most significant, man's duty as *imitatio christi*.[35] References to the significances of man's emulation and assimilation of moral models punctuate the satirist's descriptions of both visits, in fact. In his frustrating dialogue with the bore, for example, he pointed out that Aretino provides a poor model for satire:

> "Aretines pictures have made few chast;
> No more can Princes courts, though there be few
> Better pictures of vice, teach me vertue." (70–72)

Such pornographies remain all *vituperatio* and no *laus*,[36] offering no models worthy of imitation. Parading emblems of vice, "Spartanes fashion" (68), before courtiers only provides them subjects that they foolishly emulate—as the hanging in the Presence Chamber of the tapestry depicting "the seaven deadly sins" (232) attests. The courtiers' play provides another example (like that of the libellous bore's histrionics) of the imitation of inadequate models or imitations of right models for the wrong reasons. The courtiers debase, pervert, and misapply, in fact, the types of religious ceremonies and gestures that were created for their spiritual regeneration. Even though their actions may seem to be the religious actions natural to fallen man, they are actually only blasphemous perversions because of the courtiers' unregenerate motives and proud intentions: "their fruits [are] bastard all" (174).[37] Like the words of the bore, the actions of the courtiers observed during the satirist's second visit disclose the *absence* of spiritual self-knowledge and responsiveness to the Word in the "Presence" Chamber.

Illustrative of the degenerate manners and morals of the courtiers is Glorius, whose name itself signals the duplicity of the court while pointing ironically to the Christian virtue conspicuously absent from it. Glorius, the *miles gloriosus* who "commands like law" (228) in the court through terror and crudeness, imitates the wrong biblical figures, making his face "as ill, / As theirs which in old hangings whip Christ" (225–26). And the other courtiers participate in the same kind of perverse imitation. Macrine parrots the conduct proper to the confessional, forcing his clothes to "confesse not only mortall / Great staines and holes; . . . but veniall / Feathers and dust" (201–03) before he dares to engage in the court's daily play. He enters the court "As a young Preacher at his first time goes / To preach" (209–10) and once there imitates Catholic prayer,

> whisper[ing] "by Jesu," so'often, that A
> Pursevant would have ravish'd him away
> For saying of our Ladies Psalter. (215–17)

Once he spies the actual "Lady" whose wanton "grace" he desires, he

> protests protests protests
> So much as at Rome would serve to have throwne
> Ten Cardinalls into th'Inquisition. (212–14)

The play that the courtiers perform daily in the waxen garden (169) of the court, then, is a ludicrous parody of the gestures that should remind them of their precarious position in the scheme of grace. They may indeed "doe as well / At stage, as court" (212–14), but their play remains a chaotic uncreating of the spiritual dimensions of man's life.

The "Presence" of Justice is still evident even in their morally vacant Chamber, however, just as it was in the satirist's original fall into the court during his first visit, for the end result of their derelict performance is that "they each other plague" (218). The men's outrageous compliments only make the ladies fear their "drugs ill laid, [their] haire loose set" (196). And all their elaborate preparations are frustrated by the intentional rudeness of Glorius, who "Jeasts like a licens'd foole" (228). Their courtly theatrics and overriding concern with proper clothing, manners, and decorum are all subverted by this recalcitrant bore who "only doth / Call a rough carelessenesse, good fashion" (220–21): he "spits on / He cares not" whom (222–23). Glorius' clothing, manner, and actions repudiate the standards sought by Macrine and the court ladies; but it is *his* threats, and not those of eternal damnation, that keep "all in awe" (227). Thus the careful but vapid choreography of the courtiers serves only to make the court a perpetual hell of frustration for those who abide there, a prefiguration of the *poeni damni* of those who fail to respond to the moral models provided for man's reformation. "The wicked are scourged for God in this life, . . . their afflictions have begun already here," Dean Donne pointed out, "in this world, there are *Dòlores inferni*, Sorrowes that have begun hell here" (*Sermons*, IX, 394).

Glorius provides example also of another perversion of man's "gift of utteraunce." Similar to the bore in appearance and manner, he too scourges the ostentatious courtiers with his aloof denigrations and aggressive uncivility. He speaks like a "licens'd foole" in the "rough" terms associated with satire and plagues the court fools with the "course attire" of his assaults. But, then, like the bore and unlike Donne's satirist, he is stirred only by personal ambition and greed. His ability to "command like law" in the court only substantiates the need for the satirist's zealous pity and his attempts to alert man to God's immanent *Gloria*. Glorius "keepes all in awe"—or, as the pun suggests, actually removes All from awe and denies the awe of All—but imitates not Christ but those who crucified Christ. Committed only to his own *gloria*, he bespeaks the satirist's own moral ignorance during his first visit; but the moral ignorance of his abusive satire is dramatically ridiculed by the satirist's present understanding of and response to the benefits as well as the responsibility of Christ's sacrifice. Glorius' central role in the court's daily ritual manifests the courtiers' ignorance of the importance of moral imitation and the absence of spiritual knowledge in their cupiditious travesty of religious devotion.

What the satirist "spied" during his second visit actually was, as he puns in the opening lines of the poem, a "Masse in jeste." In one sense, the courtiers' play parodies the ceremony of attendance on the Virgin Queen, perverting it into a blasphemous mockery of religious gesture by their pursuit of personal power and sexual possession. They have perverted the ritualistic, patriotic attendance on the most ceremonious of all holy monarchs into a self-serving travesty bereft of any moral or legal motive. It has become a ceremony of base appetite by immoral buccaneers and adulterous "Pirats" (126); Elizabeth's fearful privateers who defended her throne and her religion have now been replaced by courtiers who use her chamber to aggrandize their personal greed.[38]

At the same time, the daily play in the Presence Chamber is even more treasonous and more blasphemous, for that performance at the center of international Protestantism parodies a specific Roman Catholic Mass: the Mass celebrating the Feast of Presentation of Christ in the Temple. This Mass celebrates Simeon's naming and recognition of Christ at His circumcision; it is to just such a wise man as Simeon (243), in fact, that the satirist entrusts recognition of the "Canonicall" truthfulness of his own word at the end of the poem. Verbal echoes of the Presentation Mass are evident throughout the poem.[39] The Gospel for that Mass, for example, is Luke 2—Simeon's quotation of the *nunc dimittis* canticle from Psalm 97; the Communion passage is Psalm 97; and the Post Communion is as follows: "May this Communion, O Lord, *cleanse us from guilt*; and by the intercession of the Virgin, Mother of God, make us *sharers of the heavenly remedy.*" The epistle is Titus 2:11–15— "The grace of God our Savior has *appeared to all men*, instructing us, in order that, rejecting ungodliness and worldly lusts, we may live temperately and justly and piously in this world: [so that] He might redeem us from all iniquity and *cleanse* for Himself an acceptable people, *pursuing good works.* Thus speak, and exhort, in Christ Jesus our Lord." The Gradual includes Psalm 97 ("The Lord has made known his salvation") and concludes with Hebrews 1:1–2—"God, who *in diverse ways spoke in times past to the fathers by the prophets*, last of all, in these days, *has spoken to us* by His Son," which passage is followed in turn by the "Cleanse my Heart" prayer. Finally, another echo of the Mass in the poem comes from the Offertory (Psalm 88:12, 15)—"justice and judgement are the preparation of Thy throne." The order of this Mass is not followed by the courtiers, for even their parody figures in its disorderly procession the moral chaos their selfish ritual embodies. But the central stages and passages of this Mass reverberate throughout *Satyre IV*, from the disgusting mock-Eucharist (109–10) of slander and libel which the bore forces on the satirist (in accordance with his "strange . . . priesthood") to the parody of Confession which the sartorially penitent Macrine, "call[ing] his clothes to shrift" (200), undergoes before commencing his daily "role" at the Chamber. The contradictions inherent in their "Masse" mirror the courtiers' moral confusion. Macrine's parody of both "Romist" and "Anglican" gestures contrasts to Glorius' aggressive "Puritan" crudeness; Eastern, Western, Catholic, Anglican, and even ancient Roman expressions are mingled in their motley performance. Their "play" prefigures, in fact, the shapeless, formless repetition of transgressions that characterizes hell.

Contrasted to this chaos is the satirist's moral application of the stages and canticles of the Presentation Mass to his own experiences. Beginning with the *nunc dimittis*, his poem works variations, both serious and ironic, on the stages of the Mass. Instead of a celebration of the Eucharist he had to be content with the uncreating words of the bore, which (like Christ's sacrificial atonement) morally revived the satirist. But this experience proved to be only one of the diverse ways in which God speaks to men in order to "cleanse [them] of guilt" by the "pursuit of good works" such as satire. Both visits to the court confirmed for him, moreover, how "justice and judgment are the preparation of [God's] throne." The infernal "Masse" of the courtiers is transformed in the satirist's meditation into an ironic celebration of the Presentation, a private celebration of God's Presence in his own salvation as man and as satirist.

This identification of his meditation with the Presentation is perhaps the boldest stroke in the poem, for it once again associates the satirist with the recusants' stance, with their recommendation of meditations as private fulfillment of celebrations which they were forbidden to perform publicly.[40] But, then, the topicality of the Mass imagery is integrated into the satirist's exhortation to all his readers. Man's choice is one of celebration, of celebrating a "Masse in jeste" which may be legally allowable but which guarantees only his relegation to the judgment of the Old Law, or of celebrating the redemptive power of God's Presence in humble colloquy with the mercy of the New Law. Just as the satirist was forced to choose between the temporal law of the court and the eternal law of his "Mistresse Truth," so the reader is alerted by the satirist's poem to the dangers of choosing the wrong legal role to enact. All *are* players, but it is finally God's play.

The comparisons of the satirist's return to court with the heroism of Sir Bevis and the author of 2 Maccabees reinforce the idea that satire is an exemplary act of moral imitation. Like Sir Bevis, who fearfully confronted the giant Askaparts (233–34), and like the Apocryphal author, who dared to tell the simple truth about the enemies and heroism of God's people (241–44), the satirist dared the monstrous giants of the Presence Chamber in order to reveal the "wretchednesse / Of suiters at court." Fear of the court's "priviledg'd spie" and of "Becomming Traytor," which caused him to run from the court after his first visit, were overcome through his imitation of Christian models of faithful duty. He left the court after his second visit, he explains, only because he was "Tyr'd" (229). And once safely beyond the grasp of the "men that doe know / No token of worth, but 'Queenes men'" (234–35), men who may be strong enough to "throwe / Charing Cross" (233–34) but show no knowledge of the benefits or obligations of Christ's Cross, he evaluates his satire by allusion to the example of 2 Maccabees:

> Preachers which are
> Seas of Wit and Arts, you can, then dare,
> Drowne the sinnes of this place, for, for mee
> Which am but a scarce brooke, it enough shall bee
> To wash the staines away; Though I yet
> With *Macchabees* modestie, the knowne merit
>   Of my worke lessen; yet some wise man shall,
>   I hope, esteeme my writs Canonicall.   (237–44)

The similarities between *Satyre IV* and 2 Maccabees, which Anglicans did not "esteeme Canonicall," are quite significant.[41] *Satyre IV* is an adaptation of Horace's Latin satire, his encounter with the verbal monstrosity of the bore; 2 Maccabees is also an adaptation, of Jason of Cyrene's Greek account of certain conflicts between the Jewish nation and foreign defilers. The central concern of the biblical account (which one Renaissance commentator calls the strongest support for the doctrine of Purgatory)[42] is the sanctity of the Temple. How priests betrayed the nation to foreign captors and strange forms of worship, and how heroic leaders opposed the adoption of foreign ways and ousted the informants and traitors from the Temple are the major subjects of the account. It is the first book to celebrate the deeds of martyrs such as Eleazar (a nearly ubiquitous figure in recusant apologiae) who, like Donne's satirist, refused to eat the defiled meat forced upon him by informant priests and chanced execution rather than provide a poor example to the followers of God. Thus, the concern with traitors, martyrs, defiled meat, the sanctity of the nation, foreign manners and habits, and the dangers and rewards of opposing such illegitimate forms of action are shared by *Satyre IV* and 2 Maccabees. It is likely, therefore, that the satirist's reference to this apocryphal work intends to promote recognition of more similarities than just their veracity. Both are sacred histories that provide dramatic examples of the type of courage man should emulate in his daily role on the divine stage.

At the same time, Donne's poem does not underestimate the fearful difficulty of achieving such bravery; the human element is not sacrificed for or obviated by the virtue of the biblical model. The satirist is yet a man, of course, a fallen creature, but not a willful (or "pseudo") martyr; so it is natural that he "quake[d]" (like Sir Bevis) upon passing the giant beefeaters. He was fearful, he admits, that he would be discovered: "I shooke like a spyed Spie" (237). But the simile extends only to the adjective here. He *is* a spy. Returning to a court that embodies the *poeni damni* of the ninth level of hell, the *bolgia* of traitors,[43] he is a spy for the Truth, fulfilling his moral responsibility as a satirist. This is a mission for which he could be named traitor; he does not go there now to visit but to assault. Of more importance, however, is the fact that it is a mission that clears him ("wash[es] the staines away") of the charge of treason to the Truth. Therefore, unlike the end of *Satyre II*, where he jokingly suggested that he could not be prosecuted because he had simply told the truth, he is now aware of the mortal circumstances of his role in society. Now he does not saucily challenge the nation's judicial authority, enlightened as he has been by his encounter with the "priviledg'd spie" that the laws of libel are susceptible to political interpretations. Now he only humbly concludes that he has fulfilled his moral duty regardless of the consequences, "pleas'd so / As men which from gaoles to'execution goe" (229–30), ready to die if necessary, as the *nunc dimittis* of the opening lines announces.

Thus, as a meditation on his salvation or at least on his purgation as a fallen man and a Christian satirist, it is apt that his poem begins with the *nunc dimittis*. In his sermon on the biblical source of this canticle, Simeon's recognition of Christ in the Temple, Donne urged that Simeon's "example, and the characters that are upon him are our Alphabet; . . . that is, you must pursue the imitation. . . . The end of all consideration of all the actions of such leading and exemplar men, as *Simeon* was, is assimilation, too; That we may be like that man." Self-knowledge, he explained, "is nothing less than 'the application of Christ to our selves.'"[44] In *Satyre IV*, the speaker applies not only the Passion of Christ to his own condition but also the "wisdom of Simeon." Simeon's pronouncement, "Mine eyes have seen thy salvation," is applied dramatically; by tracing the history of divine wrath and mercy in his own life, his "eyes have seen [his own] salvation," or at least the terms of his own salvation as satirist and as man. His meditation on the fatal consequences that his failure to perform that mission could have on him eternally shows how moral imitation is the praiseworthy, necessary duty of fallen man. A retrospective evaluation of his movement from action (first visit) to meditation (trance) to action (second visit) to meditation (the poem), the poem provides, then, a literal testing and a symbolic clarification of the significance of zealous satire. Much more than the recitation of ideals, the creation of *bona carmina*, or a form of meditative devotion, satire is, we see, a dangerous, humbling, but essential participation in the unfolding of the Word.[45] The composition of his first visit to court as a journey to hell in which the satirist was scourged by "wraths furious rod" for his moral lassitude, the view of his second visit as a journey to what is a perpetual hell for those who "perform" there, and his present view of both visits as a "Purgatorie" for him provide, at the same time, a dramatic confirmation that man (by responding to and benefiting from God's grace) can escape the pains of hell immediately by self-knowledge about his role in God's theater. He cannot save himself eternally, of course—that is not the point. But the typological symbolism and the universal pattern of his account defend the satirist's recommitment of his will to his "Mistresse Truth" as a "Canonicall" response to and participation in the divine re-creation of fallen man.

The penultimate comparison in the poem substantiates and elaborates the satirist's stance. This comparison between the meditative satirist and the preachers is as much a contrast as a similitude. The speaker of the poem has offered a meditation, a "Masse" in miniature, in private, for the reader's own meditation and emulation. But the satirist is not so naive as to expect even "Seas" of satiric or homiletic "Wit and Arts" to "drowne" the sins of the court. (In a sense they have already been drowned, of course, in the flood of Christ's blood.) What he recommends is that the reader "wash [his own] staines away" by meaningful Christian imitation. That is, that the reader turn his own life into a "Masse," meditating on his sins and duty to God, and then enacting meaningful, erect imitations of Christian heroism. Being true to one's "Mistresse Truth," after all, finally means being true to oneself. Until each man, with God's help, begins to re-create himself *imago dei* and therein begins to transform the court of the world, England will remain an infernal "Masse in jeste" whose court "flouts [the] Presence" (171) of God's connection with His creation. It is not, then, even the preachers who will inevitably "drowne the sinnes" of the country; all their wit and arts are of no avail unless each man, "scarce brooke" that he is, begins to respond to the purifying grace of God. Donne's satirist is similar to the preachers, then, in his exegesis of man's duty; but the image of satire in the poem identifies him as well with the priest, even the Catholic priest, who invites and exhorts the reader to attend to (and attend) his meditative "Masse," *Satyre IV*.

A final word about the concluding words of the poem is appropriate. In a poem complicated by conflations of narrative time, typological symbolism, and the play motif, it is significant that it concludes with "with." The entire satire seems dominated by witty comparisons and contrasts; but in his concluding evaluation of his genre, the satirist urges that he writes not "like" but "with" the modesty of the biblical author. It is an important variation on the strategy of the poem and reinforces its central view of satire—that the satirist's experiences and his poem attest to and participate in the mysterious communion of time with eternity. Just as the Mass is a celebration and renewal of God's new covenant with man, so the satirist, "with *Macchabees* modestie," presents his poem as another testament to the fulfillment of man by God in time. Thus, the wise man, the reader who responds to *Satyre IV*, appreciates not just the wit of his "writs" but the "hand-writing" of God that animates them, the mysterious Author of all men's re-creation.

iii

In many ways, *Satyre IV* offers Donne's fullest and most daring exploration of the satiric process. As suggested by the constant references to the satirist as a traitor, spy, victim, or outsider, and the frequent comparisons of his pain, fear, or conviction to that of a recusant, the poem presents his boldest appraisal of Anglican intolerance; on one level, it exploits the cruel ironies underlying the optimism of Protestant England's "claim to have restored a golden age of imperial religion."[46] If Donne as recusant poet and heir to the More tradition speaks through the poem it is to laugh wryly at how salacious libellers, blasphemous courtiers, and vulgar politicians are given social and legal liberty to travesty the rites, rituals, and devotional practices for which sincere believers might end up on Tyburn Hill.

The issues of religious politics and the politics of religion raised in the poem were, of course, more than aesthetic concerns to Donne at the time of *Satyre IV*. The great grandnephew of Sir Thomas More, nephew of the famous Jesuit leader Jasper Heywood, son of a life-long and adamant Catholic mother (who may have been present at the planning of Southwell's *Humble Supplication*),[47] and brother of a Catholic who had recently been imprisoned for harboring a Jesuit priest, Donne acknowledged with pride his Catholic heritage on several occasions. In the preface to *Biathanatos*, for instance, he professed, "I had my first breeding and conversation with men of a surpressed and afflicted Religion, accustomed to the despite of death" (p. 5). In *Pseudo-Martyr* he writes of "certaine impressions of the Romane religion . . . early layde upon my conscience, both by Persons who by nature had a power and superiority over my will, and others who by their learning and good life, seem'd to me justly to claime an interest for the guiding, and rectifying of mine understanding."[48] As late as 1612, in a private letter to his friend Henry Goodyer, he could write that both Protestantism and Catholicism are "connatural pieces of one circle"[49] and as early as the third *Satyre*, we should recall, he wrote that

> To adore, or scorne an image, or protest,
> May all be bad; doubt wisely; in strange way
> To stand inquiring right, is not to stray.

Erskine-Hill suggests that *Satyre IV* "urge[s] upon us the experience of fearing an unjust force in the law and operations of the established state."[50] Earl

Miner says that "*Satyre IV* gives a sense that the outer world has oppressed or threatened Donne's private inner world almost to the point of destruction" and that the nightmarish social landscapes of the poem "argue a deep, obsessive fear" deriving in part from the fact that "Donne had real attachment to Catholicism."[51] Such comments correctly gauge the wry and anxious exasperation of the poem. For surely there is at least a touch of personal bitterness (and fear) in the descriptions of the preposterous "Masse in jeste" performed at the heart of Protestant England. It was in the court, after all, that the satirist spied the figures that Anglican preachers and pamphleteers repeatedly associate with the evils of Catholicism. It was in the court that he was assaulted by the Antichrist, which Protestant polemicists depicted as residing in Rome or in the uncreating words of "papist atheists."[52] It was in the Presence Chamber that he witnessed the mimetic parody of Marian worship, ironically embodied in the courtiers' "Italianate" (170) performance at the shrine of the Virgin Elizabeth. Thus, the satirist's ironic and oblique reliance on the *topoi* of Anglican antipapist polemics indicts the hypocrisy and injustice of a system that persecutes and destroys sincere devotees of a politically illegal religion at the same time that it tolerates and even fosters perversities of the devotional stances for which any devout recusant would be imprisoned, tortured, or killed.[53] The insolent abuse of God's gifts by the satirist's morally myopic countrymen is bad enough; but that their abuses are enforced and protected by informers and pursuivants and that their conduct, if not performed by people on the inside, would be labelled treasonous are the cruelest ironies of England's "Age of rusty iron" (V, 35). Such an indictment surely suggests the exasperation that must have been felt by Donne as a member of the persecuted Catholic minority.

Nevertheless, one must be careful not to overemphasize the effects of Donne's strategy in the poem. The satirist does not champion Catholic devotion *qua* Catholic devotion over Anglican devotion. His technique is to compare and contrast failures in Anglican morality with sincere Catholic morality. The difference may be slight, but it amounts to the difference between pro-Catholic polemics and Christian satire. Still, given the condition in which Donne lived, it is not surprising that he later admitted to Sir Henry Wotton that "to my satyrs there belongs some feare."[54]

At the same time, one must not overstate the autobiographical impulse in Donne's poems, regardless of how strongly it appears that personal animus entered into their motivation. Although the speaker of *Satyre IV* is a rhetorical device through which Donne speaks (however "equivocally"), the poem shows at the same time, and more fully, how the poet was able to respond artistically to his dilemma as descendant of a religious minority. *Satyre IV* captures not just the tensions and fearful circumstances of Donne's personal situation but transforms that historical situation into an expression of how satire, as the imitation of moral types, provides dramatic models of Christian devotion timeless in their applicability. The meditative satirist's initial evaluation of his experiences remains the best summary of the major impulses of the poem—his denotation of life and art as re-creation. The central action of the poem, in fact, is not the juxtaposition of controversial doctrines but the action of re-creation: the re-creation of Latin satire, personal biography, biblical typology, and even Christian meditation into zealous satire. The major addition that Donne makes to Horace's plot, in fact, is the satirist's second visit, in which he re-creates Christ's assault against the denizens of hell. It is this type of personal and artistic re-creation of the self that the poem urges the readers to imitate. Each is encouraged to follow the meditative pattern of the satirist, to redirect his will to celebration of the Word by imitating the satirist's personal regeneration. Such personal assimilation of the action of the poem is in itself, the typological symbolism urges, a participation in the re-creation of man by God's Word. The satirist washes the stains of his sin of going by writing the poem that his meditations have shown to be the act of Christian loyalty necessary for him; the reader is urged, not to imitate the specific actions presented in the plot of the poem (assault of the court), but to imitate the pattern that the satirist presents as a model for all fallen man: to transform his life into a celebration of Truth through moral imitation. Such a mode of action is to accept the benefits and the responsibility of the *effectus passionis* and the tradition of moral imitation it fulfills.

We are still left, however, with a problematic view of satire at the end of the poem. Even though *Satyre IV* endorses empirically and typologically the moral synonymity of satire and religion affirmed in the first three *Satyres*, it still presents only a process by which man *can* cure himself if he chooses, if he responds to and emulates the *laus et vituperatio* of the satirist's moral allegory. Even the image of the satire as the private celebration of the Presentation Mass offers finally a meditative model. The satirist is still, in a sense, imprisoned in the meditative privacy of his own ideas about satire, even though all doubts about zealous satire as a moral imperative have been removed by the end of *Satyre IV*. Perhaps this is the dilemma of any poet, of all poets—to be forever dependent on the ability of some wise man, some receptive reader, to "esteeme" their writs truthful. Even the most optimistic of the Renaissance poets, we might recall, after his initial hopes of creating "a gentleman or noble person in vertuous and gentle discipline" concludes his unfinished epic romance with the slanderous destructiveness of the Blatant Beast.[55] Thus, in *Satyre IV*, perhaps the most the satirist can do is meditate, re-creating his own experiences in universally relevant terms for the reader's consideration, offering his own poem as a *mediation* of the Word. He cannot activate regeneration in the reader, but can only hope and urge that the reader respond to (by imitating) the model he dramatizes and praises. He still has no arena for action other than the "Ridling" words of poetry. The manner in which the generic pattern of Christian devotion that he recommends *can* be activated—how the satirist's fiction can be re-created in the theater of the fallen world—is the subject of the final *Satyre*.

CHAPTER FIVE

The Satirist as Advisor

They judge not with justice.

Jeremiah 5:28

At the conclusion of *Satyre IV*, the satirist challenged the "Preachers which are / Seas of Wit and Arts" to direct their attention to the outrages that "swell the bladder of our court." Admitting to a false modesty about the value of his own efforts, he resolved nevertheless that for him "it enough shall bee / To wash the staines away" of his own perilous ventures there. Such a resolve did not endure, it seems, for in the fifth *Satyre* he returns to the subject of the court's corruption in order to disclose the bribery and collusion pervasive there. In a sense, then, *Satyre V* extends the satirist's previous attack on the blasphemous perversions of the court into an assault against the legal corruptions it perpetuates—but with one major and highly significant difference. In the previous poem, as in the first three *Satyres*, the satirist spoke as an outsider, a "Spie" whose complaints could be dismissed as the jealous ravings of a malcontent. Even in his elaborate defense of satire as exemplary performance in the divine play the satirist was still a meditative scourge who had no specific means to augment or enforce the actions he encouraged (except theoretically through the response of his readers to his pleas for reformation). In *Satyre V*, however, the satirist expands the possibilities and scope of his Christian satire by examining the role of satire *within* the legal machinery of the established state. Now he speaks as an insider who has the means, the opportunity, and the place to activate reform. This does not mean that the conclusions about the role of satire presented in the first four poems are overturned in this one. Rather, this final poem expands those insights by applying the satirist's established generic principles to a specific moral problem and legal situation in late Elizabethan England.

In one sense, *Satyre V* is the most occasional of the *Satyres*. It was undoubtedly composed after Donne had completed his legal training at the Inns of

Court, returned from the Islands Expedition, and entered the service of the lord keeper, Sir Thomas Egerton, as his "chief Secretary" in 1597.[1] One of the first investigations in which the poet would have participated was Egerton's examination of the outrageous fees demanded of suitors at the Chancery and the widespread bribery and corruption in the procedures of Elizabeth's courts. In Bald's words, *Satyre V* addresses itself in part to "the exactions levied on suitors by the lawyers and officials of the courts, not merely in the Star Chamber and in the law courts generally, but also in the Chancery and other offices to which those who had obtained royal grants had to go to get their grants validated" (pp. 100–101). Egerton had just begun this investigation when he hired Donne, so doubtless the young lawyer was cast immediately into an "inquiry into the machinery of the law and its working."[2] But *Satyre V* explores much more than merely the legalities of "the world of human law and its manipulators"[3]—a subject he had already treated obliquely in *Satyres II, III,* and *IV* from the perspective of his own recusancy. And it is much more than merely a hastily constructed attempt to impress his new employer,[4] even though the flattering portrait of Egerton as a figure of "righteousnes" (31) is central to its strategy. What it does present is a judicious, meditative analysis of the perversions of eternal Law endemic to the corruptions that the lord keeper was investigating and, at the same time, the capacity of satire to "know and weed out this enormous sinne" (34) in Elizabeth's courts. The biographical context of the poem reinforces its central theme: Donne's analysis of the ultimate foundations and spiritual significances of his recent appointment and initial assignment provides a personal example of the exegesis of law and Law that the satirist counsels can lead to the self-knowledge necessary for spiritual survival.

Donne's appointment to the legal staff of the lord keeper provided him the occasion and the position, then, for solving the problematic view of satire presented in the first four *Satyres*. This biographical circumstance (which, we shall see, does not have to be strictly interpreted only in terms of Donne's personal situation) allowed him to explore how the activity of satire analyzed in the first four poems can "cure these worne maladies" not just theoretically but actually. It provided the poet, in fact, an opportunity denied his Latin models. Persius, Juvenal, and even Horace, in spite of his association with Augustus and Maecenas, remain outsiders whose effectiveness as social reformers is determined by the capacity of their readers to respond rationally or emotionally to their poems—thus the constant concern in their satires with the legality of the genre. But the Egerton appointment provided Donne not just a metaphoric but an actual means by which to transform satire into law. The characterization in *Satyre V* of the satirist as "zealous" meditator, legal advisor, and textual exegete illustrates how this transformation is possible.

i

The situation and strategy of *Satyre V* are quite similar to Juvenal's *Satire XIII*, the Roman poet's ironic address to Calvinus. In fact, the description of Elizabethan England as an "Age of rusty iron" (35) is borrowed directly from this poem. Juvenal's poem is a mock *consolatio*, which uses the occasion of Calvinus' complaint that he has been swindled out of ten thousand sesterces by a perjurious friend ("fraude sacrilega") to denounce the hopelessly perverse irrationality and meretricious self-destructiveness of iron-age Rome.[5] But the classical satirist's animus is leveled as much at the moral simplicity and incipient hypocrisy of Calvinus' irate complaint as at the irretrievability of Roman justice and rationality ("posito diademate falcem / Saturnus fugiens"). Juvenal's satirist (surprisingly) rejects as philosophically and existentially inadequate the *ira* which had characterized his earlier satires in favor of a Stoic resolve to endure with a smile the slings and arrows of outrageous fortune. This dismissal of the *facit indignatio versum* credo of his first book of satires has been gradually prepared for by the programmatic poems introducing Books II, III, and IV;[6] but it receives its fullest expression in this ironic *consolatio* which initiates his last book of poems. Much closer in tone to the calmer, more detached stance of Horace, from whom Juvenal had deliberately distanced himself in his first Book through his definition of the satirist as *Lucilius ardens*, in *Satire XIII* Juvenal's satirist refuses to offer Calvinus the expected "consolations of philosophy" (great *victrix fortunae sapientia*), but instead accuses him of having lost his moral perspective. Even though the satirist assures Calvinus (quite ironically, it turns out) that no malefactor can escape the bar of his own prosecuting conscience ("quod se / iudice nemo nocens absolvitur"), he emphasizes that such a precept offers little consolation when viewed from the perspective of civilization's rapid decline and provides meager cause for satisfaction, especially to a man of Calvinus' self-ignorance.

The focus of Juvenal's mock *consolatio*, W. S. Anderson points out, is Calvinus' insistent *indignatio* as "unreal, excessive, and motivated by corrupt traits in his soul":[7]

> curentur dubii medicis maioribus aegri:
> tu venam vel discipulo committe Philippi.
> . . . .
>   quippe minuti
> semper et infirmi est animi exiguique voluptas
> ultio, continuo sic collige, quod vindicta
> nemo magis gaudet quam femina.

Not only is his plea for personal justice futile in the context of existing legal and moral decline, but it intimates that he is engaged in trivial selfishness,

committed to materialism, and has become suspiciously hypocritical. Relying on the same arguments one would use in a consolatory elegy, then, the
satirist illustrates that Calvinus' lack of self-knowledge renders him ridiculous to all: "nescis / quem tua simplicitas risum vulgo moveat"; enslaved to
possessions, he is more affected by the loss of coins than he would be by the
loss of a relative: "maiore tumultu / planguntur nummi quam funera." So
the old man is advised to learn to laugh at himself and to reject the Heraclitean anger of "chidren and women" for the Democritean capacity to laugh at
the follies and criminal madnesses of this last age ("nona aetas"). He must
learn that there is meager justice in the world, that the golden age of Saturn
is lost forever, if he is to acquire the Senecan *tranquillitas* appropriate to his
age and his generation. The only possible punishment for iron-age criminals
is their guilty consciences ("perpetua anxietas nec mensae tempore cessat").
But even this possibility is slender; for men like Calvinus' criminal, who are
unafraid of thunder and lightning (223–27) and of the gods (229–35), are
unlikely to reform or to confess their crimes under any circumstances. Following his view of the ubiquity of irreligion and immorality, in fact, it is
unlikely that the satirist believes in the efficacy of the conscience.[8] Rather,
the only probable punishment for such malefactors stems from the likelihood
that they will inevitably fall afoul of the corrupt system they have helped
pervert:

> dabit in laqueum vestigia noster
> perfidus et nigri patietur carceris uncum
> aut maris Aegaei rupem scopulosque frequentes
> exulibus magnis.

But even this glimmer of retributive justice in the workings of nature and
fortune should not occupy Calvinus' attention or bolster his hopes for vengeance, the satirist concludes.

Thus, Juvenal's ironic *declamatio* finally dismisses as insufficient the proverbial epigram with which it began ("Exemplo quodcumque malo commit-
titur, ipsi / displicet auctori")—or at least ironically turns it on his complaining addressee. Even the consolations of philosophy become objects of
ridicule, then, in the classical satirist's self-critical mock *consolatio*. Just as he
turns his back on the *saeva indignatio* which dominated his earliest poems and
displaces it here with irony, that "frame of mind which lets us accom-
modate to change and disappointment,"[9] so the satirist advises his addressee
to abandon his selfish desire for revenge and to bridge the gap between ex-
pectation and actuality with an equanimity and healthy skepticism. Such an
attitude must have been especially appealing to an Elizabethan satirist whose
own examination of the religious foundations of his own society had concluded that the safest and surest approach to life's vagaries is to "doubt
wisely."

The most obvious instance of Donne's indebtedness to *Juvenal XIII* in *Satyre V* appears in his description of late Elizabethan England as an

> Age of rusty iron! Some better wit
> Call it worse, if ought equall it;
> Th'iron Age *that* was, when justice was sold; now
> Injustice is sold dearer farre   (35–38)

—a direct borrowing from lines 28–30 of the Latin satire:

> nona aetas agitur peioraque saecula ferri
> temporibus, quorum sceleri non invenit ipsa
> nomen et a nullo posuit natura metallo.

Donne's satirist is able to discover a *nomen*—by suggesting that the worst pejorative of the ancient age has to be accommodated to fit the perversity he sees in the legal corruptions of his own day. But Donne has borrowed more than just these few lines from his Latin model. *Satyre V* is also an address to a complainant who has been defrauded and now "Beg'st right" (82) from a system he helped to corrupt. And, like *Juvenal XIII*, it is a mock *consolatio* that attacks both the illegalities preponderant in this latest age of iron and the suitor's "thrice foolish" (81) inference that he can find some relief in retribution or legal revenge. Donne's poem extends the authoritative design of Juvenal's satire, however, into an ironic and implicit defense of the Justice that the Roman satirist urged was absent from his own age. Addressed to complaining victims who are revealed to be ridiculous in their selfishness and childish pleas for vengeance, both poems conclude that human justice and rationality are absent from the world. Both satirists argue that man's natural and necessary recourse is to turn within himself for the *virtus* of soul that alone can insure his endurance; but the darker vision of the Latin poem, its insistence that there is no evidence of a final cause that will not be mocked by man's idiosyncratic desires and thefts, is transformed by the Elizabethan poem into an ironic vindication of the workings of Providence even within the worst legal system in the worst age. Part of the brilliance of Donne's poem lies in its expansion and accommodation of the dicta and approach of the Roman satire into a Christian theodicy while enforcing the ancient prescription, *nosce teipsum*.

Equally important to this philosophical adjustment to Juvenal's vision are Donne's structural additions to the Latin model. Like *Juvenal XIII*, *Satyre V* aims to edify and criticize a man who has suffered from legal corruptions; but whereas the Roman poem directly addresses the complainant, in Donne's poem he is addressed only indirectly. In *Satyre V* this address is framed as an hypothetical speech, an *example* of the advice that the complainant should receive. The direct addressee of the poem is the lord keeper. Rather than advising an outraged victim of legal fraudulence about what manner of conduct is philosophically sound, Donne's satirist counsels the most powerful legal figure in the land on the use of his power to enforce "righteousnes" (31), on the use of his "authority" (33) to "weed out" sin (34) and to initiate reform of the legal and spiritual abuses within Elizabeth's courts. On one level, then, Donne's poem is framed as an oration to the lord keeper (organized precisely according to the strategy of a formal forensic oration),[10] a formal piece of legal counsel, which contains a hypothetical address to an Elizabethan suitor.

The structure of the poem is even more complex than this, though, for the initial addressee of the poem is not Egerton but the satirist himself. The opening lines return again to consideration of the character of satire: "Thou shalt not laugh in this leafe, Muse, nor they / Whom any pitty warmes" (1-2). The nature of his own satire was also at issue in Juvenal's poem. As Anderson illustrates, when Juvenal advises Calvinus to reject *ira* in favor of a resolve to endure sardonically the irrationality of man, society, and nature, he in effect dismisses as inadequate the stance of his earlier satires.[11] Implicit in Juvenal's poem, then, is an ironic identification of the victim of his satire with the satirist of his own first book of poems. His moral advice to Calvinus, that he supplant self-righteous *indignatio* with Stoic perseverance and laughter, is exemplified by the satirist in his own rejection of the stance of the Heraclitean railer ("difficile est saturam non scribere") for that of the Democritean ironist ("ponamus nimios gemitus"). This implicit identification of the aesthetics of satire and the morality of human conduct in Juvenal's poem is developed explicitly and more fully in Donne's poem. For *Satyre V* is initially a meditation on the satirist's role now that he is no longer a legal outsider. It is the satirist (in his poem) as well as the lord keeper (in his investigation) who is "authoriz'd now [to] beginne / To know and weed out this enormous sinne" (33-34)—authorized both by his position on Egerton's staff and by his moral-aesthetic education chronicled in the first four *Satyres*. Thus, the last *Satyre*, the most complex rhetorically, is cast simultaneously as meditation and as oration. Its outer frame is meditative; its inner frame is forensic or oratorical.

The simultaneous meditative-oratorical perspective is not in itself a significant advance beyond the problematic rhetorical stance of *Satyres III* and *IV*. The crucial difference here, the addition constituting the significant advance beyond the strategies of both Latin satire and the imitations of Donne's contemporaries, is the figure of Egerton. As a figure of authority, invested with the legal power of the queen because of his "righteousnes," he is the means by which the satirist's ideas about the function of satire and about necessary legal reforms can be actualized. "By having leave to serve" the lord keeper (32), the satirist is "most richly / . . . paid" (32-33) by being granted an arena in which his satire (as counsel to Egerton) can legally enforce moral reform. Egerton becomes the activating principle of the satiric process, the means by which satire-as-idea becomes satire-in-action. Therefore, the satirist is no longer merely a meditative observer who understands right action and who hopes that the *energeia* of his poems will move the reader to "Good workes." Now the exemplary options that he dramatizes in his poems can become the means, through Egerton's authority, by which the process of Christian satire becomes the administration of law. From the satirist's point of view, then, as legal counsel to the lord keeper he has become both Horace and Trebatius. And the proposition of the poem, as denoted by the satirist's identification of his role as satirist with that as legal advisor, is for the lord keeper to become Trebatius and Horace—and, by extension, for Egerton to force the suitor to realize the same kind of ethical education. The figure of Egerton, then, provides the satirist with the capacity to *realize* on a national scale, to actualize in the fallen world, that reform that has been central to all his poems. As suggested by his identification of the aesthetic problems of the satirist and the moral problems of mankind throughout the first four *Satyres*, his ultimate goal has been not merely specific personal or national reforms but the reformation, the creation or re-creation of his countrymen, his victims, and his readers into satirists. By illustrating that the aims of satire and the aims of Egerton's investigation are identical, the satirist essentially educates the lord keeper about his role as satirist: he proposes that he *become* a satirist. Thus, the union of the satirist's moral authority and the lord keeper's legal authority provides an opportunity for the satirist to create a nation of satirists.

Obviously, such a statement does not derive from the general definition of the satirist as "*satyr*," "railer," "malcontent," or simply "attacker of vices." To create a nation of satirists means to create a nation of devout seekers and defenders of truth whose zealous union of "Kinde pitty" and "brave scorn" enacts that dutiful self-knowledge and humility about their fallen status and potential salvation that Donne's satirist has dramatized as the role of man in a providential universe. Satire, after all, is a process. As we have seen in the first four poems, it is the activity of loving sinners and hating sins, a steadfast mental attitude by which one responds to and prepares for the gift of God's grace, whether he be scholar, law student, pilgrim, courtier, poet, or lord keeper. This does not mean that it is merely a private, contemplative virtue. Rather, it is an attitude that determines a code of conduct—for scholar, courtier, poet, and lawyer—a code of devotion the principles of which are unfolded in one's public actions. In *Satyre V*, then, it is most significant that Egerton is identified as a figure who has gained power because of his righteousness. His importance to the satirist rests on his status as the embodiment of righteousness as much as the embodiment of law. That is, the implicit, rhetorical given is that since Egerton does embody righteousness, the very righteousness that is the source of his power as lord keeper, then he can deny the satirist's explication of the current legal predicament and of his own duty as lord keeper only by denying that he is indeed righteous. Therefore, rather than just a coincidental historical allusion fortuitously providing Donne a way to solve his problematic view of satire (it is precisely that in an important sense, of course), the figure of Egerton-as-righteousness advances the argument beyond the particular to the general. The argument is not that the man of righteousness will be granted legal power because of his righteousness (despite the examples of both Egerton and Donne), but that the man of righteousness will *enact* the process of satire in his own life. The argument rests not on an *either-or* proposition but a *both*. Satire is the correct conduct in this particular situation and in general. In fact, if the central contention of the poem—that legal abuses amount to abuses of the Law—is applied to the figures of the satirist and the lord keeper, then it is apparent that these figures "serve" the Law ("righteousnes") by reforming the law (as satirical legal counsel and as lord keeper): "Judges are Gods" (57) when they defend moral righteousness, whether they be lord keeper or satirist. Egerton's position as lord keeper, then, proposes an exemplary model and literal, historical, personal means by which the process of satire can be actualized—in 1597 or anytime. Through the Egerton appointment the satirist has the opportunity to remake England in his own image, to use his satiric word to redirect the nation's imitation of the Word—by turning law into satire.

ii

The specific activity in which the satirist engages in the poem, the methodology he enacts and recommends for Egerton's enforcement, is the accommodation of texts—the application of various "wise" texts to one's situation in order to understand the spiritual consequences thereof. In like manner, the satirist's analysis of his role as satirist involves the witty, ironic applicaton of the "Rules" (3) of the courtiers to his own role. For Egerton it means the interpretation of his role as the queen's agent of righteousness in terms of various humanistic and biblical texts, and to the suitor this means the exegesis of his predicament by the accommodation of classical and scriptural texts to his complicity in the corruptions about which he complains. The stages of the satirist's argument are marked, in fact, by textual allusions, whether one emphasizes the meditative or forensic rhetoric of the speaker.

The locus classicus for the satirist's methodology is Augustine's definition of the doctrine of accommodation in *De Doctrina Christiana*.[12] Its basic principle—that the believer, like the preacher and the congregation, should realize his own condition as the embodiment of the text or topic contemplated—is central also to meditations. "Study all the history, and write all the progres of the Holy Spirit in thy selfe," Dean Donne later advised, for God is both "a *direct God*, . . . that wouldest be understood *literally*, and . . . a *figurative*, a *metaphoricall* God" whose purposes can be read in the book of the world as well as in the Bible.[13] *Satyre V* provides both a literal and a metaphorical application of this technique. The satirist applies specific texts to the conditions of satirist, lord keeper, and suitor in order to explicate both the legal (literal) and divine (figurative or spiritual) law. And, at the same time, his exegeses of current abuses confirm that although the present legal system about which the suitor complains has literally become a system of injustice, there is yet a Justice at work within it that ironically punishes those who participate in legal corruption. The satirist begins each section of the poem by referring to a popular or classical text, accommodates that text to the present conditions, and then clarifies its significance with a biblical text or Christian tenet. The "pagan" condition of English justice in this "Age of rusty iron" is clarified, in other words, by application of God's law to that condition. Thus, the meditative examination of the role of satire within this system proposes both a specific address and a specific methodology by which the lord keeper can force the corrupt suitors to understand their complicity. Even the methodology of the poem—the application of texts—mirrors the process by which satire is activated. Just as the suitor is to apply specific texts to his situation in order to understand what action to follow, and just as the satirist applies specific texts to his role as satirist and Egerton's role as lord keeper, so it is proposed that the lord keeper apply a specific text to his situation in order to initiate reform—the text of the satirist's poem. And this, of course, is the process the satirist hopes to instill in all men: the man of righteousness who has understood (3) the definitions of satire as devotion and moral imitation in the previous *Satyres* will apply those texts to his own condition, thus participating personally in the satirist's and the lord keeper's efforts "To know and weed out this enormous sinne." "It is the text that saves us" (*Sermons*, V, 19).

The meditator's opening proposition (the "entraunce" of his address to Egerton) applies the "rules" of Castiglione to the satirist's "question" about satire. These rules are then clarified by his plea for "Charity and liberty" (7), the foundation of Christian ethics and morality. Explication of the Paracelsian doctrine of accommodation (9) at the start of his second Preludium (9–27)—the *narratio* of his address—is supplemented by exposition of Genesis 3:19 (19–27). After a curious apotheosis of Elizabeth and encomium of Egerton, which concludes the meditator's Preparation and contains the orator's *propositio* (28–34), the procession through the mental faculties of memory (35–42), understanding (43–63), and will (63–78) provides the "proofs" of the oration. The first of these sections explicates the general condition of justice and law in England, beginning with an application of Juvenal's epithet (35), which is amplified by reference to Ariosto (41–42). This "composition" of the place of justice in English law is confirmed by expositions of Psalm 40 (43) and Matthew 25:28 (56). Once the claims of the suitor are begun, however, this pattern is reversed, mirroring the inversion of right and wrong in his legal activities. Psalm 82 (57) and a phrase from the *Pater noster* (62) are clarified by reference to the pagan concepts of destiny (70) and fate (71); and the words of Micah (82), Numbers (83), and Esther (87) are explained by a "fable" from Aesop (89–91). Thus, the meditator's appeal to the will of the auditor and colloquy to him confute and summarize the illegitimacy of the suitor's hypothetical complaint. The poem proceeds, then, not by a "series of spasmodic efforts,"[14] but in accordance with the structure, methods, and techniques of traditional devotional and forensic principles: a thoroughly fitting mixture for a young lawyer assessing the legal, moral, and spiritual foundations of his recent appointment and imminent assignment and for a satirist evaluating the role of satire within the legal machinery of the law and the unfolding revelation of the Law.

This process of accommodation, which both St. Augustine and Dean Donne defended as a supreme form of Christian love,[15] begins with the satirist's ironic application of the rules of the courtiers' book of manners to his own satire. Similar to the opening of *Satyre II*, in which he allowed the *misomusoi* their most severe argument in order to disclose the outrageous illogic of their claims, he accepts the prescriptions of Castiglione as a defense of his own satire of the courtiers: *Il Cortegiano* "Frees from the sting of jests all who'in extreme / Are wrech'd or wicked" (5–6). The litotes here is marvelous, for, like the courtiers who pervert the spirit of the law (and the Law) while answering to its letter, the satirist "perverts" the courteous intention of their own code by allowing that he will in no way "jest" at them. As Castiglione's Bernardo prescribed, they will be "otherwise punished"[16] by him. But if he will not jest, neither will he suspend judgment—"Thou shalt not laugh in this leafe." As in *Satyre II*, then, he prepares his defense of satire by an apparent willingness to conform to the rules of his victims.

These rules are turned on the courtiers, however, by the satirist's agreement to follow only their letter, according to which he must be granted the "Charity and liberty" to satirize those who are "extreme[ly] . . . wrech'd or wicked" as long as he does not laugh at them. Castiglione's rule receives a final gibe in the satirist's sarcastic retort—"What is hee / Who Officers rage, and Suiters misery / Can write, and jest?" (7–9)—but this only validates further the satirist's apparent concession to adhere literally to the code of those he attacks. These ironic deflations of the Italian humanist's prescriptions intimate, then, the ethos of the satirist. They qualify his opening warning that his poem would contain no pity by revealing that he speaks on behalf of "Charity and liberty"; thus they enact that union of mercy and justice (*laus et vituperatio*) constituting the true quality of law and satire. And the sarcastic parenthesis about Castiglione—"(hee being understood / May make good Courtiers . . .)" (3–4)—suggests that his emphasis as a satirist is on the rectification of man's understanding. After all, the problem with the courtiers is not their ignorance of the rules of justice in the realm, but their incomprehension or refusal to acknowledge the consequences of applying the letter of the law while denying its spirit. Each of the biblical texts the satirist subsequently applies to their case, in fact, if taken only literally, could be read as a defense of their activities. But his exposition shows these activities to be perversions of the spirit of the scriptural law he cites. Thus, the satirist's ironic application of the courtiers' rules to himself both defends and exemplifies the central method and message of satire as textual exegesis and meditative counsel—the recitation of precedent laws and their applicability to one's condition.

This opening ironic defense of his satiric stance also looks beyond the topical reference to Castiglione to the authoritative formula of Horace, providing another modification of or response to Horace's explanation of his approach in *Satire I.i.* In the classical diatribe against the avarice that stirs human dissatisfaction, Horace offers the following defense of his own satiric method:

> praetera ne sic, ut qui iocularia, ridens
> percurram—quamquam ridentem dicere verum quid vetat?

These lines, Anderson points out, are probably intended to contrast his own satire with that of his famous predecessor, Lucilius, whose liberality and thoughtless jocularity are mocked throughout Horace's first book of satires and *Ars Poetica*.[17] The Lucilian satiric stance, Horace urges, is inappropriate to the more serious matter of satire. He "discards *iocularia* and *ludus* as inadequate to his purpose," anxious to insist that he begins his satire "where the Lucilian satirist presumably left off." Horace's stance is aptly summarized by Anderson: "the Horatian satirist is *doctor*, . . . a teacher instructing puerile mankind in serious elementary moral truths, but willing to coax us by his laughing, ironic manner in order to impress his truths more effectively in our hearts."[18] Horace's *ridentem dicere verum* became, in fact, an authoritative formula for satiric expression in the commentaries and annotations of Renaissance critics and scholars such as Lambinus, Britannicus, Landinum, Crinitus, John Bond, and Lubin.[19] Even Casaubon's championing of Persius over Horace and Juvenal borrowed this prescription to defend the second great Roman satirist: "Satirae proprium est ridendo dicere verum: duo igitur . . . scriptionis satiricae, reprehendere et ridere."[20] But, just as Horace found the jocularity of Lucilius inappropriate to the moral seriousness of satire, Donne's satirist once again finds the stance of Horace inadequate; it must be accommodated to suit the severe conditions of the "Age of rusty iron" in which he writes. The defense of his anger and hatred, in other words, responds ironically but seriously to Horace's defense of his "telling truths while he laughs."

Therefore, the satirist's assertion of the universal principle of accommodation—

If all things be in all,
As I thinke, since all, which were, are, and shall
Bee, be made of the same elements:
Each thing, each thing implyes or represents   (9–12)

—has already been verified doubly by his discovery of a defense of charity
and liberty in the rules of the courtiers and by his accommodation of the
ancient formula. The elemental structure of the universe, the enigmatic but
eloquent book of the world, confirms the validity of his applications; it "implyes" that he can satirize if he does not jest and represents a defense of his
using the harsh weapon of satire to punish extremity. At the same time, the
lines are another example of his accommodation of texts to identify the faults
he prosecutes. Several sources were available for the theory that "all things
be in all," Plato's *Timaeus* the most famous, the recent writings of Paracelsus
the most likely.[21] And whether Donne himself accepted the conclusions of
the philosophical science of the hermetic doctor is not the crucial point
here.[22] That the satirist assents to it, using another form of "wisdom" in his
own defense of truth and prosecution of "enormous sinne," shows him not
to be an isolated idealist who resolutely condemns the efforts of other men
to acquire truth. Rather, the satirist emerges as a judicious exegete willing to
acknowledge the possibility of truth in men's efforts in order to build on
their observations, to help others understand the spiritual consequences of
their actions, and to verify his own genre.

From the principle of accommodation both the satirist's method and subject evolve, so that his own application of texts to the workings of justice and
Justice in the world imitates the very manner in which the Word is existentially revealed to man. His satire becomes *a* word which both explicates and
imitates the workings of *the* Word in the world. To borrow Janel Mueller's
term for Donne's devotional technique, the satirist's "exegesis of experience"[23]
provides a method and an explanation of the wisdom of that method simultaneously. In this case, the satirist's amplification of Paracelsus' text by two
micro-macrocosmic analogies (13–19) delineating the "raging" fraudulence of
officers and the suicidal incontinence of suitors discloses that the same principle the satirist applied to his own function is applicable equally to the
objects of his satire. If "man is a world" (13), then the officers are seas which
drown greedy suitors; if "the world [is] a man" (17), then the suitors are the
"excrements" which the appetitive officers "voyd" (19). By applying his universal theory first to the inanimate and then the animate level of being (moving in the next lines to the human level), the satirist intimates not only that
those who participate in such a corrupt system are stupid, but also that the
justice of the suitor's suffering from willful participation in an unjust frame-
work merely "represents" how *Justice* exists in even the most corrupt system.

The speaker's observation that "All men are dust" (19) seems merely to be an extension of his amplification of Paracelsus' doctrine and the *contemptus mundi* strain of his application of it to the courtiers' situation. This appropriated image is significant mainly, however, as a scriptural text: Genesis 3:19, God's announcement of his dispensation of mortality to mankind for the original sin. In one sense, the citation compels recollection of man's spiritual condition, his participation in Adam's sin and his need for grace, just as the satirist's plight in *Satyre IV* forced him to reconsider his own "forefathers sinne." But, equally important, the implicit comparison of the treatment of the suitors by the officers to the treatment accorded mankind by God reveals that the suitors receive worse punishment than they would from God at his most "jealous." "Worse then dust" by allowing themselves "to mens lust . . . made preyes" (20–21), suitors receive a harsher sentence from the "devouring" officers than from the Eternal Judge for mankind's original "enormous sinne." And although the satirist does not in any way defend the heinous wickedness of the officers, he does point out that the suitors ironically are treated "justly" by them:

> They [the officers] are the mills which grinde you, yet you are
> The winde which drives them; and a wastfull warre
> Is fought against you, and you fight it; they
> Adulterate lawe, and you prepare their way
> Like wittals; th'issue your owne ruine is.   (23–27)

The suitors do suffer from evil judges and agents, against whom it would be both treason and improvidence to rebel; but the officers could not continue in their adulteration without the aid of the suitors themselves. In this sense, the suitors' suffering "represents" evidence of an efficacious Justice in the world. In accordance with the Providence that made "all men dust," the suitors are aptly punished for their continued participation in sin. What their misery "implyes," the application of the Genesis text shows: that they should turn their attention to the "All" who guides and directs all things in this world. As Donne later pointed out in one of his considerations of why men are not "*meere dust*," man can initiate recovery from the Fall by recognizing that the condition of his soul depends on knowledge of God's dealings with man, gained from the Bible.[24] The satirist emulates that process here by illustrating the relevance of God's law to the suitor's legal experiences.

This union of method and matter by the satirist continues in his identification of his satire with the "righteousnes" of Egerton, in which he satisfies the principle of *laus et vituperatio* by providing an exemplary alternative to the vice he attacks. There is always "a wastfull warre" being fought against God's children, the satirist warns; here he recognizes those forces of "righteousnes" with which one can align himself. Initiated by a question (as is each section of his meditation), allusion to the appointment of Egerton by the queen provides a norm against which the incontinency of the suitors can be judged. The satirist seems torn between idealizing Elizabeth in the customary fashion and accusing her of criminal neglect, between insisting that the suitors solicit their own misery and intimating that the "Greatest and fairest Empresse" (28) has contributed to their misery by failing to "know / Whose meades her armes drowne, or whose corne o'rflow" (29–30). But the emphasis of his description of her as knowing "no more then Thames calme head doth know" (29) is that even though she is "Greatest and fairest" of all temporal powers, she is helpless without figures such as Egerton. Her esteem is salvaged through her association with him—she does "righteousnes . . . love" (31). But the satirist's praise is reserved for the lord keeper as an embodiment of that law and righteousness. The attempt to idealize Elizabeth intentionally fails, it seems, in order to illustrate that man's greatest form of justice is inadequate unless it is supported by an attempt "To know and weed out" the sins of the realm. In this sense, then, the ambiguous antecedent to the word *authoriz'd* suggests that it is the satirist as well as the lord keeper who "*now* begin[s]," in the following presentation of proofs and in the formal investigation, to clarify the causes and cure for this "enormous sinne."

Therefore, since "to know" in the context of the poem means to know one's relationship to God's law, the satirist proves his case ("composes" his subject) by continuing his accommodation of classical and scriptural texts to current legal practices, offering first a view of the general condition of "injustice" and the sense of Justice which that condition perverts. Having expanded the scope of his address in the previous section, moving from the original private address to himself to include Egerton in his satirical party, the satirist adds another level of address. Thus, what is an "actuall thinking on the matter elected" for the meditative satirist and a general "proof" of the wisdom of the lord keeper's investigation becomes also hypothetical counsel to a typical suitor—a meditative example of why and how Egerton will proceed if he accepts the advice of his legal advisor.

This counsel to lord keeper and suitor borrows first the epithet of *Juvenal XIII*:

> nona aetas agitur peioraque saecula ferri
> temporibus, quorum sceleri non invenit ipsa
> nomen et a nullo posuit natura metallo.

But even the classical poet's most severe pejorative for Roman degradation has to be modified to fit the present age:

> O Age of *rusty* iron! Some better wit
> Call it some worse name, if ought equall it.
> Th'iron Age *that* was, when justice was sold; now
> Injustice is sold dearer farre.   (35–38)

The accommodation of this ancient invective in some ways supports the description of the head of the government as removed from the activities of justice (or injustice) in the realm, as when Astraea (with whom Elizabeth was often compared) forsook the world because of human corruption. That the present situation deserves such an epithet is proved by specific examples of the suitors in action. By allowing "All demands, fees, and duties" (39) to be extracted from them in hope of profit for themselves, they corrode justice. By striving for "controverted lands" (41) that they might not deserve and by permitting all judgments to be decided by "fees, and duties," these "gamsters" (39) find that such lands escape their grasp, just as Ariosto's Angelica escaped the lustful knights who fought over her (42).

That it is the suitors who bring about their own misery is confirmed by Psalm 40 ("If Law be in the Judges heart" [43]), David's admonition that the vow of man should be to "delight to do thy will, O God; thy Law is within mine heart" (verse 8). Thus, reference to the full context of the biblical source reveals not only the suitors' predicament but also the option that they should enact. Certainly, the speaker is dismayed over the perversions of justice in the current system, as his long amplification of this passage from the Psalm (46–53) makes clear. But the burden of his reminder about the legitimate source of the "Powre of the Courts below" (45)—it "Flow[s] from the first maine head" (46), from the queen and through her as deputy of God—is on the conduct required of the suitors: such corrupt manipulation of the law is self-perpetuating and endlessly frustrating to those who support its continuance with their gold. The next textual applications urge the same point. The conflation of another Paracelsian text ("All things follow their like") and Christ's parable of the talents in Matthew 25:28 ("only who have may have more" [56]) shows that the suitors have helped to create a system in which the duty of every man as prescribed by Christ has been perverted into a purely economic fiat that dooms the miserable to more misery, the poor to endless poverty, and the weak to more suffering. Suitors may complain about the officers, but they are still like them and follow their example. Like the greedy servants of Christ's parable, they merit the poverty they suffer.

The contrast between the Law and present legal practices is finally understood by applications of Psalm 82 and the *Pater noster*. Psalm 82 ("Judges are Gods" [57]), a vision of God's judgment of proud judges according to Renaissance annotation,[25] is particularly apt in the historical context of *Satyre V*'s attack on judges of the Star Chamber, supposedly a poor man's court. The psalmist insists that the function of judges is to cease to "judge unjustly and show partiality to the wicked," to "give justice to the weak and the fatherless: maintain the right of the afflicted and the destitute" (verses 2–3), and warns that such "gods . . . shall die like men, and fall like princes" (verses 6–7), their god-like powers only a temporary gift. So, rather than being a defense of the injustice of Elizabethan judges—an interpretation literal reading might imply—the passage shows that the judges will be punished eventually for failing in their charge: "n'er may / Faire lawes white reverend name be strumpeted" (68–69). Present practices *are* a perversion of the theocentric basis of justice: He who gave judges these powers to exercise after His model on earth "Meant not that men should be forc'd to them to goe" (58) through bribery. The recognition that "daily bread" (62)—the Charity that sustains the world—is and will be "Scarce to Kings" (63) reiterates, moreover, that God's Justice is yet operative on earth and "stretches" to all men regardless of worldly rank or power.

That the suitors are therefore innocent of any culpability because of the officers' tyranny is, however, denied again by the satirist's portrait of the manner in which Justice is served even through a deformed system. Just as Juvenal's satirist advised that the widespread degradation of Roman religion and law could not excuse Calvinus for his culpable hypocrisy and materialism, so Donne's satirist insists that the suitors deserve the punishment they receive. A final reminder of the temporary power of the officers and their responsibility for the present corruption is provided by reference to the pagan concepts of destiny and fate and the phrase "on earth" (71–72), but the emphasis of the satirist's counsel is that God's law continues to operate at all times (from the beginnings of time, as the reference to the ancient concepts specifies) in spite of and even through acts of human corruption. The current judges and officers will personally pay for their abuses of power, but they are yet the means through which Justice scourges the suitors for their greed. Even in their perversions of the letter of the Law, they ironically fulfill the spirit of God's Justice by providing punishment for the suitors. There is a divinity that shapes man's ends even in an "Age of rusty iron!" There may be no justice in the courts, but there is always Justice in the world:

> Shee is all faire, but yet hath foule long nailes,
> With which she scracheth Suiters; In bodies
> Of men, so'in law, nailes are th'extremities,
> So Officers stretch to more then Law can doe,
> As our nailes reach what no else part comes to.   (74–78)

Thus, the appraisal of the suitor's complaint about unfair treatment clarifies the justice of his own misery while reminding him of the Justice to which he should turn his attention:

> Why bar'st thou to yon Officer? Foole, Hath hee
> Got those goods, for which erst men bar'd to thee?
> Foole, twice, thrice, thou'hast bought wrong,'and how hungerly
> Beg'st right.   (79–82)

Having acquired goods by devious methods and then lost them to the officers, the suitor is a triple fool who begs for legal justice only after finding that prostitution of the law has failed to advance him personally. "That dole," with its suggestions of a final grief as well as a final justice simultaneously, "comes not till these dye" (82). "Dole," in fact, recalls the admonition of Micah about that "evil time" when the evil men of the world will wail "with a doleful lamentation" their inequities (Micah 2:4) and the warning of Isaiah about that "time [which] is near to come" when "houses shall be full of doleful creatures" (Isaiah 13:21–22)—Old Testament prophecies of the Day of Judgment.[26] The suggestions that the suitors will receive a "dole" (grievance) as their "dole" (justice) on that day—and not until that day if Justice will arrive "not till these dye"—summarizes the satirist's paradoxical view of the operations of Justice amidst injustice.

It is not necessary, of course, that the satirist be thinking of either of these passages for his warnings to intimate the eventual end the suitor's ill-acquired goods (80) will earn him, but Micah's warning (one of only two instances of the word *dole* in the Bible) contains in its full context striking parallels to the strategy of the satirist's argument. The Prophet, speaking of the eventual "woe to those who devise wickedness and work evil upon their beds," insists that the day shall come when such sinners "will have none to cast the line by lot." "In that day," he urges, "a parable shall be taken up among you," which, according to sixteenth-century annotation, meant that a day shall come when "the Israelites by their crying of injustices provoke God to punish them."[27] The satirist's speculation that the suitor would "lawes Urim and Thummim trie . . . for more" (83–84), that he would cast the sacred lots of the Church, is parallel to Micah's line, then, as a remembrance of the eternal governance of God and the inevitable judgment promised by his Word. Since the suitor wants "right" (82) and it "comes not till these dye," till that Day predicted by Micah, then the foolishness of his testing the holy lots is reinforced by the scriptural prophecy that evil men ultimately doom themselves to "dole."

Furthermore, the satirist's declaration that the suitor would "trie Urim and Thummim . . . for more," that the suitor would test the "clarity and integrity" of the law in order to gain his own covetous ends, is enlarged by the biblical sources for this specific allusion (Numbers 27:21, Exodus 28:30, I Samuel 7:7). Although the exact nature of these gems is not made clear in any of the half-dozen references to them in the Old Testament, it is certain from all these references that they were considered authoritative and oracular means of divining God's purposes, some sort of dice used by the Hebrew priests to discover God's intentions in judicial matters.[28] Such an interpretation would ironically accord with the satirist's earlier view of the suitor as a "gamster." But here the allusion recalls again the divine Justice operative in the world, the Law. The satirist insisted earlier that Law "tells us who must bee / Rich, who poore, who in chaires, who in jayles" (72–73). The implication here is that the suitor in effect tests and "trie[s]" Providence ("trie" meaning also to strain the justice of the Law), in accordance with Micah's prophecy of a time when fallen men's cries for justice shall "provoke God to punish" them.

The satirist's final biblical allusion also directs attention to the futility of the suitor's activity by revealing that all he has gained from them is sheets of paper that are worth no more than wrapping:

> for all hast paper
> Enough to cloath all the great Carricks Pepper.
> Sell that, and by that thou much more shalt leese,
> Then Haman, when he sold his Antiquities.   (84–87)

Actually, the suitor has gained nothing but rubbish for all his efforts—suffering an ironic inversion of the Christian paradox of man's earning most (salvation) by possessing least (earthly goods). The reference to Haman also recalls an example of how God punishes men through their own crimes; the traitorous priest sold his own treasures in order to pay off the assassins but ended up being hanged on the gallows he had erected for the faithful Mordecai. This final biblical accommodation emphasizes again that, by demanding justice after practicing injustice and by continuing to "trie" the Justice of the land, the suitor will share the fate of Haman. He will, as one of the most popular preachers at the turn of the century phrased it, become himself an example of how Providence "hoists men on their own golden chains."[29] By selling his "Antiquities," God's people and the wisdom of their religion (*O.E.D.*, II, 5, 6), Haman lost his life; the suitor "Much more shalt leese"— his soul. Once again, the satirist has found need because of the perversity of the times to modify his text in order to apply it to the present age.

His theoretical address concludes, however, not with a Christian text, but with a classical allusion, Aesop's fable of the dog who saw his shadow in a pool, dived after the bone he saw reflected there, and almost drowned. According to one Renaissance commentator, this fable was a Christian lesson to "That wauering wighte, that hopes for better fate, / And not content, his cawlinge doth despise" that he would "liue at lengthe, with losse of maine, and all."[30] This is certainly, in one sense, the condition of the suitor, but the point here is not just that the fable is a veiled Christian parable but that it is a *pagan* tale. It warns that by trying Providence, by becoming even worse than the traitorous Haman, the suitor shall, in a sense, be beyond even Christian understanding. Failure to understand, to apply to one's own case the examples of God's working as made clear by God's Words, amounts to spiritual suicide. The suitor is a wretch not just because he renders himself foolish and subhuman in action, no better than a hungry dog, but because his activities "moralize . . . tales" and make them "prophesies" (88–89). In the rhetorical context of the poem, there is no scriptural text suitable finally to describe such degradation. So, this inversion of the pattern of allusions in the poem, in which each section is clarified by a biblical reference and which relies constantly on Christian texts to add spiritual perspectives on the actions of the suitor and officers, suggests the perversity of the suitor's condition. Acting as if the Revelation has never occurred, as if Christianity had never produced examples of morality and lessons about greed, as if God does not clearly offer eloquent books through which man can understand his duties and spiritual condition, the suitor perversely "moralize[s] tales," fulfilling not the prophesies of God but those of pagan folklore. Having chosen to trust in an "iron age" system of injustice from which he receives harsher treatment than he would from the Justice of God, the suitor is aptly classified in pagan terms. Whether this cozened fool can understand that Justice has not vanished from the world by recognizing the justice of his own misery is the charge the satirist leaves with him. Whether he wishes to continue to pursue the fable of human justice or to acknowledge the eternal truth of God's immanent Word is the choice he must make.

iii

What begins, then, as another examination of the role of satire in the world and an imitation of a Latin satire becomes Donne's fullest development of the "zealous" satirist as theodicean counselor. A triple address "hovering between the public and the meditative voice,"[31] both meditation and oration, the poem illustrates not only the means but the manner in which satire can become a process of active Christian reform. In one sense, the appointment to Egerton's staff provided Donne the arena in which he could have his satire transformed into legal reform. At the same time, we must remember that Egerton is, in one sense, merely an historical metaphor, a particular embodiment of "righteousnes"—a metaphor for the actual bodying forth of the satirical process of "Kinde pitty" and "brave scorn" which the exemplary satirist has dramatized for all his readers. The view of satire as the application of texts to one's condition in the theater of God's judgments presented in the final *Satyre*, after all, does not specify only the manner in which Egerton activates satire: it also reveals how the satirist's reader, by applying this text, the *Satyres*, to his situation, can make satire the moral law of the land. This is the charge to lord keeper, suitor, and reader at the end of the fifth *Satyre*. Whether they can, as the satirist's words counsel, recognize, respond to, and rely upon the Words of Justice before they suffer the inevitable "dole" of that Justice remains the only unanswered question about the role of satire and the uses of Law (and law) at the end of Donne's book of *Satyres*. "The readiness," as another poet of the age counseled in his examinations of the workings of the Word, "is all."

The last lines of *Satyre V* encapsulate many of the central features of the *Satyres* overall—the borrowing from Aesop (and perhaps a side glance at Horace's *Satire I.i.* 69–70),[32] the modification of the ancient fabulist's warning (the dog does not drown here), the description of his satiric victim as someone who does not recognize his own image, the focus on one's precarious position in a providential world, and the reiteration that man is a product of his own creation (or re-creation), even the nod at the biblical satirists in the word *prophesies*. This complex of allusion, accommodation, and exhortation, this re-creation of ancient forms and methods, is typical of the central issue of all five poems—the transformation of the ancient modes and techniques to the rhetoric of Christian zeal in order to promote ethical reformation based on self-knowledge. The *Satyres* are, of course, excellent examples of Donne's status as a "witty" poet, as the creator in English literature of a poetry of wit; but their animating principle is the poet's profound contempt for sham and pretense, falsehood, affectation, and intolerance—in himself as well as in his satiric victims. Such an attitude necessitates above all his own discovery or creation of a voice appropriate to the conditions in which and about which he writes, a voice able to address and to admit the variety of human failures he confronts. The sequence shows that Christian satire requires a constant process of adjustment, critical adaptation, and inventive transformation, not just of the strictures and strategies of Horace and Juvenal, but to the speaker's own condition as a fallen man in and of an inconstant world. The mode of pastoral care applied to the London fop must be adjusted when facing the meretricious abuses of a Coscus; the stern admonition used for the failed religious amorists must be modified to the demands of dangerous confrontation of court blasphemers; and the advice offered the lord keeper must assume a more complex mode of address altogether. So, as the sequence depicts the satirist's discovery of a various world of folly and crime it also details his expanding awareness of the variety, strengths, and limitations of his powers as man and as poet.

Thus the central drama of the *Satyres* is less the satirist's clever ridicule of fools and knaves than it is the unfolding discovery of his own voice and genre, of the demands, decorum, and dangers of *kinde pitty* and *brave scorn*. Words, like men, like himself, he discovers, are fallen; so the satirist must always search *about*, *and about* for the ways his words can affect the moral cure he is determined to realize. And such a search requires a moral constancy and faith in language concomitant to an awareness of the protean character of men and words. It is this process of opening up and critically analyzing his own voice and genre that is the major experience of the five poems—the poet's reflexive testing of the private and public truthfulness of his own words, of the "riddlingly" complex character of man and metaphor.[33]

Donne is always the comic poet, whether focusing fearfully on the tragic immorality of the human comedy or directing attention to the fearful demands and tolerance of the divine comedy; but the spirit, the intelligence which guides that comic spirit, is distinguished by the ability to perceive keenly, in himself and in all men, the false. This is the feature of Donne's poetry that continues to charm and alert us, whether he is mocking literalistic petrarchists and dispassionate neoplatonists in his lyrics or puncturing the high seriousness and moral intolerance of social *gravitas* in his elegies, implicitly criticizing puritan smugness in the holy sonnets or undercutting platonic separations of body and soul in the love poems; and it is first distinguished in the *zealous* reflexiveness of his own *Satyres*. The clear-sighted recognition of the truth of reality is also what animates his powers of imitation and parody, and lies at the heart of his ability, in the *Satyres* most notably, to take a conventional form or mode and re-animate it, re-use it, revive it, and yet not take out its essential strengths. As most evident in his adaptations and accommodations of Roman verse satire to the demands and perception of Christian zeal, Donne's essential power as a poet lies in his ability to see and to convey the limitations and strengths of norms and forms of expression as vehicles of truth. This is the general achievement of Donne in his *Satyres*—the clear-sighted, perceptive, careful distinction of what is real.

APPENDIX A

"Carelesse Phrygius"

Stultus factus est omnis homo, à scientia.

Jeremiah 10:14

The first three figures ridiculed in the central section of *Satyre III* have been easily recognized as embodying insufficient reasons for aligning oneself with the three major parties in the Elizabethan settlement. Mirreus the Roman Catholic worships authority and tradition; Crants the Genevist Puritan adores only the most "unhansome" church; and Graius the Anglican accepts the local church because of its proximity. The fourth figure in the satirist's mimetic Choice of Paris[1] has proved to be more problematic:

> Carelesse Phrygius doth abhorre
> All, because all cannot be good, as one
> Knowing some women whores, dares marry none.

Like the first three myopic sectarians, however, the source for the satirist's ridicule is best discovered among the religious controversialists at the end of the sixteenth century.

The most frequent explanation of Phrygius is that he is an atheist, a sound annotation if one takes "All" as a punning reference to God (rather than to all churches). Such a view also seems consistent with the logic of the satirist's anatomy of current religions: the first three figures represent abusive varieties of the three choices available to Donne's Elizabethan countrymen, and Phrygius represents the next logical choice—no choice at all. Like the cynical Petrarchist who speaks "Song: Goe, and catche a falling starre," Phrygius has decided only that he knows of no true Church; all have been infected, the simile suggests, by descent from the Whore of Babylon. The puritanical aloofness of both speakers is undoubtedly undercut by the pun on the verb *knows* as sexual knowledge; both the singer and the sectarian base their atheistic principles on their exclusive "knowledge" of some whores. Certainly, in an age in which men tortured, hanged, and burned each other for doctrinal differences, Phrygius could be termed an atheist. But this does not mean that he is an atheist in the strictest technical or modern sense of the word (and Donne reveals a keen awareness of the technical meanings of theological distinctions throughout his poetry). Phrygius does not deny the existence of God, but only that any of the current churches descends unblemished from the vicarage of St. Peter.

Much to the point are Don Cameron Allen's observations of atheism as the Renaissance's "majestic term of reproach and condemnation": "Roman Catholics, convinced that doctrinal disagreement ended in disbelief, called the views of their opponents 'atheism.' Protestants pointed up their case against Rome by counting the alleged atheists in the Catholic hierarchy. Some Christians heard the bellow of atheist laughter in every street."[2] But in the scores of books which streamed from European and English presses during the Renaissance, infrequently "was the word 'atheist' used correctly, and atheism was seldom separated from heresy or even theological disagreement."[3] Although not a direct volley in the doctrinal wars of the age, Robert Burton's comments on atheism as a version of religious-melancholy are typical of the broad application of this term to a wide range of religious views with which he disagrees. Phrygius, Milgate points out,[4] would certainly have qualified as an atheist in Burton's eyes. One of the "milder sort" of that "monstrous Melancholy; or poisoned Melancholy," the ironist writes, are

> the Atheisticall spirits . . . that profess Religion, but timidly and hesitantly, tempted thereunto out of that horrible consideration of diversity of Religions, which are and have been in the world . . . besides the covetousness, imposture and knavery of Priests which . . . makes people believe less in religion, and those religions some of them so fantastical, exorbitant, so violently maintained with equal constancy and assurance; whence they infer, that if there be so many religious sects, and denied by the rest, why may they not be all false? or why should this or that be preferred before the rest?[5]

If, on the other hand, we apply the criteria for atheism of Richard Hooker to Phrygius, then he fails to fit the term. As Allen points out, Hooker, in Book III of the *Laws*, describes an atheist "to be nothing more than an atheist. Let a man think his soul immortal . . . and a belief in the creation of the world, the Providence of God, the resurrection of the dead, the joys of heaven, the endless pains of the wicked, and the authority of the Bible comes after 'as a voluntary train.'"[6]

Whether Phrygius believes in the immortality of the soul or even in the existence of God is not made clear in Donne's passage. That he does, in fact, is implied. He is not portrayed as an atheist but as some sort of purist (I dodge the word *puritan*) who believes simply that all current forms of the

Church fail to fulfill Christian principles. He does not believe in the possibility of a pure Church any more than some of Donne's lyrical personae believe in "a woman [both] true, and faire." If we consider *Satyre III* a timeless philosophical inquiry into types of religious error, then we might use Burton's subgenre of atheism and term Phrygius a Skeptic. But if the poem is an address to his contemporaries or a meditation on the religious opinions and religious errors of Donne's time, then it is more likely that the original for Phrygius can be found in the sixteenth-century English controversy over "true religion" which dominated the age. Such an approach seems more fitting since the picture of Phrygius follows the satirist's question as to where his countrymen found their versions of "faire Religion."

Deciding which or if Donne had a particular sect in mind in the creation of Phrygius is complicated by the attitudes towards the other religious sects in the age (as well as by the rapid proliferation of sects at the end of the century and the large number that were merely subspecies of each other). Once again, Burton's remarks in his *Anatomy* are representative of the tendency to draw no distinctions between the various sectaries:

> So it is with all hereticks and schismaticks whatsoever: and none so passionate, violent in their tenets, opinions, obstinate, wilful, refractory, peevish, factious, singular and stiff in defense of them; they do not only persecute and hate, but pity all other Religions, account them damned, blind, as if they alone were the true Church, they are the true heirs, have the simple fee of heaven by a peculiar donation, 'tis entailed on them and their posterities, their doctrine sound, *per funem aurem de caelo delapsa doctrina*, are to be saved. . . .
>
> . . . we have a mad giddy company of Precisians, Schismaticks, and some Hereticks . . . that out of too much zeal in opposition to Antichrist, human traditions, those Romish rites and superstitions, will quite demolish all, they will admit no ceremonies at all, no fasting days, no Cross in Baptism, no knelling at Communion, no Church-Musick, &c. . . . because Papists use them, . . . no disciplines, no ceremonies, . . . no Churches . . . but such as their own phantastical spirits dictate. . . . many times they broach as prodigious paradoxes as Papists themselves. . . .
>
> . . . What are all our *Anabaptists, Brownists, Barrowists, Familists*, but a company of rude, illiterate, capricious base fellows?[7]

Even the controversialists themselves often fail (or refuse) to distinguish various groups from one other, relying instead on a general nomenclature of disdain. George Gifford, for example, in his heated exchanges with Henry Barrow and John Greenwood, calls all the dissenters Brownists and Donatists; Richard Alison calls them just Brownists; while Robert Some prefers Anabaptists. And as might be expected, exemplified first and foremost by the Marprelate Tracts, the grand malediction *antichristian* finds a place on the title page of most of the pamphlets, printed sermons, and treatises of the controversialists. Many groups complain specifically, in fact, that their critics "blasphemously" fail to distinguish them from other, heretical sectaries.[8]

Nevertheless, given the focus of Donne's catalogue on *contemporary* religious foolishness, it is possible that the poet had a specific target in mind in the portrait of Phrygius. The English sect closest in spirit and word to the "reasoning" of Phrygius is the Seekers. They too urge that the search for "our Mistresse, faire Religion" among existing churches is futile. Replete with the language of Daniel, Canticles, and (especially) Revelations—central to the polemic of Renaissance schismatics and separatist dissenters—,[9] their apologiae are founded on the belief that one "dare marry none" (64) of the existing churches because all have inherited the corruptions of their "eldest sister," the Great Whore of Babylon, Roman Catholicism. Also known as the English Arians or Legatine-Arians (after the three Legate brothers who founded the sect), this group contends that "the powers and authorities granted to the apostles in the New Testament [have] been so corrupted and destroyed by the Church of Rome that no true church could be constituted until God raise[s] up a new race of apostles." In 1646 Thomas Edwards could report that the Seekers constituted a genuine threat to English religious harmony: "the sect of Seekers grows very much, and all sorts of sectaries turn Seekers; many leave the congregations of Independents [and] Anabaptists, and fall to be Seekers, and not only people, but ministers also."[10] Henoch Clapham refers to them in his *Antidoton* (London, 1600) as "our English Arians [who] deny all Baptisme and Ordination, till new Apostles be sent to execute those parts to the Gentiles"; and Edmond Jessop in his *Discovery of the Errours of the Anabaptists* (London, 1623) says that the Seekers "held it stiffly that their must be new Apostles before their could be a true constituted Church." The case against the Seekers is encapsulated in the Privy Council's examination of one of their company, Edward Wightman, in 1611, who is accused of holding that "Christianity is not truely sincerely and Wholly professed and preached in the Church of Englande."[11] Thus, the Seekers' belief in the inexorable defilement of the Church by antichristian heresies of Romism would accord with Phrygius' view that none of the modern claimants to St. Peter's staff can be accepted as worthy of adoration. One problem obviates this identification, however—the Seekers are simply too late a candidate for Donne's satire.

The beliefs of the Seekers did not completely originate with them, however. One of the founders of this group, in fact—Thomas Legate—was earlier a member of a sect whose beliefs and existence correspond with the imagery and date of Donne's wry portrait. In 1590 Thomas Legate was arrested for being a member of the Barrowists, one of the two sects (along with the Brownists) that especially alarmed the Establishment at the turn of the century. Founded through the collaboration of John Greenwood and Henry Barrow, by the last decade of the century this group had accepted the leadership of Barrow, apocalyptic separatist and enemy of Canterbury, Rome, Geneva, Brownists, and Anabaptists alike. It is in the tenets and current estimation of this specific group that we find consistent parallels with Donne's portrait of Phrygius.

The achievement and character of Barrow's contribution to the Separatist tradition are best summarized by Paul Christiansen. Barrow, he points out,

> synthesized the core of the separatist message, . . . cutting through layers of polemic to create a solid, lasting tool of separatist analysis. . . . Barrow gathered together most of the strands of earlier separatist criticism of the Church of England and wove them into an intelligible pattern with powerful prose. . . . [The Puritans] agreed that the Established Church contained antichristian elements, but for them it remained a true church. For Barrow, anyone who would not follow the evidence to its logical conclusion and fully condemn the English church as false deserved a place on the side of perdition.[12]

His views are most fully and eloquently articulated in *A Brief Discoverie of the False Church* (1590), from which his prosecutors drew copiously at his treason trial in 1593.[13] (He was executed the same year.) In his examination by Archbishop Whitgift he was accused of having averred "that ther is not a true church in England" (a likely charge, Leland Carlson points out, since a Barrowist, Margaret Maynerd, made such a statement when she was examined, and Barrow said as much in his *Profes of Aparant Churche*).[14] In subsequent examinations he told the Archbishop, "You have a false and antichristian ministery set over your church. . . . And your church is governed by . . . the Romish courtes and canons." "I thinke that these parish assemblies as they stand generally in England are not the true established churches of Christ," he later asserted before the Council's examiners (pp. 179, 197).

For Barrow, as would be expected, only the "reformed" church is not disqualified automatically from consideration. The Roman Church is unquestionably the Whore of Babylon. The other minor sects are only considered at all because they have been blasphemously compared to his own visionaries, and are dispatched with a succinct and consistent directness: the Brownists and Donatists are "uncharitable, . . . a damnable sect" (pp. 123, 136); the Presbyterians are "factions of our pontifical and reforming priests [that] grosly drawe al their water from the most filthie and poisoned sinke of the papistical corruption" (p. 560); the "quicksandes of Anabaptistrie" are equally "damnable, . . . wicked, . . . and condempned" (pp. 443, 316, 126); the Calvinists and English "Reformists" are "apostles of presumption . . . uncleane and corrupt . . . [both] as counterfeit, prodigious, antichristian, [and] monstrous as the [Roman] harlot their churche sitteth on" (pp. 297, 299, 335). It is "blasphemy," he insists, to "compare us to the Anabaptists and heretiks" (p. 136) that dominate England.

His main thrust, of course, is at the Anglican Church, which he characterizes as "the eldest daughter of the church of Rome . . . the harlot or great whore" (pp. 452, 446). Under Rome, he reiterates often, "the whole church growing remisse and negligent, both people and officers, that heavenly patterne left by the apostles was soone violate, and upon new pretence, more and more innovate" until it finally "became the very throne of antichrist" (pp. 273–75). Likewise, "our learned Reformists, . . . this antichristian ministrie of England" (pp. 524, 533), are nothing more than a "reforming of Babilon" (p. 444) that is "wholy corrupte" (p. 282):

> all the priestes of England have a false and antichristian ministrie upon them [and] have the markes of, and stand in subjection unto the beast. (p. 487)

> we are now being fallen into, and found in that general defection and apostacie, whereof we were warned by our saviour Christ. (p. 444)

> . . . .

> This preaching of theirs . . . is exercised in a false ministrie, a false church, as it proceedeth from the chaire of antichrist. (p. 517)

> there can be no comparison betwixt the church of Christ, and th[is] whorish idolatrous church, which hath not one part of a true church, not one pinne, naile, nor hooke, according to the true patterne. (p. 303)

There is in England, he concludes, "no lyght" (p. 65): "fle from these unholye assemblyes, this false and unholye worscip, this false and unholy minisrie, this false and unholye peopell, this false and unholye government, lest [you] be partakers of their sinnes and so of ther plages" (p. 66). Rome only "lead[s] us back to Egipt, Sodome, Babilon" (p. 443), but Canterbury "never taught or brought to the acknowledgement and raight practise of the truth" (p. 443). Thus, "al extraordinarie offices have ceased . . . and so must all the building of Christ's church and the worke of the ministrie cease, untill some second John Baptist or new apostles be sent us downe from heaven" (p. 443). Barrow and his followers, then, like Phrygius, "abhorre / All."

Why, then, did Donne choose the name Phrygius? A. J. Smith focuses on the most likely reason. Rather than designating Phrygius an atheist or nonbeliever, he suggests that the name derives from the ancient, oft-conquered tribe of Asia Minor: "Possibly Donne alludes to the multiplicity of gods which confronted the ancient Phrygians as a consequence of their subjection to several peoples in turn."[15] Overrun by Cimmerians in the seventh century, B.C., they were later ruled by Lydia, Persia, Macedon, and Rome. Smith's note locates the site of Donne's allusion, but Donne's strategy is more fully uncovered by review of Phrygian religious history after the Christianization of its people in the first century and its subsequent notoriety as home of a heretical sect later made illustrious by Tertullian.[16] Eusebius' *Ecclesiastical History* (V, 16–19) offers the fullest early account of the rise and spread of a millenarian cult in Phrygia initiated by Montanus (a former priest of Cybele, the orgiastic Earth-Mother). This group, called the Montanists, the Cataphrygian heresy, or the "Phrygian frenzy," began sometime during the first century in a village near Philadelphia, spread throughout the land, and remained strongly entrenched in the Tembris Valley until around the fourth century.[17] Emphasizing the imminent return of Christ and inauguration of the New Jerusalem, devotees believed that in the trances and utterances of Montanus and his disciples were heard the Paraclete announcing the new age. Outraged at the terrors of Domitianic oppression, the Phrygians identified their Roman conquerors with the Babylonian captors, castigated the Roman Church on many grounds, and anxiously accepted the "new apostle's" vitriolic outcries for aggression against the satanic foe in these "last days." In the first centuries of the Christian era, then, the Phrygians, those noble warriors who joined Priam in battle against the Amazons (*Iliad* iii. 187), since subjected to a number of foreign gods and mystery cults, became identified with millennial prophecy and widespread discontent with Babylonic Roman rule—similar to the prophetic voices arising in England at the end of the sixteenth century from radical groups such as the Barrowists.

More than one Renaissance writer does associate, in fact, the ancient cultists with contemporary sectaries. Most eminent among these is Thomas Rogers, chaplain to Archbishop Bancroft, in his "Exposition of the Thirty-Nine Articles" (*The Catholic Doctrine of the Church of England* [London, 1586]), a work that originally "met not with that welcome entertainment, which seemed due to the author's endeavours, [especially among] the two extremes, Papists and Schismatics, who were highly enraged."[18] Commenting on the 17th Article ("Of Predestination and Election"), Rogers lists Phrygians among his adversaries:

> This truth ["In our actions the word of God, which is his revealed will, must be our direction"] is gainsaid by the *Phrygians*, *Montanists*, and Messalians, also by Enthusiasts, Anabaptists, and Family of Love, which leave the written word of God, and rely upon their own dreams, visions, and lying revelations. Hence proceedeth the *contempt of* God's written word, and of the preachers, and *all religious exercises* thereof. For saith the Family of Love, "No difference is there between a ceremonial either letter-doctor christian and an uncircumcised heathen."[19]

I have been unable to find documentation that the Separatists, the Barrowists in particular, were called the modern Phrygians in the period. But the attacks of Rogers and Gifford affirm, I believe, the basis of Donne's allusion in *Satyre III*. "Carelesse Phrygius" is not, in the technical sense of the word, an atheist but an "atheistic" Separatist, most likely a Barrowist. In his anatomy of the late sixteenth-century body of religious controversy, after ridiculing myopic Catholics, Genevists, and Anglicans, Donne uncovers the extreme skepticism of another English sectarian, the Barrowist-Separatist who finds "All" churches descended in filth from the Romish Whore and therefore "dares marry none." There was undoubtedly a wide streak of healthy skepticism in the young satirist himself. As he advises later in the poem, doubt is essential to the search for Truth, and "He's not of none, nor worst, that seeks the best" (75). But one "must one and . . . but one allow" (70). "Carelesse" in his arrogant aloofness from the search for true religion and in his short-sighted, radical intolerance, Phrygius, as the Barrowists, does not "doubt wisely" (77).

It is not only a contemptuous regard for the established church that the Montanists and Barrowists share with Phrygius. The ancient heretics, Rogers writes, "like the Arians," did not believe in holy matrimony: they "too basely and badly think of matrimony," adjuring none to marry, "utterly condemn[ing] marriage."[20] Barrowists evince the same prejudice; for them marriage is only a civil ceremony, an "ordinance of the second table" (p. 454) transformed into "execrable idolatrie" by the "Reformistes" (p. 454). One member of the sect, Christopher Bowman, urged that "marriage in a howse without a mynister, by consent of the parties and friends, is sufficient."[21] This, of course, was heretical to the Establishment: "as of *Montanus*, the *Montanists*," says Gifford, they with the Barrowists/Brownists "agree together, as even as two peeces of cloath that are of the same wooll, the same threed, colour, working & breadth: and that an Egge is no liker to an Egge, then they be each to other." Montanist/Donatist: Barrowist/Brownist—this is "their eloquence . . . which differing in words, containeth the same reasons . . . [they are] damnable and . . . wicked Schismatics" all.[22]

Finally, just as the Barrowists based their criticisms of all churches on the exclusivity of their own private vision and understanding of the Scriptures—"we have receaved a most sure word of the Lord our God," says Barrow (p. 269)—so the Phrygian Montanists drew their inspiration from a visionary who claimed a direct conduit to the Holy Ghost. Montanus, says Archdeacon John Philpot, "said . . . he was the Holy Ghost and the apostle of Jesus Christ."[23] In an age replete with sectaries claiming a "fee simple" to divine truth, the Barrowists are no more unique than were the Montanists in a period rife with millenarian prophets; but the similarities in regard to tenets about marriage, the corruption surrounding them, and the urgency of non-conformity mark the Elizabethan Separatists as likely candidates for the title of modern Phrygians. It is on such similarities that Donne focuses in his satirical character sketch of Phrygius.

One final caveat—it is risky to insist that Donne had *only* the Barrowists in mind when he created Phrygius. As shown by the selections from Burton, Rogers, Gifford, and the other controversialists and the disclaimers of association with other sects by Barrow, many Elizabethans did not maintain strict lines of demarcation among Separatist groups. But Separatism was a major concern at the time of Donne's poem, so important that Parliament in 1593 transformed the 1581 statute against Catholic recusants into a rigid assault against the growing threat of the sects. In debate about that statute, in fact, Sir Walter Ralegh, although arguing against the severity of the proposed bill, estimated that there were over 20,000 Separatists in England.[24] Many of these groups did overlap in their doctrinal insistences (as in their membership); and most were nearly as extreme in their attacks on the Established Church and in their millenarian "prophesyings" as the Barrowists. Donne could have had only Separatist in mind in his portrait. But if the poet did intend a specific group, then the Barrowists, because of their extremity, their similarities to the features of "Phrygian frenzy" and Montanist heresy, and their "alarming" popularity, provide the most likely target of his ridicule. Either allusion—to Separatism or to Barrowism—is more likely in Donne's ironic portrait than the age's more general, and hence more slippery, malediction, *atheism*.

"Becomming Traytor"

you rise against my people as an enemy.

Micah 2:8

As suggested above, the boldest and most perilous stroke in *Satyre IV* is the association of the satirist with the recusant stance, or at least with recusant attitudes and sympathies. Donne must have found satire an apt metaphor for his personal situation in the 1590s; but in addition to the personal reasons for this provocative portrait (which are almost subsumed by the *imitatio christi* motif), there is also a generic tradition which complements the general features of Donne's portrait, examination of which uncovers (at least) a significant analogue and (at most) a possible source for the second half of *Satyre IV*.

One of the central concerns of Roman satirical apologiae is the legality of satire; the XII Tables and the ancient strictures forbidding the use of powerful incantations are obstacles around which the ancient satirist always carefully maneuvers—usually by variations on the claim that the laws of satire do not actually violate the laws of the state or by promises not to attack the living or to name names. But always the implicit admission is that the satirist is treading dangerously the borders of illegality and sedition. Robert Elliott points out that "by Quintilian's day satire had broken cleanly from its remote past. Its magical encumbrances have been cast off [so that when] Horace or Juvenal hurls threats in Archilochean terms, we understand the threats in a special sense: language which was once believed capable of magically inflicting death, now kills in a metaphorical sense only."[1] However, the myth is still there in their apologiae: "sophisticated as Roman satire is, it still retains a connection, enigmatic though it be, with its primitive past."[2] The "riddlingly" evocative satirist still stands on the edges of society, as a bold figure in a precarious position, always daring to tell even the king about his new clothes, or his old obligations.

Even when the myths about the forbidden "charmes" and "harmes" of the satiric word have become only metaphors for the power of satire to instigate moral reformation or to rip away the veil of illusions, the inherent dangers of the genre remain. Maybe satire cannot kill its victims,[3] but it can alienate and place in dire peril its bold spokesman. By Donne's day, belief in the dangers of riddles, the power of words to transform patriots into traitors, the faithful into equivocators, was retained in what Steven Mullaney calls "the ritual and representation of treason in the age."[4] As John Stubbes discovered, satire was yet a dangerous undertaking for, as always, those in power retained the prerogative of determining who was lying like truth and who was speaking the truth in the riddles of satire. Even the "licens'd foole," as Shakespeare reminds us, faced the possibility of being hanged.

The metaphorical and literal dangers of the genre are of considerable concern throughout Donne's *Satyres*. More than any of the other self-conscious satirists in the age, Donne confronts directly the precarious position of the satirist in society. Guilpin, for example, evades the issue with a display of wit, hiding behind the persona of the *satyr* and the pose of comic indifference, posturing as a witty schoolboy playing the game of the *satyr* for his clever friends.[5] His witty "scourge, the Tamburlaine of vice" (*Satyre Preludium*, 89), merely "keeps *Decorum* to the time" (*To the Reader*, 69). He may dare to imitate that "whip of fooles, great *Aretine*" (I, 143), but the "mad-cap stuffe" of his "unmannerly" Muse is safely distanced by the generic conventions that he keeps before the reader's eyes. In the same vein, Hall always elaborately documents the personal integrity that stirs his thrusts, carefully explains that he follows Juvenal's authoritative precedent, and specifically defends his satisfaction of, and necessary adjustments to, the conventions of the genre. Even Marston's ill-tempered satirist at his most swaggeringly contemptuous reminds us that his pose is conventional and well within the established rules of the game. As R. B. Gill phrases it, "Marston's fervent tone admits no smile [and] his seeming belief in the pose gives his dark moral judgments an intensity that most other Elizabethan satires lack,"[6] but it is still a self-conscious pose that protects him from prosecution while it accentuates or shows off his virtuosity with and within the conventions. Only Donne, especially in his last two *Satyres*, confronts directly the issue of the legality of satire and the dangers of satire directly and fully. No other satirist goes so far as to suggest that the law become satire, that the monarch's appointed agent of "righteousnes" assume the role and duty of the satirist, as Donne does in his last poem; and no satirist before Pope accepts and uncovers the dangers inherent for the satirist in his genre as fully as Donne does in his fourth poem.

In one sense, in *Satyre IV* Donne has merely modified the conventional stance of the satirist as outsider, renegade, and aloof moral scourge into its most extreme form—the satirist as spy. He could easily have turned to Juvenal as precedent and model for such a technique; in fact, the last section of *Satyre IV* (the satirist's report of his second visit to court) recalls in particular the imagery, themes, and dangerous satirical stance of the classical satirist's third satire. Even the portrait of the Elizabethan *garrulus* as "like a priviledg'd spie," as an italianized malcontent traveler and mendacious flatterer whose allegiance can be acquired by "the prerogative of [anyone's] Crowne" seems closer to Juvenal's diatribe against the meretricious "strangers" who dominate Roman culture than to Horace's comic depiction of the bothersome bore. Beginning his poem with an imitation of Horace's *Satire I.ix*, and then dramatically rejecting the satirical stance of Horace as an inadequate response to the resolute immorality and devious maliciousness of the court, Donne could well have discovered in Juvenal's account of Umbricius' scornful attack on Roman self-betrayal a classical form and therein a traditional precedent for the expression of his "unlicens'd" and potentially "traitorous" doubts about the English court's morality and patriotism. The last section of *Satyre IV* does not follow the plot and situation of Juvenal's poem as closely as the Horatian narrative was followed in the first section, but the description of the court as a theatrical parody of national values and the portrait of the speaker as a patriotic expatriate alienated by his convictions about the moral and ethical foundations of his civilization recall especially Juvenal's *Satire III*.

The classical satire recounts Umbricius' apologia for his abandonment of Rome. It is dominated by the stage motif and by the insistence that Roman civilization has betrayed itself through subjection to alien models of behavior, perverting its natural strengths and rituals into vain instruments of greed and lust. Rome has become a nation of actors, Juvenal's "confusus amici" complains: "natio comoeda est"—all are players. And the play performed at the center of his civilization is identified as a travesty of the nation's spiritual and cultural foundations: "Praeterea sanctum nihil est ab inquine tutum." Rome has become "Graecam urbem," a parody of its former eloquence and integrity, an alienated and alienating welter of foreign strumpets, informers, spies, and bullies; "picta lupa barbana mitra. . . . omnia novit / Graeculus esuriens." Only actors and equivocators, liars and braggarts can survive (and thrive) in such a circus of lust and greed: "rides, maiore cachinno / concutitur. . . . adulandi gens prudentissima. . . . sermo / promptus et Isaeo torrentior. . . . omnia Romae / cum pretio. . . . quantum quisque sua nummorum servat in area, tantum habet et fidei." Men like Umbricius (and Juvenal), men devoted to the truth and to the truth of Roman civilization, are doomed to hellish frustration, "miserum," and the constant threat of physical discomfort and violent death. "Quid Romae faciam?" the xenophobic "civiem" asks, "mentiri nescio: librum, / si malus est, nequeo laudare et poscere." Unable to abide the ridiculous and the unworthy—unable to praise or to read with pleasure the parody that the art of Roman civilization has become through the adoption of foreign styles—the good man and the good Roman is forced to desert this unnatural Rome of Greeks and hellenized Orientals: "cedamus patria." So Umbricius prepares to withdraw to Cumae, the Greek colony; only there, in the land of his cultural enemies, can he live by the ancient code of Roman *virtus*.

Satire III is not just an exaggerated and episodic attack on the sprawl of urban immorality; as W. S. Anderson points out, it is carefully constructed by a series of contrasts (*laus et vituperatio*). Umbricius' defense of *solum* and *unus* is not just a personal longing for solitude or an outcry against his isolation from the spirit of his country, but identifies him as *vir bonus atque Romanus*, as the isolated patriotic upholder of the Roman moral tradition of righteousness, individuality, and liberty. Rome, on the other hand, has become a vulgar monster ("vulgus") of noise, fearful intrigue, and suffocating indifference, its sacred strengths and beauty violated by foreign aggrandizement:

hic, ubi nocturnae Numa constituebat amicae,
nunc sacri fontis nemus et delubra locantur
Iudaeis, quorum cophinus faenumque supellex.

Like the sacred grove of Cumenae, the city has been turned into an alien marketplace, "lonely and wretched because it has ceased to be Roman . . . totally bad, because totally un-Roman."[7] The true Roman is thus forced by his patriotic faith to become an expatriate: "non est Romano cuiquam locus est."

The most problematic feature of *Satire III* is the figure of Umbricius, which some readers suggest is an ironic persona undercut by his own hyperbole, ineptitude, and unproductive nostalgia. According to this view, Juvenal carefully distances himself from the character by rendering Umbricius' attack on Rome as a reported conversation and by a level of overstatement that can be interpreted as mockery of his *indignatio*. Richard A. LaFleur argues, for example, that Umbricius is a "*doctor ineptus*" who offers only "irrational, unproductive solutions" to Rome's problems;[8] and S. C. Fredericks suggests that he represents "the futility of reactionary Romanism," for "beneath [Juvenal's] apparent nostalgia for a lost age of idealism, there is a deeper self-awareness on the part of the satirist that his fiery vehemence is acutely decadent."[9] Such a view would seem to be substantiated by the initial description of the alienated speaker as "confusus" and by the self-effacing stance he assumes in retreating to the Greek colony. This figure cannot be totally associated with the poet. But, at the same time, total rejection of Umbricius is unnecessary. It seems more likely that Juvenal distances himself from his speaker, not because he rejects the extremity of his complaints, but because of the *dangerous* attitudes that the poem expresses. This is what Rome has become *according to Umbricius*, Juvenal urges—you must judge whether such outrage is justified. Juvenal has simply and carefully modified the traditional stance of the satirist as outsider or renegade to an extreme—the satirist as expatriate patriot, the legal and social outsider who yet believes in the spiritual laws of the nation. Satirical personae, we should remember, are masks *through which* poets speak.

Donne's speaker in *Satyre IV* is also characterized as a legal outsider, alienated from the heart of his civilization, in this case because of its perverse transformation of the Presence Chamber into a "strange" parody of English spiritual and moral culture. Just as Juvenal contrasts Umbricius' Roman fortitude with the posturing and meretriciousness of hellenized Romans, so Donne contrasts the satirist's commitment to his "Mistresse Truth" with the pernicious espionage and mendacious flattery of the malcontent court popinjay/informer, the threatening histrionics of Glorius, and the spiritual poverty of such miserable creatures as Macrine. To counter the "privileg'd spie[s]" and "licens'd foole[s]" of the court, Donne's satirist must become a "Spie" against the court, just as Umbricius retreats from the Graecian Rome to the Greek colony. Juvenal's Rome proves unbearable to the true Roman; the English court of Sir Bevis and other Christian knights and martyrs has become a parodic theater of lust and greed, overrun by Aretines and Askaparts. Thus, in both poems the speaker seeks to fulfill the spiritual obligations of the sacred, civic roles which are literally perverted by the alien "priests" who control the nation's civic cathedral. Like the mythical Daedalus, Umbricius flies to Cumae to prove his Roman dignity and valor; like the author of the *apocryphal* second book of Maccabees, Donne's satirist simply relates the truth (and Truth) as he has experienced it, withdraws to his home, and awaits the nation's "wise" response. To act like a Roman, Umbricius must withdraw; to fulfill his role in the divine play of English civilization and the unfolding pageant of divine Truth, Donne's satirist must dare being "nam'd . . . Traytor" and becoming "a spyed Spie." The extremity of their reactions—the desertion of Rome, the association with the recusant stance—does not undercut the validity of the satirists' outrage so much as it endorses the strength and depth of their commitment to national and spiritual integrity. Umbricius' fond and nostalgic plea that Rome become Rome again and the Elizabethan satirist's plea that England return to the "Canonicall" religious principles of its heritage suggest that such extreme acts are valid responses of the defender of Truth when confronted by national fraud.

Thus, Juvenal's third satire provides a classical analogue and perhaps a strategic and imagistic model for Donne's own ironic, anti-epic[10] portrait of the "Presence" Chamber as a "strange" embodiment of "Vanitie" outstanding for its *absence* of English virtue and sense. As Milgate points out, it is difficult "to put a finger on specific lines in the Latin satirists which Donne is referring to or copying." But the similarities in strategy, speaker, and imagery suggest that, at the very least, the Roman poet's Umbricius provides a classical precedent for Donne's portrait of the satirist as a spiritual fugitive from the egregious absurdities that threaten to refashion and uncreate the national character. In Juvenal's Umbricius Donne could well have found classical authority to support and endorse his own "illegal" outrage at his nation's betrayal of its spiritual strengths and foundations.

NOTES

INTRODUCTION

1. Pope's comment is recorded by Joseph Spence, *Anecdotes*, ed. S. W. Singer (Carbondale: Southern Illinois Univ. Press, 1964), p. 144. See note 4 for Jonson's opinion.

2. See, for example, Louis Martz, "Donne's *Anniversaries* Revisited," in *That Subtle Wreath*, ed. Margaret W. Pepperdene (Atlanta: Agnes Scott College, 1973), pp. 29–50.

3. Whether Donne or Joseph Hall, as he claims, was in fact first cannot be definitely determined; see Arnold Stein, "The Second English Satirist," *Modern Language Review*, 28 (1943), 273–78.

4. "Conversations with William Drummond of Hawthornden," in *Ben Jonson*, ed. C. H. Herford and Percy Simpson (Oxford: Clarendon, 1925), I, 135.

5. *The Anniversaries*, ed. Frank M. Manley (Baltimore: Johns Hopkins Press, 1963).

6. I borrow the term from Aubrey L. Williams, review of *Satires Against Man: The Poems of Rochester* by Dustin H. Griffin, *Seventeenth-Century News*, 33 (1975), 28.

7. Hugh Richmond, *Shakespeare's Sexual Comedy: A Mirror for Lovers* (New York: Bobbs-Merrill, 1971), p. 44.

8. Thomas Nashe, *Christes Teares over Jerusalem* (London, 1593), in *Works*, ed. R. B. McKerrow (London: Sidgwick and Jackson, 1904), II, 87.

9. Frank Kermode, *The Sense of an Ending: Studies in the Theory of Fiction* (New York: Oxford Univ. Press, 1967).

10. This is the brief definition of decorum provided by George Puttenham, *The Arte of English Poesie*, book 3, chapter 27, in *Elizabethan Critical Essays*, ed. G. Gregory Smith (Oxford: Oxford Univ. Press, 1904), I, 173.

11. "The association of satire and satyr is the fundamental assumption made by nearly all Elizabethan satiric authors," Kernan contends. "[To] them a poem in which the writer wore the mask of the satyr and displayed the appropriate savage characteristics was by definition a satire. . . . From approximately 1590 on," he concludes, "every author of satire labored to create the biting satyr" (*The Cankered Muse: Satire of the English Renaissance*, Yale Studies in English, vol. 142 [New Haven, Conn.: Yale Univ. Press, 1959], pp. 89–90). Patterson suggests, on the other hand, that there is "a direct causal link between the *style* of Juvenalian satire in England and the Ideas of Reproof defined by Hermogenes—Asperity, Vehemence, and Vigor" (*Hermogenes and the Renaissance: Seven Ideas of Style* [Princeton, N.J.: Princeton Univ. Press, 1970], p. 97).

12. Kernan, p. 118. He notes that Donne's five poems are the most notable "modification" of the "cankered" satirist so popular in the period.

13. Mary Claire Randolph, "Thomas Drant's Definition of Satire, 1566," *Notes and Queries*, 180 (1941), 416. The citation refers to Drant's *A medicinal moral*, which prefaces his translation of Horace's *Satires*. See also Peter Medine's study of Drant in his introductory essay to Drant's *Horace, His Art of Poetic, Pistles, and Satyres Englished* (Delmar, N.Y.: Scholars' Facsimiles and Reprints, 1972). He says that for Drant "both the Roman poet and the Hebrew prophet shared the aim of the Christian preacher, to enlarge the audience's understanding" (p. x).

14. Medine, "Praise and Blame in Renaissance Verse Satire," *Pacific Coast Philology*, 7 (1972), 50. Randolph first pointed out that "the positive, rational mode of procedure advocated or unmistakably implied in a satire" balances and opposes "the vice or folly ridiculed". "The Structural Design of the Formal Verse Satire," *Philological Quarterly*, 21 (1942), 368–84; rpt. in *Essential Articles for the study of English Augustan Backgrounds*, ed. Bernard N. Schilling (Hamden, Conn.: Archon Books, 1961), pp. 262–80.

15. W. Milgate, ed., *John Donne: The Satires, Epigrams, and Verse Letters* (Oxford: Clarendon, 1967), p. xvii. All citations of the *Satyres* are from this edition.

16. Many of the echoes of and direct borrowings from the classical satirists in Donne's five poems have been pointed out by Raymond Alden, *The Rise of Formal Verse Satire in England Under Classical Influence*, University of Pennsylvania Publications, Studies in Philology, Literature, and Archaeology, VII, No. 2 (Philadelphia: Univ. of Pennsylvania Press, 1899), pp. 75–90; Niall Rudd, "Donne and Horace," *Times Literary Supplement*, 23 March 1963, p. 208; and Howard Erskine-Hill, "Courtiers out of Horace," in *John Donne: Essays in Celebration*, ed. A. J. Smith (London: Methuen, 1972), pp. 273–307.

17. This view is, of course, a commonplace of Platonic aesthetics in the Renaissance, as fully documented by Bernard Weinberg, *A History of Literary Criticism in the Italian Renaissance*, 2 vols. (Chicago: Univ. of Chicago Press, 1961); and William Kerrigan, *The Prophetic Milton* (Charlottesville: Univ. of Virginia Press, 1974).

18. William Harrison, *The Description of England*, ed. Georges Edelen (Ithaca, N.Y.: Cornell Univ. Press, 1968), pp. 110–11.

19. *Marlowe's 'Tamburlaine': A Study of Renaissance Moral Philosophy* (Nashville, Tenn.: Vanderbilt Univ. Press, 1941), p. 86.

20. Herschel Baker, *The Wars of Truth: Studies in the Decay of Christian Humanism in the Earlier Seventeenth Century* (Cambridge, Mass.: Harvard Univ. Press, 1952), p. 14.

21. The thoroughness and volume of what amounted to an apocalyptic clamor has been fully documented by Helen White, *Social Criticism in Popular Religious Literature of the Sixteenth Century* (New York: Macmillan, 1944); Baker, *Wars of Truth*, chapter 1; C. A. Patrides, *The Grand Design of God* (Toronto: Univ. of Toronto Press, 1972); Don Cameron Allen, *Doubt's Boundless Sea* (Baltimore: Johns Hopkins Press, 1964); and Victor Harris, *All Coherence Gone* (Chicago: Univ. of Chicago Press, 1949), chapter 4. For treatment of sermons concerned with the imminent end of the world see Carroll Camden, "'The Wonderful Yeere,'" in *Studies in Honor of DeWitt T. Starnes*, ed. Thomas P. Harrison (Austin: Univ. of Texas Press, 1967), pp. 163–79; and Patrides, "Renaissance and Modern Thought on the Last Things: A Study in Changing Concepts," *Harvard Theological Review*, 51 (1951), 169–85. The influences and changing directions of homiletic literature in the age are studied fully by Millar Maclure, *The Paul's Cross Sermons 1534–1642* (Toronto: Univ. of Toronto Press, 1958), and J. W. Blench, *Preaching in England in the Late Fifteenth and Sixteenth Centuries: A Study of English Sermons* (New York: Barnes & Noble, 1964).

22. (London: A. Islip, 1597), sig. A³.

23. (London: R. Newberry, 1581), p. iii.

24. *Christes Teares Over Jerusalem*, in *Works*, II, 87.

25. *Lectures Upon Jonah, delivered at Yorke, in the Year of Our Lord 1594* (Oxford: Joseph Barnes, 1597), p. 6.

26. Adam Hill, *The crie of England* (London: Ed. Allde for B. Norton, 1595); Timothy Tymme, *A Plaine discourse of ten English Lepers* (London: T. C., 1592); Thomas Playfere, *The Meane in Mourning* (London: Widow Orwin for Andrew Wise, 1596); Thomas Drant, *Three godly and learned Sermons* (London: W. Jaggard, 1584); Tobias Bland, *A Baite for Momus* (London: John Wolfe, 1589); Henry Bedel, *A Sermon exhortyng to pitie the poore* (London: John Audely, 1572); and James Bisse, *Two sermons preached the one at Paules Crosse* (London: Thomas Woodcocke, 1581). For the minorities' opinions see Elliot Rose, *Cases of Conscience: Alternatives open to Recusants and Puritans under Elizabeth I and James I* (Cambridge: Cambridge Univ. Press, 1975); Thomas H. Clancy, *Papist Pamphleteers: The Allen-Persons Party and the Political Thought of the Counter-Reformation in England, 1572–1615* (Chicago: Loyola Univ. Press, 1964); and Paul Christiansen, *Reformers and Babylon* (Toronto: Univ. of Toronto Press, 1978).

27. *Lectures Upon Jonah*, pp. 6, 7.

28. Baker, *Wars of Truth*, esp. chapter 2; Owst, *Preaching in Medieval England* (Cambridge: Cambridge Univ. Press, 1926); and *Literature and Pulpit in Medieval England* (Cambridge: Cambridge Univ. Press, 1933); and White, *Social Criticism*.

29. As Arthur Barker phrases it, the approach to the literature of the period merely through economic theories of boom or bust "leaves the English poetic renaissance of the sixteenth and seventeenth centuries as a kind of dumb-show commercial performed when the transitional economic drama had ended" ("An Apology for the Study of Renaissance Poetry," in *Literary Views*, ed. Carroll Camden [Chicago: Univ. of Chicago Press, 1964], p. 33).

30. In *The Myth of the Golden Age in the Renaissance* (Bloomington: Indiana Univ. Press, 1969), Harry Levin points out that, in fact, Renaissance thinkers saw their own age as a contrast to the Golden Age as much as a revival. Nor did momentary elations such as that upon the defeat of the Armada blunt the growing alarm at the end of the century. As Paul A. Jorgensen illustrates, "Even in the flush of military victory, the Elizabethans were a reflective people. . . . Their divines never let them forget that ultimately the real war would come; meanwhile they must be grateful for a short reprieve. That it would be brief was evident from biblical signs. There were rumors of war, never before so general; the world was in its declining and latter days. . . ." "Elizabethan Religious Literature for Time of War," *Huntington Library Quarterly*, 37 (1973–74), 15–16.

31. In his sermons Donne often points to biblical figures and biblical literature as models for contemporary conduct, of course: "The Psalmes," he urges in one place,

> are the Manna of the Church. As Manna tasted to every man like that that he liked best, so doe the Psalmes minister Instruction, and satisfaction, to every man, in every emergency and occasion. *David* was not onely a cleare Prophet of Christ himselfe, but a Prophet of every particular Christian; He foretels what I, what any shall doe, and suffer, and say. . . .[these] Catholique, universall Psalmes, that apply themselves to all necessities, . . . these five Psalmes are my Gomer, which I am to fill and empty every day of this Manna. (*Sermons*, ed. George R. Potter and Evelyn M. Simpson [Los Angeles: Univ. of California Press, 1953–61], VII, 51–52.)

For fuller studies of Donne's debt to biblical aesthetics, see Louis L. Martz, *The Poetry of Meditation*, rev. ed. (New Haven: Yale Univ. Press, 1962); Barbara Kiefer Lewalski, *Donne's Anniversaries and the Poetry of Praise: The Creation of a Symbolic Mode* (Princeton, N.J.: Princeton Univ. Press, 1973); and Raymond B. Waddington, *The Mind's Empire: Myth and Form in George Chapman's Narrative Poems* (Baltimore: Johns Hopkins Press, 1974).

32. *Aggeus and Abdias Prophetes, the one corrected, the other newly added, and both at large declared* (London: W. Series, 1562), p. 6.

33. Thomas Becon, "The Demands of Holy Scripture," in *Prayers, and Other Pieces*, ed. Jo. Ayre, The Parker Society (Cambridge: Cambridge Univ. Press, 1844), p. 612. Italics are mine. Likewise, Bishop Hooper, in a sermon on "the office of every true Christian," argues at length that "there is great virtue in this word 'zealous.' It is not sufficient to work well except that the justified man with a godly zeal and ardent desire follows this good work begun" ("A Godly and profitable treatise conteinying a declaration of Christ and his office," in *Later Writings*, The Parker Society [Cambridge: Cambridge Univ. Press, 1852], p. 94). Bishop Sandys, in the same vein, explains that "the law of love and charity requireth zeal; and this neither taketh away the sword from the magistrate, nor the rod from the minister; but that each of them severally according to the order of his vocation may punish sin, as he must punish sinners" (*The Sermons of Edwin Sandys*, ed. Jo. Ayre, The Parker Society [Cambridge: Cambridge Univ. Press, 1841], p. 107). Bishop Jewel offers a similar definition of the term:

> albeit there is much likeness between the rage and fury of hypocrites and the godly zeal of good men, yet there is a difference: godly zeal is tempered and seasoned with charity. . . . The godly when they see any disorder, they mourn in their hearts to see that the truth is not received, and to see the minds of their brethren so obstinately hardened. . . . Yet through such zeal for God's house Christ whipped out the buyers and sellers, David shed forth tears abundantly, and Moses dashed in pieces the tablets of God's commandments. All men ought to be patient and gentle in matters pertaining to themselves; but in God's cause no man must yield or be patient. (*The Works of John Jewel*, ed. Jo. Ayre, The Parker Society [Cambridge: Cambridge Univ. Press, 1845], II, 1008–9.)

34. "The True Triall of the Spirits," in *The Sermons of Master Henry Smith gathered in one volume* (London: Thomas Orwin for Thomas Man, 1592), p. 137.

35. *Works*, II, 1008.

36. *Sermons*, pp. 247–48.

37. *Sermons*, p. 135.

38. Hill, *The crie of England*; White, *A sermon preached at Paules Crosse* (London: Francis Coldock, 1578); Tyrer, *Five godly Sermons* (London: I. H. for John Harrison, 1602); Anderson, *The*

138

Shielde of our safetie (London: H. Jackson, 1581); Drant, *Three godly and learned sermons*. Other equally harsh sermons include: Bishop John Bridges, *A Sermon, preached at Paules Cross* (London: Henry Binneman, 1571); Edward Deringe (who once preached a sermon of royal chastisement to the queen's face), *XXII Lectures or Readings* (London: Lucas Harrison, 1576); William Kethe, *A Sermon made at Blandfor Farm* (London: John Daye, 1571); John Stockwood, *A Sermon Preached at Paules Crosse* (London: Henry Bynneman, 1578); Thomas Gibson, *A fruitful sermon preached at Occham* (Mauldon: Robert Waldegraue, 1584); and Edward Topsell, *Times Lamentation: an exposition of the prophet Ioel* (London: John Windet, 1596).

39. *A sermon of repentence* (London: John Harrison, 1583), sig. Biv.

40. Keckermann, *Rhetoricae Ecclesiasticae* (Hanover, n.d.); Hyperius [Andreas Gerardus], *The practis of Preaching* (London: J. Ludham, 1577). Likewise, Nicholas Hemmingsen's *The Preacher, or the methode of Preaching*, trans. I. H. (London: T. Marsh, 1576), includes prescriptions for "the chiding sermon," in which "the corupt maners of men are harshly reproued" (p. 83). And Leonard Wright's "The Patterne for Pastors," which is annexed to his *A Summons for Sleepers* (London: Henry Bynneman, 1596), recommends "Chiding, fearing, and admonishing" as techniques of digression in sermons (p. 10). "The proper duty of preaching," Gerardus maintained, "is the reproof of vice, and beyond reproof, the threat of divine fury and future punishments."

41. *A medicinall moral, that is the two books of Horace his satyres Englished: The Waylyngs of Hieremiah* (London: T. Marsh, 1566), sigs. a2ᵛ–3.

42. Daneau, *A Fruitful Commentarie upon the twelve Small Prophets*, trans. J. Stockwood (Cambridge: J. Legatt, 1594), pp. 6, 71ff; Downame (London: G. Simson for W. Jones, 1600), pp. 4–19, 30–64; Greenham, "Of Zeale," in *Works* (London: F. Kingston, 1599); *Glass* (London: Iohn Wolfe, 1587); and Tossanus, *The Lamentations and holy mourninge of the Prophete Ieremiah*, trans. Thomas Stocker (London: Iohn Windet, [1587]), sigs. B⁴–6.

In the same vein are some of the earlier works of John Parkhurst and Robert Crowley, as Peter E. Medine points out. In the *Ad lectorem* of *Ludicra sive epigrammata juvenalia*, for example, Parkhurst points to the letters of St. Paul and the preaching of Christ as sanctification of Christian satire: "quicquid est certe nec primus hoc, nec sine exemplo feci. Nam vt taceam, eos a Paulo, stultus, canes ventres, inimicos, et hostes cruci Christi appellari, Christus ipse eos caecos, sepulchra nitentia, progenies viperarum vocat" (sig. A4ᵛ). Crowley claims the authority of Saint John— "It pleased myn author to geve me of name / The voice of the laste trumpe (as Sainte Iohn doeth wryte)" (The Voyce of the Laste Trumpet, [1549])—of Saint Paul (*One and thyrte Epigrammes* [1550]), and of Isaiah ("as Esaye hath bydden," in *Epigrammes*). Medine elaborates on these and other "moralistic" satirists in "Contexts of Renaissance Verse Satire: Moralistic and Moral," Ph.D. dissertation, Univ. of Wisconsin, 1970, pp. 26, 29–33.

43. See, for example, Sister Mary Bonaventura Mroz, *Divine Vengeance* (Washington, D.C.: Catholic Univ. Press, 1941), and Lila Hermann Friedman, "Satiric Personae: A Study in Point of View in Formal Verse Satire in the English Renaissance from Wyatt to Marston," Ph.D. dissertation, Univ. of Wisconsin, 1955, for studies of the classical and patristic attitudes towards useful wrath.

44. *The Wrath of God*, in *Minor Works*, tr. Sister Mary Francis McDonald (Washington, D.C.: Catholic Univ. Press, 1965), pp. 101–2.

45. "All Attest His Writs Canonical: The Texts, Meaning and Evaluation of Donne's Satires," in *Just So Much Honor: Essays Commemorating the Four-Hundredth Anniversary of the Birth of John Donne*, ed. Peter Amadeus Fiore (University Park: Pennsylvania State Univ. Press, 1972), p. 252.

46. A. F. Bellette, "The Originality of Donne's *Satires*," *Univ. of Toronto Quarterly*, 44 (1974–75), 130–40.

47. "Praise and Blame," p. 50.

48. Ibid.

49. See Milgate's textual introduction, and Alan MacColl, "The Circulation of Donne's Poems in Manuscript," in *John Donne: Essays in Celebration*, pp. 28–46.

The evidence of the manuscripts and early editions suggests that the *Satyres* circulated as a group, in what Drummond called their present "nomber & order." As Milgate and Shawcross point out, the five poems appear so in all editions 1633–68, and (using the stemma established by Helen Gardner in her edition of the divine poems) in all the Group I manuscripts (except *H 49* which omits the fifth), and some Group III manuscripts. The Group II manuscripts vary the order of the poems (with a sixth not by Donne added sometimes); the Group III manuscripts vary greatly in number and order. The highly authoritative Westmoreland manuscript, copied by Donne's friend, Rowland Woodward, has the five *Satyres* in the standard order; Milgate urges that it "has a text of the Satires which was in existence by about 1598, and also that this text is of great authority" (p. xlvii). In the most thorough accounts of the manuscripts, Milgate concludes that "the *Satires* too circulated as a set of poems, and that the absence of one or more Satires from a collection is due either to accident or to conscious selection by the copyist" (p. xlv), and Shawcross concludes that "perhaps . . . they had circulated as a unit" and ought to be arranged in their usual order ("All Attest His Writs," p. 247). Although Shawcross agrees that the Group I manuscripts are derived from a collection made around 1614, he does not accept Milgate's "speculation that Donne revised the text of his satires at a specific time and for a specific person (the Countess of Bedford)" (p. 250). Declaring the dates of the *Satyres* is problematical. Most readers and editors argue, along with Grierson and Milgate, that the poems were composed in the last decade of the century, 1593–1598. Shawcross suggests that "they all may have been written in the years 1597–98 when Donne was first in Egerton's employ" (p. 251). For an argument on a later date (1619) for *Satyre III*, see Paul R. Sellin, "The Proper Dating of Donne's 'Satyre III,'" *Huntington Library Quarterly*, 43 (1979–80), 275–312; but A. J. Smith finds allusions to the poem as early as 1611 (by Jonson) and 1618 (in Anon., *The Mirrour of Majestie*): *John Donne: The Critical Heritage* (London: Routledge & Kegan Paul, 1975), pp. 35, 41.

50. This topos was prominent in Renaissance thought, of course, as Samuel C. Chew has fully documented in *The Pilgrimage of Life* (New Haven, Conn.: Yale Univ. Press, 1962). These examples are merely the most popular instances of this scheme. See also Thomas B. Stroup, *Microcosmos: The Shape of the Elizabethan Play* (Lexington: Univ. of Kentucky Press, 1965), p. 206, for illustration that this "testing pattern" is central to the structure of Elizabethan drama.

51. McGrath, p. 560.

52. That the term *zeal* did not yet have the pejorative connotations of mere enthusiasm it later acquired is evinced by the particular fondness which Donne shows for it in his sermons. He uses this term more than 170 times there and usually in wholly complimentary tones, as pointed out by Madelon E. Heatherington, "'Decency' and 'Zeal' in the Sermons of John Donne," *Texas Studies in Literature and Language*, 9 (1967), 307–16. In these sermons Donne points out that "zeale" is the feature of the Old Testament Prophets (*Sermons*, X, 121) and usually defines it very similarly to the definition of Becon and earlier commentators:

man's impatience with sin comes from "the force, the vehemence of God's grace, in the vehemence of his zeale" (*Sermons*, I, 258);

"zeale" and "godly anger" are "not improper" in the "cause of true religion" (*Sermons*, X, 167);

"that vehemence of *zeale* which the apostle found, we hope not for; . . . yet we cannot deny, . . . that though it were accompanied with many inconveniences, it testified a vehement devotion" (*Sermons*, X, 131–32);

"in many cases, where there is no *anger*, there is not much *zeal*" (*Sermons*, II, 77);

man must speak "with a holy vehemence, with a zealous animosity, as indeed belongs to the denouncing of Gods judgements" (*Sermons*, IX, 403);

"God gives good men zeale; zeale to make good their station; zeale to conserve the integrity and sincerity of Religion" (*Sermons*, VIII, 263);

"Truth in the beginning, Zeale all the way, and Constancie in the ende make up a Christian" (*Sermons*, VII, 425).

The view of satire as zeal continues well into the seventeenth century, of course. In "An Apology Against a Pamphlet," for example, Milton cites Christ, John the Baptist, St. John, Ezekiel, and "the true Prophets of old" as sanctions for the use of "the invincible Zeale [which is] a sanctifi'd bitternesse against the enemies of truth" (*Complete Prose Works of John Milton*, ed. Don M. Wolfe et al. [New Haven, Conn.: Yale Univ. Press, 1953], I, 901, 903). Thomas Kranidas, "Milton and the Rhetoric of Zeal," *Texas Studies in Language and Literature*, 6 (1965), 423–32, shows how "the language of zeal becomes the medium for the exposure and castigation of false devotion" in Milton (p. 431). Likewise, Pierre de La Primaudaye, in his highly influential *French Academie* (London: for T. Adams, 1618), refers to Joel, Isaiah, and Paul to the Corinthians as examples of that "religion, that zeale" which comes from the "contrary affections [of] indignation . . . and compassion [being] mingled together [to] breed a third affection, which in holy Scripture is called Zeale" (p. 504).

<h2 style="text-align:center">CHAPTER ONE</h2>

1. Milgate, Hughes, Shawcross, and S. F. Johnson ("Donne's Satires," I, *Explicator*, 11 [1953], item 53) view the poem as a version of the traditional debate of body and soul. Andreasen ("Theme and Structure in Donne's *Satyres*," *Studies in English Literature*, 3 [1963], 60–66) urges that the poem contrasts constancy and inconstancy, a largely thematic reading extended by the perceptive study of Geraldine ("Donne's *Notitia*: The Evidence of the Satires," *Univ. of Toronto Quarterly*, 36 [1966], 24–27) and Sicherman ("The Mocking Voices of Donne and Marvell," *Bucknell Review*, 17 [1969], 38–40). In the most recent study—"Two Hollow Men: The Pretentious Wooer and the Wayward Bridegroom of Donne's 'Satyre I,'" *Seventeenth-Century News*, 23 (1975), 10–13—Barbara L. Parker and J. Max Patrick insist that the speaker is a "spiritual caricature . . . defined primarily by his self-righteous moralizing, his priest-like manner coupled with a slavish preoccupation with sin . . . and his lofty concept of fidelity" (p. 13).

2. "Courtiers out of Horace," p. 274.

3. "The wise man," says Dame Folly, "retreats to the books of the ancients, and there learns mere verbal trifles. The fool plunges into the thick of things, staring danger in the face, and in this way (unless I am badly mistaken) he acquires true prudence" (*The Praise of Folly*, trans. Clarence H. Miller [New Haven, Conn.: Yale Univ. Press, 1979], p. 42).

4. Erasmus, *The Enchiridion*, trans. Raymond Himelick (Bloomington: Indiana Univ. Press, 1963), p. 96.

5. Eugene Rice, *The Renaissance Idea of Wisdom* (Baltimore: Johns Hopkins Univ. Press, 1958), p. 160.

6. *Works*, ed. John Bruce, The Parker Society (Cambridge: Cambridge Univ. Press, 1842), p. 83.

7. *The Treasure of Truth, touching the grounde worke of man his salvation, and chiefest pointes of Christian Religion*, trans. John Stockwood (London: Thomas Woodcocke, 1581), p. 60.

8. *The Voyce of the laste trumpet, blowen bi the seueth Angel . . . calling all estates of men to the ryght path* (London: R. Crowley, 1550), 11, 665–72.

9. For similar delineations of the role of the Christian scholar see Sandys, *Sermons*, pp. 368, 426; Pilkington, *Works*, ed. James Sutherland (Cambridge: Cambridge Univ. Press, 1842), p. 81; and Becon, *Early Works*, I, 321. Similarly, Dean Donne urges that "man is not placed in this world onely for speculation; He is not sent into this world to live out of it, but to live in it; *Adam* was not put into Paradise, onely in that Paradise to contemplate the future Paradise, but to dresse and to keep the present; God did not breathe a soule towards him, but into him; Not in an obsession, but a possession; Not to travaile for knowledge abroad, but to direct him by counsell at home. . . . Our body also must testifie and expresse our love, not onely in a reverentiall humiliation . . . when we present our selves at Gods Service, in his house, but in the discharge of our bodily duties, and the sociable offices of our callings, towards one another" (*Sermons*, VII, 104).

10. By the end of the century, for example, *Nature's Secretary* was also a derisive term, a scornful invective for the theoretical scientism of scholasticism; see Hiram Haydn, *The Counter-Renaissance* (New York: Scribner's, 1950), pp. 76ff.

11. *De moribus ecclesiae Catholicae et de moribus Manichaeorum*, I, 17, 31.

12. The phrase is a grand pun, of course, applicable in many ways to the speaker, his adversary, and his poem. The speaker wears the *coarse* attire that is natural to fallen man (*course*, "natural," *OED*, II) and to the meditator (*course*, "prescribed prayers for canonical hours," *OED*, IV.22b). His poem has the rough, *coarse* texture germane to verse satire and is prescribed as *cor*, *cors*, or *core satire*. As *cor satire*, it attacks one who shares man's fallen nature with the speaker (Lat. *cors*, "fellow, cohort") but who is yet a "humorist" (Lat. *cors*, "heart, as seat of the emotions or humors") devoted to the fashionable "course" (*OED*, I.10). Both the subject of the poem,

especially of this passage on man's natural apparel and his need for marital union with the Truth, and his choice of attire intimate man's share in Adam's sin; so, his poem is also *core satire* and *core's attire* (*core*, "allusion to Adam's sin" [*OED*, 1b]; and Donne, *Sermons*, IX, 396, 398: "The coare of *Adams* apple is still in their throat. . . . If thou turne from God that made thee, that was adultery . . . ; every departing from that contract which you made with God, is Adultery"). In subsequent poems, the satirist's poems will become *cour satire* (Fr. *cour*, "of the Court"). On the conventional roughness of satire, see Arnold Stein, "Donne's Harshness and the Elizabethan Tradition," *Studies in Philology*, 41 (1944), 390–409; "Donne's Obscurity and the Elizabethan Tradition," *ELH*, 3 (1946), 98–118.

13. "A Dissuasion from Pride, and an Exhortation of Humility," in *The Sermons of Master Henry Smith*, p. 208. Francis Elizabeth Baldwin, *Sumptuary Legislation and Personal Regulation in England*, Johns Hopkins University Studies in Historical and Political Science, vol. 44 (Baltimore, 1926), points out that the last two decades of the century witnessed a large increase in attempted, proposed, and regulated sumptuary laws.

14. "The Jewel of Joy," in *Works*, III, 438.

15. Pilkington, *Works*, p. 385.

16. "The Jewel of Joy," p. 440.

17. Gervase Babington, *A Very fruitful Exposition of the Commandements by Way of Questions and Answers for greater plainenesse* (London: R. Robinson, 1596), p. 153. Donne evokes the same image often in his sermons, e.g., "Assoon as we were clothed by God, our very apparell was an Embleme of death" (*Sermons*, IV, 52).

18. Hill, *The crie of Englande*, p. 40; Babington, *Very fruitful Exposition*, p. 133.

19. "Against excesse of Apparell," in *The Second Tome of Homilies* (London: John Bill, 1623).

20. *The Sermons of Master Henry Smith*, pp. 208–9. See also Tymme, *A plaine discoverie of Ten English Lepers*; Allen, *A treasurie of catechisme or christian instruction* (London: R. Field for T. Man, 1600); Joye, *A contrarye (to a certain manis) consultacion: that adulterors ought to be punished wyth death* (London: J. Joye, 1549); Sandys, "A Sermon Made at York," in *Sermons*; Bullinger, "The Second Decade: Tenth Sermon," in *The Decades of Henry Bullinger*, ed. Thomas Harding (Cambridge: Cambridge Univ. Press, 1849); Hooper, "A Declaration of the Ten Holy Commandments of Almighty God," in *Early Writings of John Hooper*, ed. Samuel Carr (Cambridge: Cambridge Univ. Press, 1843). Donne, *Sermons*, IX, 399, urges that "Even in nature you are made for that marriage. . . . And every departing from that contract you made with God . . . is an Adultery. . . . If thou turne from God that made thee, to those things that he made, this is an adultery."

21. Milgate, p. 118.

22. *Summa Theologica*, II, ii, 3, 1.

23. *Certaine Sermones*, p. 11.

24. For a definition of Christian liberty in precisely these terms, see John Bradford, *Writings*, ed. Aubrey Townsend (Cambridge: Cambridge Univ. Press, 1848), I, 377.

25. *Christian Prayers and Holy Meditations, As Well for Private As Public Exercise* (London: Henry Middleton, 1570), pp. 106–7.

26. Milgate, p. 124.

27. Ibid., p. 125.

28. *The crie of Englande*, p. 39.

29. (London: W. Jaggard, 1607).

30. *The Epic of the Beast, Consisting of English Translations of "The History of Reynard the Fox" and Physiologus*, ed. William Rose, trans. John Carlill (London: George Routledge, n.d.), p. 158.

31. *Sacrorum Emblematatum Centuri Una* (Cambridge: John Legate, 1591), cited in Rosemary Freeman, *English Emblem Books* (London: Chatto & Windus, 1948), pp. 64–65.

32. *Historie of Foure-Footed Beastes*, unpaginated.

33. *The Epic of the Beast*, p. 203.

34. Cited in Freeman, *English Emblem Books*, p. 6. S. H. Atkins, "Banks' Horse," *Notes and Queries*, 179 (1934), 28–30, has collected the contemporary references to the highly popular performing horse to which Donne may be alluding.

35. H. W. Janson, *Apes and Ape Lore in the Middle Ages and the Renaissance* (London: Warburg Institute, Univ. of London, 1952), documents this topic thoroughly.

36. *The Epic of the Beast*, p. 203.

37. *The Progress of the Soul: The Interior Career of John Donne* (New York: William Morrow, 1968), p. 25.

38. Erwin Panofsky, *Studies in Iconology* (New York: Harper & Row, 1962; rpt. of 1939 ed.), chapter 3, provides an illuminating analysis of the figure of Time in the Renaissance.

39. "A Dissuasion from Pride," in *Sermons of Master Henry Smith*, p. 212.

40. Providence, points out Peter Baro, is "that perpetuall disposition and administration of all things that be" (*A Speciall Treatise of Gods Providence* [London: J. L[udham], 1588]); "all things in heaven, and under heaven, be continually governed and provided for, according to the state of their nature," affirms Edwarde Cradocke, *The Shippe of assured safety, . . . a discourse of Gods Providence* (London: H. Bynneman, 1572), p. 274. See Donne, *Sermons*, I, 229; II, 67; III, 193, 201; VI, 214, for the view of calamities as the work of Providence.

CHAPTER TWO

1. Typical of modern opinion of the poem is Milgate's judgment that it "fall[s] apart badly" and that the "figure of Coscus enables Donne to give [only] some appearance of unity to his satire" (*The Satires*, pp. xxiv, 128). "I am not sure how poetasters and lawyers got to be objects of satire in the same poem," Doniphan Louthan writes, "except that in Donne's time many young men ostensibly studying law, must have been primarily interested in letters" (*The Poetry of John Donne: A Study in Explication* [New York: Bookman, 1951], p. 100). Hallett Smith suggests that the poem is an attack on "the extravagances of love poetry, especially of those verses which it was fashionable for the young men at the Inns of Court to write"; but he finds no acceptable similarity between the satirist's ridicule of the poets and his proceeding "to the more serious charges against lawyers of social parasitism and of larceny" (*Elizabethan Poetry: A Study in Conventions, Meaning and Expression* [Cambridge, Mass.: Harvard Univ. Press, 1952], p. 224). J. B. Leishman admits the validity of a satire on "both poets and lawyers" but says that the unsatisfactory union of the two subjects in the poem affords such an "abrupt and obscure transition" that the resulting piece shows Donne to be "far more concerned with the working out of his ingenious similes than with the subject (whatever it be) which they profess to be illustrating and illuminating" (*The Monarch of Wit: An Analytical and Comparative Study of the Poetry of John Donne* [New York: Harper & Row, 1965], pp. 114, 116). Richard Hughes offers one of the most severe attacks on the poem; he suggests that it is "ironically suicidal, . . . merely a compendium, an assembling of leftover victims that the first satire missed . . . a gallery of follies raced through without any particular finesse" (*The Progress of the Soul*, pp. 25, 26). This is "one of the less successful" of the *Satyres*, says Howard Erskine-Hill; "it lacks the immediate narrative and dramatic interest of *I* and *IV* . . . is not united, like *Satyre III*, by the exposure of a central theological and human dilemma," and achieves at best only "a largely formal sense" of unity ("Courtiers out of Horace," pp. 274–75). Wilbur Sanders summarizes the concern over the unity, persona, and imagery of the poem by suggesting that it exhibits "a sureness of touch . . . Donne of course couldn't sustain . . . the fanatical proliferation of startling and insane comparisons . . . an art which is . . . *inventive* rather than *creative*" (*John Donne's Poetry* [Cambridge: Cambridge Univ. Press, 1971], pp. 36–37). In the most recent study of the *Satyres*, Richard C. Newton suggests that the apparent weaknesses of *Satyre II* are essential to Donne's exploration of "his own character as a satirist . . . Donne's struggle to comprehend and to contain this impulsive and turbulent character"; but his identification of Donne with the speaker of the poem and his suggestion that the poem relies on "evasive maneuver[s]" to deny "the real, and frightening, implications of his hate" differ from my own reading of the significance of the satirist's strategy in the poem ("Donne the Satirist," *Texas Studies in Literature and Language*, 16 [1974], 429, 434).

2. Many readers have observed similarities between the spirit of Donne's poems and the spirit of Shakespeare's *Hamlet*, especially between the angry tone of the satirist and the dramatist's melancholic prince. The phrase quoted here is from Richard Foster's study of the play ("Hamlet and the Word," *Univ. of Toronto Quarterly*, 30 [1960–61], 229), in which he illustrates that *Hamlet* is concerned with an "articulation of the mystery of the Word in the country of profanation." The situation facing the avenging prince as delineated by Foster—the decay of forms of human intercourse and communication—is the same as that which Donne's satirist

confronts in *Satyre II*. The application of the principles of Thomas Wilson's *Arte of Rhetorique* to this problem (which follows below) is also indebted to Foster's study.

3. The name is common in early Renaissance satires on lawyers and could derive from the legacy-hunter of Juvenal's tenth satire, Cossus. Etymologically, Gertrude Drake has pointed out for me, it raises two associations. The Latin *quisqiliae* ("refuse") is related to the Greek *Koskul* ("scraps of flattery"); also, Donne could have in mind *Koskim*, related to "sieve."

4. As A. Bartlett Giamatti points out, for the Renaissance

> words were units of energy. Through words man could assume forms and aspire to shapes and states otherwise beyond his reach. Words had this immense potency, this virtue, because they were derived from and were images of the Word, the Word of God which made us and which was God. . . . Because words, like men, were fallen, however, they contained, as we do, shapes of evil within them. Fallen words, like men, are unstable elements; thus they are, as we are, such dangers to us. . . . This is simply to say that the power of words and the power in words reflect our fallen state. ("Marlowe: The Arts of Illusion," *Yale Review*, 61 [1971–72], 532.)

I am also indebted to Giamatti's essay, "Proteus Unbound: Some Versions of the Sea God in the Renaissance," in *The Disciplines of Criticism: Essays in Literary Theory, Interpretation, and History*, ed. Peter Demetz, Thomas Greene, and Lowry Nelson, Jr. (New Haven, Conn.: Yale Univ. Press, 1968), pp. 437–76.

5. These similes actually portray that "crowd of malefactors" which is germane to verse satire. As Kernan explains, "The scene of satire is . . . packed to the very point of bursting. . . . Pick up any major satiric work and open it at random and the immediate effect is one of disorderly profusion. . . . The scene of formal satire, despite the attempts of the author to make it appear a piece of reporting, is . . . a selection of significant and interrelated details, a symbolic world" (*The Cankered Muse*, pp. 7–8, 13).

6. This view of Sebond appears in Rosalie Colie's *Paradoxia Epidemica: The Renaissance Tradition of Paradox* (Princeton, N.J.: Princeton Univ. Press, 1966), pp. 482–83.

7. Robert Elliott, in *The Power of Satire: Magic, Ritual, Art* (Princeton, N.J.: Princeton Univ. Press, 1960), traces the persistence of this old Irish belief in English satire. This view of the satirist is related, of course, to the idea of the poet as *magus*, as described by Giamatti, "Proteus."

8. For fuller treatment of this idea, see Marshall MacLuhan, "Cicero and Renaissance Training for Prince and Poet," *Renaissance and Reformation*, 6 (1970), 38–42; O. B. Hardison, "The Orator and the Poet: The Dilemma of Humanist Literature," *Journal of Medieval and Renaissance Studies*, 1 (1970), 33–44; and especially Aubrey L. Williams, *Pope's Dunciad: A Study of Its Meaning* (London: Methuen Press, 1955), pp. 104–23. Two recent studies, published after my own was written, examine the ramifications of the breakdown of this central humanist tenet: James L. Calderwood, "Elizabethan Naming," appendix to *Metadrama in Shakespeare's Henriad* (Los Angeles: Univ. of California Press, 1979), and Patrick Grant, *Images and Ideas in Literature of the English Renaissance* (Amherst: Univ. of Massachusetts Press, 1979). Donne's poem, on one level, presents a vivid reaction to the split of *verba* and *res* in his society.

9. MacLuhan, "Edgar Poe's Tradition," *Sewanee Review*, 52 (1944), 25. The seminal statement of this principle is Cicero's *De Oratore*, I, viii, 33: "eloquence is so potent a force that it embraces the origin and operation and developments of all things, all the duties, all the natural principles governing the morals and minds and life of mankind, and also determines their customs and laws and rights, and controls the government of the state, and expresses everything that concerns whatsoever topic in a graceful and flowing style" (trans. E. W. Sutton and H. Rackham [Cambridge: Harvard Univ. Press, 1942]). He also emphasizes the power of eloquence "to gather scattered humanity into one place . . . to lead it out of its brutish existence in the wilderness up to our present condition of civilization" (I.viii.33).

10. Thomas Wilson, *The Arte of Rhetorique*, ed. G. H. Mair (Oxford: Clarendon, 1909), sig. Aiii.

11. Giamatti, "Arts of Illusion," p. 532; this concern with the loss of linguistic credibility was especially acute at the time Donne writes, of course, when the shift from a "verbal fideism to scepticism" was well underway. The shift from a sacramental ontology of words to a verbal skepticism in the Renaissance is outlined by Calderwood, *Metadrama*, pp. 183–220.

12. The structure and strategy of the programmatic apologiae of Horace, Juvenal, and Per-

sius are delineated by Lucius Shero, "The Satirist's *Apologia*," *Classical Studies in Language and Literature*, Series 2, Univ. of Wisconsin Studies in Language and Literature, No. 15 (Madison: Univ. of Wisconsin Press, 1922), pp. 148–67.

13. Ibid., p. 159.

14. *The Arte of Rhetorique*, sigs. Aii-Biii.

15. Puttenham, *The Arte of English Poesie*, in *Elizabethan Critical Essays*, II, 6.

16. *The Arte of Rhetorique*, sig. Aiii[r].

17. *Dr. Faustus*, V.i.25, as discussed in Giamatti, "Arts of Illusion."

18. *Apologie for Poetrie*, in *Elizabethan Critical Essays*, I, 187. Sidney shares Donne's contempt for those "*Mysomousoi*, Poet-haters . . . who seek a prayse by dispraysing others . . . [with] obiections . . . [to poetry which] are full of very idle easines. . . . deserue they no other answer, but, in steed of laughing at the iest, to laugh at the iester" (I, 181).

19. Ibid., I, 187.

20. *The Schoole of Abuse*, ed. Arthur F. Kinney, in *Markets of Bawdrie: The Dramatic Criticism of Stephen Gosson*, Salzburg Studies in English Literature, Elizabethan Studies, No. 4 (Salzburg: Universitat Salzburg, 1974), pp. 99, 77. In the introduction to this edition, Kinney contends that, in fact, Gosson's application of the dicta of Plato, Lucretius, and Plutarch in *The Schoole* results in a disputation which accords with the central tenets of Sidney's later disputation (pp. 26–51).

21. *Directions for Speech and Style* (1580), ed. H. H. Hudson (Princeton, N.J.: Princeton Univ. Press, 1935), p. 2.

22. This distinction between Horatian "fools," whose crimes are revealed to be folly by the punishment which accompanies their errors, and Juvenalian "knaves," whose unpunished evil spurs the satirist's *saeva indignatio*, is explained in Ronald Paulson's *The Fictions of Satire* (Baltimore: Johns Hopkins Univ. Press, 1967), pp. 20–31. Such a distinction, modern classicists such as W. S. Anderson and Niall Rudd have revealed, overstates the differences between the two ancient satirists, but it was a common distinction in Renaissance commentaries.

23. St. Thomas, for example, explains that "love is due our neighbor in respect of nature and grace, but not in respect of what he has of himself and from the devil, that is, in respect of sin and lack of justice. Consequently, it is lawful to hate the sin in one's brother, and whatever pertains to the defect of Divine Justice. . . . Now it is part of love of our brother that we hate the fault and the lack of good in him, since desire for another's good is equivalent to hatred of his evil." *Summa Theologica*, II, i, 29. For fuller treatments of this idea in the writings of the Church Fathers see the studies of Mroz and Friedman.

24. Augustine, *The Teacher*, trans. Robert P. Russell (Washington, D.C.: Catholic Univ. Press, 1968), sects. 38–39, expounds this idea.

25. Gilbert Skene, Doctor of Medicine, in *Ane Breve Description of the Pest* (Edinburgh: Robert Kekprevite, 1568), for example, submits that "the first and principle cause [of the plague] may be callit, and is an scourge and punishment of the moist iust God" (sig. A3). The most famous surgeon of the day, Ambroise Paré, offers the same diagnosis in his *Traicte de la Pest* (1568), in *Les Doeuvres d'Ambroise Paré* (Paris: G. Buon, 1598), pp. 78f. The earliest piece of evidence of the attack on the stage in England—*A Sermon Preached at Pawles Crosse on Sunday the third of Nouember 1577* . . . by T. W[hite] (London: F. Coldock, 1578)—viewed the plague in the same terms, as a divine visitation for sin. The authoritative statements for this view are in the official *Book of Homilies*, especially "An Exhortation Concerning Good Order and Obedience" and "An Homilie of Whoredome and Unclennesse." See, also, the elaborate explanations of dearth as a divine scourge in Lodovike Lauatere, *Three Christian Sermons*, trans. W. Barlow (London: Thomas Creede, 1596).

26. In 1593, Henry Donne was arrested for harboring the lay priest, William Harrington, placed in the Clink, and then suddenly transferred to Newgate Prison, where the plague was raging; he died a few weeks later. This specific allusion to the statute which he violated and the general brunt of this poem's attack on the manipulations of law and lawyers suggest that it was this event rather than the anonymous *Zepheria* which stirred the original composition of *Satyre II*. The events surrounding Henry Donne's death are evaluated more fully by Fr. John Morris, "The Martyrdom of William Harrington," *The Month*, 20 (1874), 411–23; R. C. Bald, *John Donne: A Life* (Oxford: Oxford Univ. Press, 1970), pp. 58ff; and my own study, "Henry Donne, John Donne, and the Date of *Satyre II*," *Notes and Queries*, n.s. 24 (1977), 524–27.

27. The image cluster of "slings," "mov[ing] Love," "singers . . . to Lords, . . . for meat" (not manna)—the view of their efforts as a parody of the creative, life-giving function of poetry (which is recalled even in the mention of the "organ," the instrument of divine musical harmony)—points ironically to the Davidic role of the poet which these poets have abnegated.

28. For an excellent evaluation of the methods and aims of irony in satire, see Sister Geraldine Thompson, *Under Pretext of Praise: Satiric Mode in Erasmus' Fiction* (Toronto: Univ. of Toronto Press, 1973), pp. 3–50. She points out, for instance, the pedagogical aims of satiric irony and that the satirist is essentially a teacher, not an interpreter, who aims to "awaken perceptiveness in others to recognize what is being taught in Scripture, in nature, and in art" (p. 26).

29. Don Cameron Allen, "The Renaissance Antiquarian and Allegorical Interpretation," in *Medieval and Renaissance Studies 1967*, ed. John M. Headley (Chapel Hill: Univ. of North Carolina Press, 1968), pp. 3–20. Here is the popular Physiologus' explanation of the bird-lime metaphor:

> In this manner does the Devil, the great hunter, chase us. He comes into the world and brings with him the lime of sin, for sin is like bird-lime. And he shows man how to blind his eyes and darken his mind, and draws him on from sin to sin and from evil to evil, and he makes a great snare of rope, for sin is insatiable, and the man becomes spotted with it, body and soul. (*The Epic of the Beast*, p. 185.)

30. *Plodding* or mere diligence through the performance of large quantities of moots was one way of gaining admission to the bar. See Philip J. Finkelpearl, *John Marston of the Middle Temple: An Elizabethan Dramatist in His Social Setting* (Cambridge, Mass.: Harvard Univ. Press, 1969), p. 9.

31. Lucille E. Cobb, "Donne's 'Satyre' II: 49–57," *Explicator*, 15 (1956), 8, points out that the words Coscus uses in his appeal would be used only in a case in which someone already had a legal claim to the contested property. Also implicit in Coscus' plea for "love" from his judge is the characterization of his speech as a parody of Marian prayer: he has "returne[d] . . . in Lent" to beg his "Lady" to "remit" "grace" to him, to restore the relationship they originally shared— just as the *Ave Maria* to the "Queene" of heaven asks her to obtain the grace of Christ's love which restores man to God. Indeed, if Coscus' plea is within one year of the "*tricesimo*'of the Queene" (50), that is, in 1589, then the image of him as invader, returning one year after the Armada (when the threat did remain), is reinforced by this characterization of his supplication as parodic Catholic prayer. As such, it supports the satirist's view of Coscus' verbal abuses as an embodiment of the "alien religion" most harmful to English civilization. The English ironically had withstood the onslaught of the Catholic Spaniards only to fall victim to a perversion of the Spanish malady—a plague of diseased words.

The satirist's application of the *topoi* of anti-Papists and anti-Spanish polemics to the abuses of Coscus is also evident in this focus on the lawyer's sexual appetite. See, for example, Thomas Wright, *An sit licitum . . .* , in Strype's *Annals* (New York: B. Franklin, 1968), III, ii, 592, and *The Passions of the Minde* (Urbana: Univ. of Illinois Press, 1971); Lord Burghley, "Letter to Mendoza," in *Somers Tracts* (London: T. Cadell and W. Davis, 1809), I, 450ff; and especially the virulent attacks of the dissident Appellant Anthony Copley, *Another Letter of Mr. A. C[opley] to his dis-iesuited kinsman* (London: n.p., 1602); the pamphlets of J[ames] L[ea]: *A True and perfecte description of a straunge Monstar borne in the City of Rome in Italy, in the yeare of our Salvation. 1588. Vnder which is described the originall and triumphant state of the Holy League, and also the sodain and desperate fall thereof in the yeare 1588* (London: John Wolfe for Walter Dight, 1590), which views the Catholics as the embodiment of noise and verbal confusion (sigs. B3ff), and *The Birth, Purpose, and Mortall Wound of the Romish holie League* (London: Thomas Cadman, 1589).

32. This is a constant theme of anti-Papist polemics from Fox onwards, a charge extended from the Italians to the Spanish during the last two decades of the century. See Clancy, especially chapter 7, and Rose, especially chapter 6.

33. The Sclavonian simile recalls, again, the "barbarism" that English homilists, pamphleteers, and officials identified with the Spanish threat. See, for example, Edward Daunce, *A Briefe Discourse of the Spanish State* (London: Richard Field, 1590), sigs. Aiiᵛ, pp. 2, 11, 34; Timothy Tymme, *A preparation against the prognosticated dangers of this yeare 1588* (London, 1587); J[ames] L[ea], *The Birth, Purpose, and Mortall Wound of the Romish holie League*.

34. With a poet as fond of word play as Donne it is not impossible that "Peecemeale," immediately following the phrases "Relique-like" and "wedding gear," is an ironic allusion to the

Eucharist. Such an interpretation would accord with the portrait of Coscus as Uncreating Word whose "woods" mirror the spiritual vacuity of his "words."

35. Milgate, p. 137.

36. As cited in Donne, *Sermons*, VII, 230.

37. This is the same satiric plot as Pope's characterization of Dulness in *The Dunciad*: see Williams, *Pope's Dunciad*, and Kernan, "*The Dunciad* and the Plot of Satire," *Studies in English Literature*, 2 (1962), 260–66.

38. Apparently, these practices were so abandoned that they required official order: see the royal proclamation, "Enforcing Orders against Dearth; Ordering Hospitality Kept in Country" (2 Nov. 1596), in *Tudor Royal Proclamations*, ed. Paul L. Hughes and James F. Larkin (Oxford: Clarendon, 1967), III, 169–72.

39. The analogy is a favorite with Donne, as pointed out by Joan Webber, *Contrary Music: The Prose Style of John Donne* (Madison: Univ. of Wisconsin Press, 1963), pp. 123–42; and Winfried Schleiner, *The Imagery of John Donne's Sermons* (Providence, R. I.: Brown Univ. Press, 1970), pp. 94–103. Webber points out that "Donne's view of language is intimately connected with the traditional concept of the Word, which not only inspires the sacramental treatment of Scripture, but is also closely related to the symbolic reading of the world that . . . helped to shape the metaphor of medieval theology and homiletics" (p. 123). "Symbolic readings of the word were commonplace," she explains, "but Donne is unusual in so stressing that most familiar commonplace, the Book of Creatures, as continually to imply that man is a word speaking words, a book within a book" (p. 125).

40. "One possible reason for the emergence of the noun 'animal' in England at the beginning of the seventeenth century, to replace the hitherto universal 'beast,' is that the latter was acquiring too specific a sense as the equivalent of Antichrist" (Christopher Hill, *Antichrist in Seventeenth-Century England* [London: Oxford Univ. Press, 1971], p. 40).

The dire prophecies concerning 1588, especially the influential forecasts of Regiomantus and the English reaction to his warnings, are surveyed by Garrett Mattingly, *The Armada* (Boston: Houghton Mifflin, 1959).

41. Alexander Sackton, "Donne and the Privacy of Verse," *Studies in English Literature*, 7 (1967), 69.

42. Hallett Smith suggests, for example, that Donne "was too impressed, philosophically and imaginatively, with the degeneration of the world to make much of an art of satirizing it" (p. 227).

43. Kenneth Reckford, *Horace* (New York: Twayne, 1969), pp. 37–38, says that Horace's reference is to the Roman prescriptions against incantations; R. E. Smith, "The Law of Libel at Rome," *Classical Quarterly*, n.s. 1 (1951), 169–79, traces it to the *Lex Cornelia*. "Tabula VIII. 1a. . . . Si quis occentavisset sive carmen condidisset, quod infamiam faceret flagitiumve alteri. . . .1b. . . . Qui malum carmen incantassit . . ." *Remains of Old Latin*, ed. and trans. E. H. Warmington [Cambridge: Harvard Univ. Press, 1938], III, 474).

44. In one of his sermons Donne calls Horace "the best Poet" (*Sermons*, IV, 476). Wide support for such a view of Horace-the-satirist is found in the Renaissance. As Thomas Maresca points out, Horace was considered a "nearly unimpeachable moral arbiter and guide, on the level of authority almost with the Scriptures to which his sentiments were so often compared" (*Pope's Horatian Poems* [Columbus: Ohio State Univ. Press, 1966], p. 15). For example, Thomas Sagittarius adapted Horace's epistles and satires to specific themes in his *Horatiis Christianus*; Octavio van Veen produced an emblem book, *Horatius Emblematus*, which illustrated parallels between the ancient poet's denunciations and biblical and patristic complaints; and in his essay, *De Q. Horatii Vita ac Scriptis*, Torrentinus attested that Horace contains "all the rules that enable profane man to progress towards living in a right, holy, peaceful, and blessed manner" (cited in Maresca, p. 33). In fact, as Soens points out ("Criticism of Formal Satire"), the view of Horace's satires as providing exemplary moral instruction compatible with and supportive of Christian doctrine is a commonplace of Renaissance annotations and scholarship: see the editions of Stephano (1575), II, 41, 51; Drant (1567), pp. 250–51; Glareanus (1576), fol. 166ᵛ; Lambinus (1566), fol. 18ʳ⁻ᵛ; Landinus (1579), fol. 55; Gualterus (1594), p. 550; and Bond (1606), pp. 150–51.

45. W. S. Anderson, "Imagery in the Satire of Horace and Juvenal," *American Journal of Philology*, 81 (1960), 242–44, and "The Roman Socrates: Horace and His Satires," in *Critical*

Essays on Roman Literature: Satire, ed. J. P. Sullivan (London: Routledge and Kegan Paul, 1963), pp. 30–33; Eduard Frankel, *Horace* (Oxford: Clarendon, 1957), pp. 147–53; and J. S. C. Teijeiro, "Apostillas jurisdicas a una satira de Horacio," *Arbor*, 31 (1955), 65–76.

46. John Aden, *Something Like Horace* (Nashville: Vanderbilt Univ. Press, 1969), p. 9.

47. A. E. Voss, "The Structure of Donne's *Anniversaries*," *English Studies in Africa*, 12 (1969), 30. Voss illustrates that, in one sense, *The First Anniversary* is a defense of the poet's medium as a version of God's creative word.

48. The view of poetry as a prophetic mission, implied at the start of *Satyre II*, is drawn more fully in the closing lines of the *Anniversaries*. The poet's "song" continues the "great office" of Moses (*First Anniversary*, 468) and therefore should be recognized as "The Trumpet, at whose voice the people came" (*Second Anniversary*, 528).

CHAPTER THREE

1. *The Complete Works of Alexander Pope*, ed. William Warburton (London: J. & P. Knapton, 1751), IV, 247.

2. Andreasen, "Theme and Structure," suggests that the poem is a soliloquy. Thomas O. Sloan, "The Persona as Rhetor: An Interpretation of Donne's *Satyre III*," *Quarterly Journal of Speech*, 51 (1965), 14–27, analyzes it in terms of the rhetorical art of *dispositio*, as a deliberative oration intended "to persuade and exhort a specific audience toward honorable action and away from merely expedient ones," addressed "to young men close to the Queen." Camille Slights, "'To Stand Inquiring Right': The Casuistry of Donne's 'Satyre III,'" *Studies in English Literature*, 12 (1972), 85–101, contends that the poem is "a dramatization of a case of conscience" (p. 86). Clarence H. Miller and Caryl K. Berrey, "The Structure of Integrity: The Cardinal Virtues in Donne's 'Satyre III,'" *Costerus*, 1 (1974), 27–45, urge that it is structured according to the pattern of the four cardinal virtues. Typical of disagreement about the tone of the poem are two most recent studies, by John R. Lauritsen, "Donne's *Satyres*: The Drama of Self-Discovery," *Studies in English Literature*, 16 (1976), 117–30, and by Emory Elliott, "The Narrative and Allusive Unity of Donne's *Satyres*," *Journal of English and Germanic Philology*, 75 (1976), 105–16. Lauritsen finds *Satyre III* "at once the least satirical and, for the satirist, the darkest of the *Satyres*" (pp. 125–26), while Elliott suggests that the speaker "discovers an answer to his struggles and those of mankind" (p. 113). My own reading accords more with the observation of Louis Martz, *The Poetry of Meditation* (New Haven, Conn.: Yale Univ. Press, 1962), that "meditation struggles to convert the methods of Roman satire" in the poem (p. 211).

3. *Sermons*, V, 149.

4. Ibid. St. Bernard, Donne's acknowledged source for his analysis of the mental faculties in this sermon, offers a similar critique of the condition of man. "This sacred trinity," he writes, "chose a fall by the force of its own will, rather than to stand by the grace of God through free choice. It fell, therefore, by suggestion, delight, consent from that supreme and beautiful trinity, namely power, wisdom, purity, into a certain contrary and ugly trinity, namely weakness, blindness, impurity; for the memory became impotent and weak, the reason imprudent and obscure, the will impure" (*Xenia Bernardina* [Vienna, 1891], I, 911, as trans. and cited by George Bosworth Burch, *The Steps of Humility by Bernard, Abbot of Clairvaux* [Notre Dame: Univ. of Notre Dame Press, 1963], p. 11).

5. *Sermons*, IX, 85. This entire sermon, on Genesis 1:26, is concerned with how "The Sphear then of this intelligence, the Gallery for this Picture, the Arch for this statue, the Table, and frame and shrine for this Image of God, is inwardly and immediately the soule of man . . . in the naturall reason, and other faculties of the immortall Soule of man" (79, 81).

6. "Hymne to God my God, in my sicknesse," line 4.

7. Helen White, "John Donne and the Psychology of Spiritual Effort," in *The Seventeenth Century*, ed. Richard Foster Jones (Stanford, Calif.: Stanford Univ. Press, 1951), pp. 355–68, examines this aspect of Donne's poetry and prose. Ruth Wallerstein's unfinished study of patristic influences on Donne also illustrates the poet's reliance on the psychology of the Church Fathers: "Studies in Donne by Ruth Wallerstein," ed. Barbara Hillyer Davis, Ph.D. dissertation, Univ. of Wisconsin, 1962, esp. pp. 77–115.

8. *Sermons*, V, 149.

148

9. The studies of *Juvenal X* that I have found most helpful are those of W. S. Anderson, "The Programs of Juvenal's Later Books," *Classical Philology*, 57 (1962), 145–60; "Anger in Juvenal and Seneca," *Univ. of Calif. Pub. in Class. Phil.*, 19 (1964), 127–95, and "Juvenal and Quintilian," *Yale Classical Studies*, 17 (1961), 1–93; Bernard F. Dick, "Seneca and Juvenal 10," *Harvard Studies in Classical Philology*, 73 (1969), 237–46; Gilbert Lawall, "*Exampla* and Theme in Juvenal's Tenth Satire," *Transactions of the American Philological Association*, 89 (1958), 25–31; and D. E. Eichholz, "The Art of Juvenal and his Tenth Satire," *Greece and Rome*, 2nd series, 3 (1956), 61–69.

10. "Anger in Juvenal and Seneca," pp. 178–83.

11. This particular view of the mixed tone of the poem differs from the conclusions of Anderson; it is more indebted to the reading of Lawall.

12. This thematic structure of Juvenal's poem was first delineated by J. de Decker, *Juvenalis declamans* (Ghent, 1913), p. 132; and is elaborated by Dick, pp. 239f.

13. Anderson, "Anger in Juvenal and Seneca," p. 179.

14. Lawall, p. 31.

15. I have relied on the *scala meditatioria* of Johan Gansfort, as popularized by Joannes Mauburnus (1494) and translated by Joseph Hall (*The Arte of Divine Meditation*), because of its use in the sixteenth and seventeenth centuries as a prototype for the meditational scheme. Both works are reproduced by Martz, pp. 334–37, from which all subsequent citations that describe the various stages of the meditation are taken. For examinations of the influence of the Gansfort-Mauburnus *scala* on the development of both Catholic and Protestant meditational practice see Martz, pp. 62–63, 331–52; and Lewalski, *Donne's Anniversaries and the Poetry of Praise*, esp. pp. 85–107.

16. Norman Knox, *The Word Irony and Its Context: 1500–1755* (Durham, N.C.: Duke Univ. Press, 1961), pp. 190–92.

17. The importance of memory as a function of prudence and of prudence as a result of the correct use of the memory (both artificial and natural memory) in Aristotle, *Ad Herennium*, Albertus Magnus, and Aquinas are delineated by Frances A. Yates, *The Art of Memory* (Chicago: Univ. of Chicago Press, 1966), esp. chapter 3.

18. *Saint Bernard His Meditations*, trans. "W. P." (London, 1631–32), Pt. 2, p. 6, as cited in Martz, p. 36.

19. In one of his Lincoln's Inn sermons, Donne offered this view of the memory: "The memory, sayes *St. Bernard*, is the stomach of the soul, it receives and digests, and turns into good blood, all the benefits formerly exhibited to us in particular, and exhibited to the whole Church of God. . . . [so] we may be bold to call it the Gallery of the soul, hang'd with so many, and so lively pictures of the goodness and mercies of thy God to thee, . . . [and] to instruct thee in all thy duties to him" (*Sermons*, II, 236–37). Even "he that hears no Sermons, he that reads no Scriptures," Donne pointed out in another sermon, "hath *all* in his memory. . . . He hath a *Genesis* in his *memory* . . . even to the *Revelation*" (II, 74).

20. *Sermons*, II, 74.

21. Gulielmus Gratarolus, *The Castel of Memorie*, trans. William Fulwood (London: 1562), sigs. Bv-vi. The same view is expressed by Ralegh in *The History of the World*, I, i, 10, 367.

22. "John Donne and the Mindes Indeavours," *Studies in English Literature*, 5 (1965), 116. She sees the poem also as having three definite movements, which are concerned with "three kinds of intellectual bankruptcy"—*inconsideratio, ignorantia*, and deliberate manipulation of others.

23. Hallett Smith, *Elizabethan Poetry*, points out, for instance, that on one level the poem is an argument that "the Elizabethan courage which expressed itself in war, traffics, and discoveries, a bold defiance of the dangers of unknown countries and distant shores, the stout maintenance of the point of honor in duels, should be devoted to the greatest venture of all and the most significant—that search for truth which would determine the real future, not the fading, short-lived future of the world" (p. 224).

24. Thomas V. Moore, "Donne's Use of Uncertainty as a Vital Force in *Satyre III*," *Modern Philology*, 67 (1969), 44.

25. H. J. C. Grierson, ed., *The Poems of John Donne* (Oxford: Oxford Univ. Press, 1912), II, 114, makes the same point about these lines.

26. The comparison here is ironic, of course. The three children of Daniel 3:11–30 were thrown into the fires because they refused to accept a false religion, specifically, to worship the

"golden image"; Donne's adventurers, on the other hand, seem to worship gold ("gaine") and dare the fires of the equator in order to worship this goddess.

27. Bernard, *The Steps of Humility*, pp. 246–47. See also Donne, *Sermons*, I, 226, 237–38; V, 298; VIII, 2, 262ff., for a view of imprudence as a failure to recall one's origin and eventual end; on fear of hell as "greate courage," see *Sermons*, VI, 111–12.

28. *The Franciscan Vision. Translation of St. Bonaventure's Itinerarium Mentis in Deum*, trans. Father James (London: Burns Oates and Washbourne, 1937), pp. 36–37.

29. "Postdate the whole Bible," Donne preached, "and whatsoever thou hearest spoken of such, as thou art, before, beleeve all that to be spoken but now, and spoken to thee" (*Sermons*, VI, 220). For a full exposition of the emphasis of Renaissance devotionals and homiletics on "finding the whole of salvation history traced in one's own soul," see Lewalski, pp. 100ff. Augustine's explanations of the "intellectual" functions of memory are in *De Trinitate*, X, and *Confessions*, X, 9–16.

30. *Saint Bernard His Meditations*, Pt. 2, p. 6, as cited in Martz, p. 36.

31. *Sermons*, VIII, 364–65.

32. *De Trinitate*, XII, 14. The continuity of Augustine's distinction into the Renaissance is discussed by Eugene Rice, *The Renaissance Idea of Wisdom*, and Manley, in his edition of *The Anniversaries*. They both cite this explanation of Luther, which focuses on the differences between "knowledge of this world" and "true wisdom":

> Those therefore who are wise in and concerning visible things . . . understand nothing and are wise in nothing, that is, they are neither intelligent [*intelligentes*] nor wise [*sapientes*], but foolish and blind. And though they may think themselves wise men, yet they have become fools. For they are wise, not in the wisdom of secret, hidden things, but of that which can be found in a human way.

33. Slights, p. 95.

34. Lynette McGrath, "Studies in the Norms and Techniques of Sixteenth-Century Satire from Skelton to Donne," Ph.D. dissertation, Univ. of Illinois, 1968, first made this point. She illustrates that each of the lovers "isolates and perverts one element in the satire's final statement about the proper search for truth" (p. 550).

35. Mauburnus-Hall defines *Tractation* as "An extending the thing considered to other points, where all questions of doubts are discussed." The *Dijudication* provides "an estimation of the worth of the thing thus handled," and the *Causation* is the "confirmation of the estimation thus made."

36. Milgate, notes, and McGrath, p. 560.

37. Milgate, pp. 290–92, provides a survey of suggestions that have been made about the source of Donne's image. I have examined the similarity of Donne's image to Petrarch's description of his "allegorical" ascent of Mont Ventoux in "Donne's 'Hill of Truth,'" *English Language Notes*, 14 (1976), 100–105.

38. This paragraph is indebted to John Freccero's discussions of spiral structure and imagery in Dante and Donne: "Dante's Pilgrims in a Gyre," *PMLA*, 76 (1961), 168–81, and "Donne's 'Valediction: Forbidding Mourning,'" *ELH*, 30 (1963), 335–76. The earliest source for this *topos*, he points out, is Plato's *Timaeus*, and it is reiterated and modified in the works of Chalcidius, Albertus Magnus, Boethius, the pseudo-Dionysius, St. Bonaventure, Aquinas, and Dante. An illuminating modern application of this image is contained in chapter 5, "The Spiral of History," of Jaroslav Pelikan's *The Shape of Death* (New York: Abingdon, 1961).

39. John R. Roberts, "Donne's *Satyre III* Reconsidered," *CLA Journal*, 12 (1968), 113.

40. Donne makes the same point in his first sermon as Dean of St. Paul's:

> Divers men may walke by the Sea side, and the same beames of the Sunne giving light to them all, one gathereth by the benefit of that light pebles, or speckled shells, for curious vanitie, and another gathers precious Pearle, or medicinall Ambar, by the same light. So the common light of reason illumins us all; but one imployes this light upon the searching of impertinent vanities, another by a better use of the same light, finds out the Mysteries of Religion. (*Sermons*, III, 359)

For an exposition of the celebration of reason in Donne's later works see Bruce Henricksen, "The Unity of Reason and Faith in Donne's Sermons," *Papers on Language and Literature*, 11

(1975), 18–30. Augustine's appraisal of the reason relies on the same image: "For your reason which converses with you promises that it will make God known to your mind just as the sun is shown to the eyes" ["R: Promittit enim ratio quae tecum loquitur, ita se demonstraturam Deum tuae menti, ut oculis sol demonstratur"]. *Soliloquies*, ed. Thomas F. Gilligan (New York: Cosmopolitan Science & Art, 1943), I, vi, 12.

41. In a letter of 1612, on the conflict between the Sorbonnists and the Huguenots in France, for example, Donne tells Henry Goodyer, "you will pardon my extravagances in these relations. I look upon nothing so intensively as these things. . . . I doe (I thank God) naturally and heartily abhorre all schism in Religion so much, as, I protest, I am sorry to find the appearance of schism amongst our adversaries in the Sorbonnists": *Letters to Severall Persons of Honour* (London: J. Flesher, for Richard Marriot, 1615), p. 132. For a fuller discussion of this issue, see the essays of Battenhouse and Flynn on Donne's recusant sympathies, a view reiterated by Earl Miner, *The Metaphysical Mode from Donne to Cowley* (Princeton, N.J.: Princeton Univ. Press, 1969).

42. *Meditations upon the Mysteries of our Holie Faith*, as cited in Martz, p. 35.

43. *Nicomachean Ethics*, trans. W. D. Ross (Oxford, 1925), V, 11, as cited by Charles S. Singleton, *Dante Studies 2: Journey to Beatrice* (Cambridge, Mass.: Harvard Univ. Press, 1958), p. 58.

44. *Summa Theologica*, I–II, q. 113, a. 1, as cited in Singleton, p. 59.

45. Donne applies the same Psalm more fully to the practices of the courts in *Satyre V*, 57–63. See also *Sermons*, VI, 297ff.

46. The homilist in the *Certaine Sermons* "Concerning Good Order and Obedience to Rulers and Magistrates," for example, insists that

Almighty God hath created and appointed all things, in heaven, earth, and waters, in a most excellent and perfect order. In Heaven, hee hath appointed distinct and severall orders and states of Archangels and Angels. In earth hee hath assigned and appointed kings, Princes, and other governours under them, all in good and necessary order.

The Scriptures, the homilist continues,

perswade and command us all obediently to bee subject, first and chiefly to the Kings Majestie, supreme governour over all, and the next to his honourable counsells, and to all other noble men, Magistrates, and officers which by GODS goodnesse, be placed and ordered.

"Therefore let us all feare," he concludes, "the most detestable vice of rebellion, every knowing and remembring, that he that resisteth or withstandeth common authority, resisteth or withstandeth GOD and his ordinance." (*Certaine Sermons*, pp. 69–70). The concluding exhortation of *Satyre III* concurs.

Equally strong directives prohibiting attack on ordained princes, even if they are tyrants, come from the recusant press. Although English pamphleteers argue that the pope's excommunication instructed Catholics to proceed against the queen, the Catholic polemics urge nothing of the sort. John Azor's *Institutionum Moralium*, for example, and Navarrus' *Enchiridion* instruct Catholics that citizens owe allegiance to their king: "co-operation with a tyrannous regime in the conduct of normal governmental responsibilites is perfectly proper," they argue. Even Molanus, who says that tyrants should be removed, points out that "they may not be removed by private authority" (Rose, pp. 97, 101).

47. Milgate, pp. 222–23, suggests 1597 as the most probable date of this letter. In one manuscript it is identified as "A Letter of Doctor Dunne to one that desired some of his papers." Among those "papers," lines 4–6 of the epistle suggest, were some of the *Satyres*. The verse letter's elaboration of Persius' "tecum habite" can be read, then, as a gloss on the *nosce teipsum* directive of *Satyre III*.

CHAPTER FOUR

1. Gransden, *Tudor Verse Satire* (London: Athlone, 1970), p. 170; Bald, *Donne: A Life*, pp. 86, 193; Jensen, "The Wit of Renaissance Satire," *Philological Quarterly*, 51 (1972), 407.

2. Erskine-Hill, "Courtiers out of Horace," pp. 273–307; Geraldine, "Donne's *Notitia*," pp. 29–31. Erskine-Hill's balanced view of the poem illustrates that both Donne and Pope succeeded in their individual approaches, that each of the poems is "humanly admirable in its courage and

independence" (p. 307). Even in the largely sympathetic study of Addison C. Bross, however, Donne's poems are said to illustrate "a tangle of obscurity," "a choppy mass . . . smother[ing] the reader," suffering generally from a "weakening of wit" because they supposedly do not exhibit Pope's "keen sense of order" or "perfect control": "Alexander Pope's Revisions of John Donne's *Satyres*," *Xavier University Studies*, 5 (1966), 133–52. Another view is presented by Ian Jack, "Pope and 'The Weighty Bullion of Dr. Donne's Satires,'" *PMLA*, 66 (1951), 1009–22.

3. Those familiar with Patrick Grant's study of the iconographic tradition of the *effectus passionis* and its importance to Book One of *The Faerie Queene* will recognize my debt to his study, *Image and Idea*, chapter 2.

4. A. C. Hamilton, *Sir Philip Sidney: A Study of His Life and Works* (London: Cambridge Univ. Press, 1977), p. 84.

5. This strategy is in itself a sort of ironic play on the Catholic plea of *communicatio in sacris*. Like *Satyre II*, where the satirist applied the *topoi* of government's view of the Spanish and the *misomusoi*'s view of the poets, here the satirist applies the common pamphlet descriptions of the Catholics and Statutes to the court. The *communicatio in sacris*, as defended most notably by Robert Persons' *A Brief Discourse* (1580), shows that Catholics had no option but to refuse attending church in England because it would force them to communicate with heretics. This was an old-established principle, Elliot Rose illustrates, "deep embedded in canon law, which forbade *communicatio in sacris* with pagans, heretics or schimatics." The pope had invoked it as early as 1562; its fullest contemporary defenses come from Persons, in *A Brief Discours* and *Quaestionis Duae*. See Rose, *Cases of Conscience*, pp. 73–80; F. W. Maitland, *Historical Essays* (Cambridge: Cambridge Univ. Press, 1957), pp. 224ff; and Clancy, *Papist Pamphleteers*, esp. chapters 6–7. Grierson claimed in his edition that "Donne is always, though he does not state his position too clearly, one with links to the persecuted minority" (II, 121); and, more recently, Erskine-Hill argues that "if Donne is not writing as a Catholic, this does not mean that he is writing as if he had never been one" (p. 282), and Clay Hunt notes that Donne's "Catholic bias is still in evidence" in *Satyre IV* (*Donne's Poetry: Essays in Literary Analysis* [New Haven, Conn.: Yale Univ. Press, 1954], p. 172). The most thorough treatment of Donne's recusancy is Dennis Flynn, "Donne's Catholicism," *Recusant History*, 13 (1975), 1–17, 178–95. On English anti-Catholicism as the product of "fear and frustration [and] an obsessively gloomy fear of disorder" which led to "apocalyptic" anxieties, see Carol Z. Weiner, "The Beleaguered Isle: A Study of Elizabethan and Early Jacobean Anti-Catholicism," *Past and Present*, 51 (1971), 27–62. She shows that the Protestant polemicists depicted the Catholics as possessors of inordinate Circean powers of persuasion (nets, snares, crosses, and forms of spiritual bribery and ransom being their common weapons) and that travellers were especially suspect of having succumbed to the Romist enchantments.

6. *Biathanatos*, ed. J. William Hebel (New York: Facsimile Text Society, 1930), p. 5.

7. A. J. Smith, "The Poetry of John Donne," in *English Poetry and Prose 1540–1674*, ed. Christopher Ricks (London: Barrie & Jenkins, 1970), pp. 139, 140.

8. In "Horace, the Unwilling Warrior: Satire I, 9," *American Journal of Philology*, 77 (1956), 148–66, Anderson points out that Horace "uses the martial context of the *Iliad* to show the incongruous aggressiveness of a typical man. . . . [T]he satirist perceives, through his controlled irony, the elements of epic battle" in his confrontation with the *garrulus*. Erskine-Hill provides a summary of the common features of Horace's satire and Donne's poem:

> In each poem the speaker is encountered in a public place by a stranger who runs and engages him in conversation. In each poem the stranger proves an intrusive and tactless talker, who praises his own accomplishment, seizes the speaker by the hand with offensive familiarity, and, because he will not be shaken off, causes the speaker to sweat with exasperation, and feel like a fool and a beast of burden. In each poem almost all the speaker says is an attempt to get rid of his unwelcome companion. In each poem a crowd fills the scene as the speaker is finally free. (pp. 277–78)

9. Anderson, "Unwilling Warrior," p. 159.

10. It is possible that the verbal assaults and the reciprocating quips of the satirist are supposed to be, in addition to their typological tenors, a sort of "polite" *duello*. The weapons of the match are "tongues"; and the allusions to the bore's conversation as "thrusts," "crosses," and "blunt iron"—all forms of Spanish and Italian duelling introduced into the court by what George Silver calls the *strangers*—suggest that the satirist now recognizes that his seemingly

innocent conversation was actually a duel in which he could have lost his life (if the informant does manage to incriminate him as a "Traytor"). Such a level of significance would accord with traditional allegories of duelling and with the central concerns of the poem. As Rosalie Colie points out, duelling is the popular metaphor for both intellectual debate (the pursuit of Truth which the satirist should be enacting) and "total risk" (which he actually undertook in that first visit). In his essay on the nothingness of this world, "An Apologie for Raymond Sebonde," Montaigne likens his paradoxical defense of nescience to the last desperate trick of the duellist. George Silver prefaces his ridicule of the popular Italian rapier by comparing fencing to the pursuit of Truth. Certainly Shakespeare had such connotations in mind in the final scenes of *Hamlet*. See Colie, *Paradoxia*, chapter 16, and Silver, *Paradoxes of Defense* (London: E. Blount, 1599), sigs. A3–A4.

11. For discussions of the many variations of the *meditatio mortis* see Martz, pp. 135–44, and Robert Collmer, "The Meditation on Death and its Appearance in Metaphysical Poetry," *Neophilologus*, 45 (1961), 323–33.

12. A penal law, Rose points out, is basically a "police measure to discourage an essentially indifferent action." This, in fact, was the recusant interpretation of the fines for not attending Anglican worship services. Naravvus' *Enchiridion* (1581), the "textbook" for moral theology at the Douai seminary, urged that the offender had fulfilled the complete intention of the law once he had paid the fine. And several recusant authors pointed out that the queen fully *expected* such fines to continue, often promising future revenues from such fines as rewards to courtiers. See Rose, pp. 66–70.

13. "[T]he Dev'l would have it so," admits Pope's satirist, "Since 'twas no form'd Design of serving God: / So was I punish'd" (*Imitations of Horace*, ed. John Butt, vol. 4, The Twickenham Edition [New Haven, Conn.: Yale Univ. Press, 1939], 14, 18–19).

14. McGrath, p. 571.

15. This traditional identification of Satan as idle "roamer" dressed in "strange" clothing is outlined by Elizabeth Marie Pope, *Paradise Regained: The Tradition and the Poem* (New York: Russell & Russell, 1962), chapter 4. These were commonplaces of Anglican and Catholic polemics, Clancy points out in chapter 7.

16. Milgate's edition reads "one language"; I have returned to the Grierson text on this one occasion.

17. These are the characteristics that were applied to the Catholics especially: see George B. Parks, "The First Italianate Englishman," *Studies in the Renaissance*, 8 (1961), 197–216; and Z. S. Fink, "Jaques and the Malcontent Traveler," *Philological Quarterly*, 14 (1935), 237–52. Donne's portrait of the bore, with its associations of Circe, monsters, foreign influence, unnaturalness, papistry, and moral decay, draws on the *topoi* first described by Ascham in his portrait of the "inchantments of *Circes*." On Catholics as menacing "strangers" of satanic intent, see the official *Declaration of great troubles pretended against the Realme by a number of Seminairie Priestes and Jesuites . . . , Oct 18, 1591*, in *Tudor Proclamations*; and Cecil's *The Execution of Justice in England* (London: C. Barker, 1583), *passim*.

18. The frequency of this image in Donne's prose and its scriptural and patristic elaborations on which he drew are examined by Schleiner, pp. 68–85.

19. In *Metempsychosis*, destiny is described as "the Commissary of God, . . . Knot of all causes" (31, 35).

20. Deriving, of course, from Matthew 6:28.

21. This is from Edward Fenton's English translation, *Certaine Secrete wonders of Nature, containing a description of sundry strange things, seming monstrous* (London: Henry Bynneman, 1569), sig. A4.

22. Joseph Wybarne, *New Age of Old Names* (London: J. Windet for W. Barrett and H. Fetherstone, 1609), p. 113; and Clement Pamen, *The Taverne*, cited in Milgate, p. 149.

23. Randolph, "The Medical Concept in English Renaissance Satiric Theory: Its Possible Relationships and Implications," *Studies in Philology*, 38 (1941), 127–62.

24. See, for example, Southwell's *Exercitia*: "Indeed I am to thinke it an especial mark of God's favour to me if I am burdened with perpetual afflictions and wearied with constant difficulties, especially as in this manner alone may I become like unto Christ" (*Spiritual Exercises and Devotions*, trans. P. E. Hallet [London: Sheed & Ward, 1931], pp. 35–36); and Loyola's "Exercises for Week Three," *The Spiritual Exercises of Saint Ignatius of Loyola*, trans. W. H. Longridge (London: A. R. Mowbray, 1919).

25. The tradition of Christ as a "Patient" is examined by Georgia Ronan Crampton, *The Condition of Creatures: Suffering and Action in Chaucer and Spenser* (New Haven, Conn.: Yale Univ. Press, 1974), chapter 1.

26. In his sermons, Donne relies frequently on this image: "Christ was a Savior as he paid God a ransome for all" (*Sermons*, VIII, 258); "[I]f thou be defective in [faith] . . . thou wilt be cast into that prison, where thou must pay the last farthing; thou must; for, Christ dyes not there, and therefore there thou must lie, till there come such another ransome as Christ. . . . This then is the Christians case, and this is the abridgement of his Religion; *Sic loquimini, sic facite*; to speak right, and to doe aright; to profess the truth, and not be afraid nor ashamed of that . . . " (VIII, 354). On another level, the term *ransom* was used by recusants to describe the fines imposed by tbe government for their recusancy; see Southwell's *Supplication*, for example.

27. *Of the Imitation of Christ*, II, 12, 4, trans. Abbot Justin McCann (New York: Mentor, 1957), p. 69; as cited in Grant, *Images*, p. 52.

28. This is Erasmus' "seventeenth rule" in *The Enchiridion*, referred to by Grant, *Images*, p. 218, n. 26.

29. Joseph A. Mazzeo's description of the peregrinations of Dante's pilgrim apply equally to adventure of the satirist; both pilgrims learn the source of their talent through "confrontations which are also self-confrontations [and] are constrained to reflect on the complex and paradoxical relations which obtain between a man's destiny as a man and a man's destiny as an artist": "Dante's Three Communities," in *The World of Dante: Six Studies in Language and Thought*, ed. S. Bernard Chandler and J. A. Molinaro (Toronto: Univ. of Toronto Press, 1966), p. 72.

30. Terence Cave's valuable study of devotional influences on Renaissance French poetry elaborates this idea, showing how meditations on the Passion engage in part in a type of "penitential self-deprecation" (p. 55) so that contemplation of the "instrument of his redemption" arouses "the meditator's compassion" (p. 48): *Devotional Poetry in France c. 1570–1613* (Cambridge: Cambridge Univ. Press, 1969).

31. In *Meditations on the Life of Christ*, for example, St. Bonaventura (or pseudo-Bonaventura) says that "to him who searches into this mystery with an earnest mind and all the affection of his heart, many unhoped-for things happen, from which he receives a new compassion, a new love, new consolations, and consequently, as it were, a new state of soul, which seems to be a presage and share of eternal glory" (trans. Sister M. Emmanuel [London: B. Herder, 1934], p. 329). On the effects of contemplation of the *gloria passionis* and trances see Erich Auerbach, *Literary Language and Its Public in Late Latin Antiquity and in the Middle Ages*, trans. Ralph Manheim, Bollingen Series 74 (New York: Pantheon, 1965), pp. 67–82.

32. Grant, p. 40.

33. Milgate, p. 158.

34. Milgate notes that the reference to the time accuses the courtiers of laziness, and cites *The Courtier's Library* as a gloss on the line: "sleep, which you must not shake off, as a rule, till after ten o'clock" (Evelyn M. Simpson edition [London: Nonesuch, 1930], p. 41). McGrath's explanation is equally appropriate; "the consequences of the Fall in the loss of timeless and static perfection," she explains, "are underlined by the persona's next reference to the clock" (p. 580). Another possible implication of the reference is suggested by Walton's note in his *Life of Herbert* that Morning Prayers were regularly said at ten o'clock; if Donne has this association in mind, then the courtiers are attacked not just for arriving at court from "the Mues, / Baloune, Tennis, Dyet, or the stewes" (176–77) but for arriving from these activities instead of from Morning Prayers (Izaak Walton, *Lives* [London: Oxford Univ. Press, 1927], p. 302).

35. Stroup, *Microcosmos*, esp. chapter 1. "The world is the Theatre that represents God, and where every man may, nay must see him. The whole frame of the world is the Theatre, and every creature the stage . . . our *Medium* the Ordinances of the Church," preached Donne (*Sermons*, VIII, 224, 231); see also II, 207; VI, 108; VIII, 220f.

36. These pictures were actually by Giulio Romano but were attributed often to Aretino during the Renaissance because he defended them and the sixteen obscene sonnets (*Sonnetti lussuriosi*) which accompanied the engravings (Milgate, p. 155).

Aretino is the apt analogue here for many reasons. Self-proclaimed "*flagello de' principi*" and proud bearer of the medallion given him by Francis I with the exergue, "Lingua eius loquetur mendacium," the Italian "condottiere" of literature (as Titian called him) was legendary in the age as a slanderer, libeller, and blackmailer who extorted money from his victims. Aretino's comedy, *La Cortegiana*, with its satirical attacks on the Papal Court, and his obscene dialogues,

Ragionamenti, strike notes quite similar, in fact, to the features of the court "praised" by Donne's *garrulus* and condemned by Donne's speaker in the account of his second visit; especially does Captain Tinca, the *miles gloriosus* of *La Cortegiana*, resemble Glorius. Assailed by Doni as "an Antichrist, a limb of the Great Devil," Aretino (or at least the popular myth of Aretino) provides an apt object for the English satirist's attack on the pagan, myopic heuristics of "Spartanes fashion," especially when preceded immediately in the poem by allusion to Cicero's "Numquam minus solus" (67–68).

37. "By their fruits ye shall know them"—Matthew 7:20; 12:33. Appropriately, the biblical allusion recalls Christ's purging of the Temple—just as the satirist prepares to enter the court once more (the court that is a "Purgatorie" for him) to purge it of its travesties and pharisaic, legalistic ignorance.

38. Given the strong *passionis* imagery in the poem, this comic view of the courtiers as "Pirats" that "board" the "weak" vessels of the court, in addition to its saucy ridicule of the libidinous proclivities of the court, may also intend to recall ironically the conventional Renaissance association of ships with the Cross, as epitomized in Augustine's sermon on Matthew 14. See Grant, pp. 46f. for elaboration on this iconographical tradition.

39. *The Sacrum Missal (in English)*, trans. Frederick E. Warren, ed. Vernon Staley (London: De La More Press, 1911). This is a translation of the 1526 Missal. The structure of the Presentation Mass has not changed—see the contemporary translation in The St. Joseph Missal.

40. John R. Roberts points out that the dichotomy between the aims of devotional works and controversial works was not made by the recusants: they hoped that "a return to the life of intensive prayer and penance might bring about the same result that the controversial literature had attempted to effect—namely, the conversion of heretical, obstinate England to the Catholic religion" (*A Critical Anthology of English Recusant Devotional Prose, 1558–1603*, Duquesne Studies, Philological Series, 7 [Pittsburgh: Duquesne Univ. Press, 1966], p. 3). In his "Preface unto all Deceaved Protestants," for example, John Heigham introduced his translation of Puente's *Meditations upon the Mysteries of our Holie Faith* as follows:

> I will humblie implore in thy behalfe, the helpe of heaven . . . to make both thee and me, men of prayer, & true contemplatives. Finallie, to effect this, for the love and zeale which I beare to my native soyle, if every fingar on my hand, and every haire on my head, were a severall Heigham, I would (by Gods assistance) expose them all to a million of martirdomes, to see these virtues in publique practice in my contrie of England. . . . This if I might be so happie to live to see, I would ioyfully singe with holy Simeon, his *Nunc dimittis*, saying, Now dismisse they servant o Lord! according to they word in peace, because myne eyes have seene thy salvation. Which he indeed should see, who should see renewed, the pious practice of Contemplation: which having seen with holie Simeon, and ended by dittie, I would desire after such a sight, with that holie Patriarche imediately to depart and dye. ([Omers, 1619], sig. A2r)

Likewise, Richard Hopkins, in the dedication of his translation of Granada's *Of Prayer, and Meditation* (Paris, 1582), said that he offered the work because he believed that "more spirituall profite wolde vndoubtedlie ensewe thereby to the gayninge of Christian sowles in our countrie from Schisme, and Heresie, and from all sinne, and iniquitie, than by bookes that treate of controuersies in Religion . . . " (cited in Roberts, *Anthology*, pp. 4–5).

41. The varying status of this book is traced by Bruce M. Metzger, ed., *Apocrypha* (New York: Oxford Univ. Press, 1965), whose edition I quote.

42. Jean Veron, *The Huntynge of Purgatorye to death, made Dialogewyse* (London: John Tysdale, 1561), fol. 298i.

43. The ninth *bolgia* was also guarded by giants, those figures Philo Judaeus calls "those who take the pleasures of the body for their quarry, who make it their practice to indulge in them and enjoy them and provide the means by which each of them may be promoted" (*De gigantibus*, xiv, trans. F. H. Colson and G. H. Whitaker, in *Philo* [Cambridge, Mass.: Harvard Univ. Press, 1929], II, 477). Louis Eugene Startzman's commentary on these lines is especially helpful. The giant beefeaters, he suggests, "seem similar to those giants Dante encountered at the center of Hell, i.e., Nimrod, Ephialtes, and Antaeus"; "they represent the strong physical presence which supports the court, [enforcing] the doom of nonsense, violence and triviality which has overtaken a court given over to perpetuating its own folly rather than serving God" ("Images of Evil in the

Formal Verse Satires of Joseph Hall, John Marston, John Donne and Alexander Pope," Ph.D. dissertation, Ohio University, 1970, p. 98).

44. *Sermons*, VII, 289, 280–81. See also IV, 76f., "God proposes to thee in his Scriptures, and otherwise, Images, patterns, of good and holy men to goe by."

45. See, for comparison, Donne's description of the "Canonicall" character of the sermon (*Sermons*, V, 56): "Our errand [is] to heare, and to heare all the words of the Preacher, but, to heare in those words, the Word, that Word which is the soule of all that is said, and is the true Physick of all their soules that heare. . . . Take a delight in Gods Ordinance, in mans preaching, and thou wilt finde Gods Word in that. . . . in those words, I have heard the Word."

46. Frances A. Yates, "Queen Elizabeth as Astraea," *Journal of Warburg and Courtauld Institutes*, 10 (1947), 38.

47. Appendix 3 of R. C. Bald's edition of Robert Southwell, *An Humble Supplication to Her Maiestie* (Cambridge: Cambridge Univ. Press, 1953), pp. 70–80.

48. (London: W. Stansby for Walter Burre, 1610), sig. B2ᵛ.

49. *Letters to Severall Persons of Honour*, p. 29.

50. "Courtiers out of Horace," p. 283.

51. *Metaphysical Mode*, p. 34.

52. Ascham, *The Schoolmaster*, in *English Works*, ed. William Aldis Wright (Cambridge: Cambridge Univ. Press, 1904), p. 232.

53. As in the previous poems, the satirist applies to the Protestant court a charge its polemicists commonly applied to the Catholics, the condemnation of the Catholic Mass as mere blasphemous histrionics. Typical of the Protestant attack is Tyndale's description of the Mass as a "play [of] juggling sophistry." John Philpot urges that "this your goodly mass [is] plainly the invention of men. . . . For where hath Christ ordained it, that any one person, clothed after the manner of players and counterfeited . . . and decked, to play as it were a part in an interlude"; and John Bradford, in his treatise on "The Hurt of Hearing Mass," says that "going to church where mass is . . . is no small sin, but such a sin as breaketh all God's laws generally, and every commandment particularly. . . . [S]uch massmongers . . . continueth in nothing," he argues; "they are traitors, and guilty of high treason against God." The blasphemous "Mass in jeste" performed under the tapestry of the seven deadly sins in the Presence Chamber, where "All are players," ironically fits the Protestant polemicists' attacks on the Catholic Mass.

Tyndale, *Doctrinal Treatises*, ed. Henry Walter, Parker Society (Cambridge: Cambridge Univ. Press, 1848), p. 149; Philpot, *Examinations*, p. 408; Bradford, *Writings*, pp. 326, 327. On the same subject see D. Douglas Waters, *Duessa as Theological Satire* (Columbia: Univ. of Missouri Press, 1970), and C. W. Dugmore, *The Mass and the English Reformers* (London: Macmillan, 1958).

54. Quoted in Evelyn M. Simpson, *A Study of the Prose Works of John Donne* (Oxford: Oxford Univ. Press, 1924), p. 316.

55. A. Leigh DeNeef, "'Who now doth follow the foule Blatant Beast': Spenser's Self-Effacing Fictions," *Renaissance Papers 1978*, ed. DeNeef and Hester (Durham, N.C.: Southeastern Renaissance Conference, 1979), pp. 11–21.

CHAPTER FIVE

1. Walton, *Lives* (Oxford, 1675), as cited in Bald, p. 93. Bald provides a detailed account of Donne's activities and duties as Secretary to the lord keeper, chapter 6, esp. pp. 99–102.

After the recusant tenor of *Satyre IV*, the question of Donne's employment by an official of the Anglican Establishment must undoubtedly arise. Perhaps a few facts about the lord keeper's past intimate why he was willing to employ this young man who had been so highly recommended by members of Egerton's own family. As Flynn points out, Egerton, too, had been a Catholic until his days at Lincoln's Inn, was disbarred for recusancy in 1569, listed as a recusant as late as 1577, and conformed in 1581. "Thus, in 1597, Donne came to work for a man who like himself had wavered, wrestled with the religious dilemma of the nation, but one who had at length decided not only to conform but to seek high position within the Establishment. . . . Moreover, in Egerton's household Donne would not feel that his Catholic background was a vulnerable point; such shared experience may even have formed part of his attraction to Egerton" (p. 11). Bald notes that "Egerton's own early recusancy doubtless gave him sympathy and understanding for Donne's religious predicament" (*John Donne*, p. 94). Thus, the bitter references to pursuivants and to Topcliffe in this poem may not have fallen on unsympathetic ears; even as an official examiner of Catholics, Egerton need not have necessarily found the methods of the court's cruel and unscrupulous officers defensible.

2. Geoffrey Bullough, "Donne the Man of Law," in *Just So Much Honor*, p. 65. A popular aphorism of the period, J. E. Neale points out, was that "as a man is friended, so the law is ended." One of Lord Burleigh's panegyrists summarized the existing conditions as follows: "I will forbear to mention the great and unusual fees exacted lately by reason of buying and selling offices, both judicial and ministerial, as also the privileges granted unto private persons to the great prejudice and grievance of the common people." ("The Elizabethan Political Scene," in *The Age of Catherine de Medici and Essays in Elizabethan History* [London: Jonathan Cape, 1963], p. 164). Professor Neale explains that the practice of selling and buying offices and the exacting of huge fees for the most ordinary judicial consideration were originally fostered by the queen herself, but had gotten badly out of hand in the last years of her reign. Her aims, "to see that her own discretion was not undermined by corrupt conspiracy between suitors and courtiers, and to ensure that bribery did not get the wrong person into office," had been greatly perverted by the late 1590s (p. 155).

3. Bullough, p. 64.

4. Milgate says the poem "has the air of a rather hastily-put-together occasional piece" (p. 165), and Leishman suggests that "the particular abuse Donne professes to be satirizing is merely a topic for the display of his wit" (p. 120).

5. The following interpretation of Juvenal's satire is based on that of Anderson, "Anger in Juvenal and Seneca," pp. 127–96; S. C. Fredericks, "Calvinus in Juvenal's Thirteenth Satire," *Arethusa*, 4 (1971), 219–31; and Mark Morford, "Juvenal 13," *American Journal of Philology*, 94 (1973), 26–36. All citations of Juvenal are from the Loeb edition, edited by G. G. Ramsey.

6. Anderson, "The Programs of Juvenal's Later Books," pp. 145–60.

7. "Anger," p. 184.

8. Lowell Edwards, "Juvenal's Thirteenth Satire," *Rheinisches Museum für Philologie*, 115 (1972), 59–73, points out that the satirist's view of "criminality [as] the way of the human race as a whole" intimates that his poem "deals with the conscience . . . only to raise the question whether conscience is strong enough to restrain or 'punish' men in a time when religion and law are corrupt" (pp. 70, 59–60).

9. Donald R. Howard, *The Idea of the Canterbury Tales* (Los Angeles: Univ. of California Press, 1976), p. 125.

10. Quotations describing the stages of the formal oration are taken from Wilson's *Arte of Rhetorique*.

11. Anderson, "The Programs of Juvenal's Later Books." He also delineates fully the rhetoric of indignation central to Juvenal's first book of satires ("Studies in Book 1 of Juvenal," *Yale Classical Studies*, 15 [1957], 31–90).

12. Full examinations of this doctrine and its application and modification by Donne in his prose works are provided by Dennis Quinn, "Donne's Christian Eloquence," *ELH*, 27 (1960), 276–97, and "John Donne's Principles of Biblical Exegesis," *Journal of English and Germanic Philology*, 61 (1962), 313–29; Thomas F. Merrill, "John Donne and the Word of God," *Neuphilologische Mitteilungen*, 69 (1968), 597–616; and Janel Mueller, "The Exegesis of Experience: Dean Donne's *Devotions Upon Emergent Occasions*," *Journal of English and Germanic Philology*, 67 (1968), 1–19. For a list of over thirty examples of medieval and Renaissance defenses of the theory of accommodation see C. A. Patrides, "*Paradise Lost* and the Theory of Accommodation," *Texas Studies in Literature and Language*, 5 (1963–64), 60, n. 9; 61, n. 13.

13. *Sermons*, II, 59; *Devotions*, p. 113.

14. Milgate, p. xxiv.

15. *De Doctrina Christiana*, I, 40, 60; Donne, *Sermons*, II, 277; IV, 211–14; V, 40–45; VI, 85–86, 91–93; VII, 394–400; X, 49–60.

16. The specific rules to which the satirist refers are from *Il Cortegiano*, in which Castiglione's Bernardo says that "it provoketh no laughter to mock and scorne a sillie soule in miserie and calamitie, nor yet a naughtie knave and common ribaulde, because a man would thinke that these men deserved to be otherwise punished, than in jesting at" (*The Book of the Courtier, Done into English by Sir Thomas Hoby Anno 1561* [London: E. P. Dutton, n.d.], pp. 138–39).

17. "The Roman Socrates," pp. 22–24.

18. Ibid., p. 23.

19. Maresca, *Pope's Horatian Poems*, esp. pp. 15ff; and Soens, "Criticism of Formal Satire," pp. 160ff.

20. Cited in Soens, p. 162.

21. *Coelum Philosophorum, The First Canon*, in *The Hermetic and Alchemical Writings of . . . Paracelsus*, ed. Arthur Edward Waite (London: James Elliott, 1894), I, 21; first noted by Grierson, II, 126. The idea of the world as a book is yoked with the microcosm-macrocosm idea in Paracelsus' *Labyrinthus medicorum errantium*, as Schleiner points out (pp. 99–101).

22. Several studies have illustrated Donne's familiarity with the theories of Paracelsus: Schleiner, pp. 97–103; E. H. Duncan, "Donne's Alchemical Figures," *ELH*, 9 (1942), 257–85; W. A. Murray, "Donne and Paracelsus," *Review of English Studies*, 25 (1949), 11–23; Joseph A. Mazzeo, "Notes on John Donne's Alchemical Imagery," *Isis*, 48 (1957), 103–23; and Eluned Crawshaw, "Hermetic Elements in Donne's Poetic Vision," in *John Donne: Essays in Celebration*, pp. 324–48. But none determines whether he accepted the basic principles of this science; even the references to Paracelsus in the sermons (II, 76, 93; VI, 116; IX, 136; X, 170–71) are noncommittal. As Crawshaw concludes, "alchemy offer[ed Donne] a sort of symbolic shorthand whose terms evoke a certain way of approaching some of his major preoccupations, and when he uses its language he does it with the seriousness and precision of the alchemists themselves" (p. 348).

23. P. 1. In his prose works Donne often describes God as an artist. The frequency of this trope in his works has been documented by Webber and Schleiner.

24. Mueller, p. 4.

25. Calvin, for instance, notes: "as kings, and such as are invested with authority, through the blindness which is produced by pride, generally take to themselves a boundless liberty of action, the Psalmist warns them that they must render an account at the bar of the Supreme Judge, who is exalted above the highest of this world. . . . Although God has invested judges with a sacred character and title . . . this will afford no support and protection to wicked judges . . . ; they themselves also must one day appear at the judgement-seat of heaven to render up an account" (*Commentary on the Book of the Psalms*, trans. Rev. James Anderson [Grand Rapids: William B. Erdmans, 1949], III, 327–38, 334–35).

26. The chapter in Isaiah is described in the Douai Bible, for example, as "a Prophecy . . . of Destruction" and Micah 2 as a prophecy of how "injustices provoke God to punishe them."

27. Ibid.

28. Richard Beck, "Urim and Thummim," *Notes and Queries*, n.s. 4 (1957), 28. He discusses the possible sources of this allusion: Numbers 27:21; Exodus 28:30; I Samuel 14:41, and Josephus, *Antiquities*, III, 8–9.

29. Henry Smith, *Sermons*, p. 212. Renaissance typological interpretations of Haman often view him as a parodic "remembrance" of the sacrifice of Christ and a vision of the union of love and grace: see E. W., "The Crucifixion of Haman," *Journal of Warburg and Courtauld Institutes*, 1 (1938), 245–48.

30. Geoffrey Whitney, *A Choice of Emblems* (Leyden, 1586), ed. Henry Green (New York: Benjamin Blom, 1967), p. 39. His motto at the head of the emblem illustrates that the fable was considered an exhortation to moderation and patience, "Mediocribus vtere partis."

31. Martz, *The Poem of the Mind* (New York: Oxford Univ. Press, 1966), p. 15, applies this description to *Satyre III*.

32. "Quid rides? mutato nomine de te / fabula narratur"; this is suggested by Medine, "Contexts of Renaissance Verse Satire," p. 151.

33. My own understanding of Renaissance genres has been greatly influenced by the study of Rosalie Colie, *The Resources of Kind: Genre-Theory in the Renaissance* (Berkeley and Los Angeles: Univ. of Calif. Press, 1973).

APPENDIX   A

1. Bernard Harris, "Dissent and Satire," *Shakespeare Survey*, 17 (1964), 130.

2. *Doubt's Boundless Sea*, pp. 1–2, 3–4.

3. Allen, p. 4.

4. *Satires*, p. 145.

5. *The Anatomy of Melancholy* (New York: Tudor, 1927), p. 298 (Part III, sect. iv, memb. 2, subs. 1).

6. *Laws of Ecclesiastical Polity*, III, 19–22, in Allen, p. 7.

7. *Anatomy*, pp. 401, 424, 390, as cited in William R. Mueller, *The Anatomy of Robert Burton's England* (Los Angeles: Univ. of California Press, 1952), pp. 79, 82, 76.

8. Gifford, *A Short Treatise against the Donatists of England, whome we call Brownists* (London: J. Windet f. T. Cooke, 1590), and *A Plaine declaration that our Brownists be full Donatists* (London: [T. Orwin] f. T. Cooke, 1590); Alison, *A Plaine Confutation of a Treatise of Brownisme* (London: T. Scarlet f. W. Wright, 1590); and Some, *A Godly Treatise* (London: G. B[ishop], 1589). William P. Holden points out in *Anti-Puritan Satire 1572–1642* (New Haven, Conn.: Yale Univ. Press, 1954) that not all commentators make these errors, but for most "*Anabaptist*, a rather vague and terrifying word, describes all varieties of dissenters; *Brownist* has similar emotive force; and *Familist* serves as a substitute for 'sexually promiscuous'" (p. 42).

9. Paul Christiansen, *Reformers and Babylon* (Toronto: Univ. of Toronto Press, 1978).

10. Cited in Michael R. Watts, *The Dissenters* (Oxford: Clarendon, 1978), p. 185.

11. Cited in Champlin Burrage, *The Early English Dissenters* (Cambridge: Cambridge Univ. Press, 1912), I, 215, 216, 219.

12. Christiansen, pp. 73, 88, 89.

13. I have used Leland Carlson's edition of the works of Barrow: *The Writings of Henry Barrow 1587–1590*, English Nonconformist Texts, vol. 3 (London: George Allen and Unwin, 1962). All citations of Barrow are from this edition and will be indicated by page number in parentheses.

14. *Barrow*, p. 96, n. 3. For the same comment by Barrow, see his most important work, *A Brief Discoverie*, esp. pp. 65–66, 79, 85, 96, 184, 187, 205, 227, 234ff.

15. Donne, *The Complete English Poems* (London: Allen Lane, 1971), pp. 483–84.

16. Roy J. Deferrari points out that after his contact with Montanism Tertullian's "harshness increases steadily and brings him into conflict with the authorities" frequently. In works such as *The Chaplet* and *Flight in the Time of Persecution* his extremism is especially evident: Tertullian, *Disciplinary, Moral and Ascetical Works* (New York: Fathers of the Church, 1959), pp. 7–10.

17. W. M. Calder points out that the earliest references to Montanism refer to them simply as the Phrygians, that the area became identified with the sect ("Philadelphia and Montanism," *Bulletin of the John Rylands Library*, 5 [1922–23], 309–54).

18. The Parker Society (Cambridge: Cambridge Univ. Press, 1854), p. vi.

19. P. 158; italics added.

20. Pp. 261, 306.

21. Cited in Carlson, p. 455, n. 1.

22. *Concerning the Brownists*, pp. 2, 41, 46.

23. *The Examination and Writings of John Philpot*, Parker Society (Cambridge: Cambridge Univ. Press, 1842), p. 421.

24. In *Elizabeth I and her Parliaments 1584–1601* (New York: Jonathan Cape, 1958), J. E. Neale points out that two anti-Catholic bills were committed in the 1593 Parliament. The more severe of the two—"An Act to retain the Queen's subjects in obedience"—was changed into an act against Protestant sectaries, namely the Barrowists and Brownists. It was during the heated debate over this bill, in fact, that the bishops arranged for Barrow and Greenwood to be taken out of prison "early and secretly" and hanged. Originally a reissue of the 1581 bill against Catholics, the bill finally aimed more at the growing threats of the nonconformists, redefining *recusant* as "whosoever, being an obstinate recusant, should hold that we had no church, that we had no true sacraments, nor true ministry, . . . this man solely to be within the law" (p. 290). The bill was rushed without trouble through the Lords, subject to considerable rancor and debate among the Commons, but finally passed, not least of all because the queen by this time "had coupled Protestant nonconformity with Catholicism as a menace to the State" (p. 287). In its final form, in fact, the bill was harsher on the Protestant nonconformists than on the Catholic recusants.

APPENDIX B

1. *The Power of Satire*, p. 129.
2. Ibid., p. 119.

3. Gerald L. Bruns, "Allegory and Satire: A Rhetorical Meditation," *New Literary History*, 11 (1979), 121–32, suggests that "the deepest wish of every satirist . . . is not merely to correct but to kill, or to correct by killing" (p. 129).

4. "Lying Like Truth: Riddle, Representation and Treason in Renaissance England," *ELH*, 47 (1980), 32–47.

5. For Guilpin I have relied on the edition of D. Allen Carroll (Chapel Hill: Univ. of North Carolina Press, 1974); for Hall and Marston, I have used the editions by Arnold Davenport (Liverpool: Liverpool Univ. Press, 1969, 1961 respectively).

6. "A Purchase of Glory: The Persona of Late Elizabethan Satire," *Studies in Philology*, 72 (1975), 417 to which I am indebted for these views of Guilpin and Hall also.

7. "Studies in Book I of Juvenal," pp. 58–59.

8. "*Amicitia* and the Unity of Juvenal's Book," *Illinois Classical Studies*, 4 (1979), 164.

9. "Irony of Overstatement in the Satires of Juvenal," *Illinois Classical Studies*, 4 (1979), 183. See also Anderson, "Anger in Juvenal and Seneca," pp. 132–35.

10. In the introduction to his translation of Juvenal's *Satires* (Ann Arbor: Univ. of Michigan Press, 1965), Richard E. Braum calls Juvenal "the ironist of anti-epic" (p. 15).

BIBLIOGRAPHY

DONNE EDITIONS

The Anniversaries. Ed. Frank M. Manley. Baltimore: Johns Hopkins Univ. Press, 1963.

Biathanatos. Ed. J. William Hebel. New York: Facsimile Text Society, 1930.

The Complete English Poems. Ed. A. J. Smith. London: Allen Lane, 1971.

The Divine Poems. Ed. Helen Gardner. Oxford: Clarendon, 1952.

The Elegies and the Songs and Sonnets. Ed. Helen Gardner. Oxford: Clarendon, 1965.

Letters to Severall Persons of Honour. London: J. Flesher f. Richard Marriot, 1615.

The Poems of John Donne. Ed. H. J. C. Grierson. 2 vols. Oxford: Oxford Univ. Press, 1912.

Pseudo-Martyr. London: W. Stansby f. W. Burre, 1610.

The Satires, Epigrams and Verse Letters. Ed. W. Milgate. Oxford: Clarendon, 1967.

Sermons. Ed. George R. Potter and Evelyn M. Simpson. 10 vols. Berkeley and Los Angeles: Univ. of California Press, 1953–62.

"A Variorum Text of the Satires of John Donne." Ed. Marian Dickinson Campbell. Ph.D. dissertation, Yale Univ., 1907.

PRIMARY WORKS

Abbot, George. *An exposition upon the prophet Jonah.* London: Richard Field, 1600.

Alison, Richard. *A Plaine Confutation of a Treatise of Brownisme.* London: T. Scarlet f. W. Wright, 1590.

Allen, Robert. *A treatise of Catechisme or Christian instruction.* London: R. Field f. T. Mann, 1600.

Anderson, Anthony. *The Shielde of our safetie.* London: H. Jackson, 1581.

Apocrypha. Ed. Bruce M. Metzger. New York: Oxford Univ. Press, 1965.

Aquinas, Thomas, Saint. *Summa Theologica.* Trans. A. C. Pegis. New York: Modern Library, 1948.

Aristotle. *Nichomachean Ethics.* Trans. W. D. Ross. Oxford: Oxford Univ. Press, 1925.

Ascham, Roger. *English Works.* Ed. William Aldis Wright. Cambridge: Cambridge Univ. Press, 1904.

Augustine, Saint. *Confessions.* Trans. J. G. Pilkington. New York: Heritage, 1963.

———. *Godly meditations made in the forme of prayers.* London: J. Daye, [n.d.].

———. *Selected Works.* Trans. John J. Gavigan. Washington, D.C.: Catholic Univ. Press, 1947.

———. *Soliloquies.* Trans. Thomas F. Gilligan. New York: Cosmopolitan Science and Art, 1943.

————. *The Teacher.* Trans. Robert P. Russell. Washington, D.C.: Catholic Univ. Press, 1968.

————. *The Trinity.* Trans. Stephen McKenna. Washington, D.C.: Catholic Univ. Press, 1963.

Babington, Gervase. *A Very fruitful Exposition of the Commandements by Way of Questions and Answers for greater plainenesse.* London: R. Robinson, 1596.

Baro, Peter [Andreas Gerardus]. *A Special Treatise of Gods Providence.* London: J[ohn] L[udham], 1588.

————. *The Practis of Preaching.* London: J[ohn] Ludham, 1577.

Barrow, Henry. *The Writings of Henry Barrow 1587–1590.* Ed. Leland Carlson. English Nonconformist Texts 3. London: George Allen and Unwin, 1962.

Batman, Stephen. *Cronicle of Doome, or Warning to Gods Judgement.* London: R. Newberry, 1581.

Beard, Thomas: *Theatre of Gods Judgements.* London: A. Islip, 1597.

Becon, Thomas. *The Catechism.* Ed. John Ayre. Parker Society. Cambridge: Cambridge Univ. Press, 1844.

————. *Papers and Other Pieces of Thomas Becon.* Ed. John Ayre. Parker Society. Cambridge: Cambridge Univ. Press, 1844.

Bedel, Henry. *A Sermon exhortyng to pitie the poore.* London: John Audely, 1572.

Bernard, Saint. *St. Bernard His Meditations.* Trans. "W. P." London: E. A[llde] f. R. Allot, 1631–32.

————. *The Steps of Humility by Bernard, Abbot of Clairvaux.* Trans. George Bosworth Burch. Notre Dame, Ind.: Univ. of Notre Dame Press, 1963.

Beza, Theodore de. *The Treasure of Truth, touching the grounde worke of man his salvation, and chiefest pointes of Christian Religion.* Trans. John Stockwood. London: Thomas Woodcocke, 1581.

Bisse, James. *Two sermons preached the one at Paules Crosse.* London: Thomas Woodcocke, 1581.

Bland, Tobias. *A Bait for Momus.* London: John Wolfe, 1589.

Boaistuau, Pierre. *Certaine Secrete Wonders of Nature, containing a description of sundry strange things, seming monstrous.* Trans. Edward Fenton. London: Henry Bynneman, 1569.

Bonaventura, Saint. *The Franciscan Vision: Translation of Itinerarium Mentis in Deum.* Trans. Father James. London: Burns Oates and Washbourne, 1937.

———— (Attributed to). *Meditations on the Life of Christ.* Trans. Sister M. Emmanuel. London: B. Herder, 1934.

Bradford, John. *Writings.* Ed. Aubrey Townsend. Parker Society. Cambridge: Cambridge Univ. Press, 1848.

Bridges, John. *A Sermon Preached at Paules Crosse.* London: Henry Bynneman, 1571.

Bull, Henry (comp.). *Christian Prayers and Holy Meditations, As Well for Private as Public Exercise.* London: Henry Middleton, 1570.

Bullinger, Henry. *The Decades.* Ed. Thomas Harding. Parker Society. Cambridge: Cambridge Univ. Press, 1849.

Calvin, Jean. *Commentary on the Book of Psalms.* Trans. James Anderson. Grand Rapids, Mich.: William B. Erdmans, 1949.

Castiglione, Baldessare. *The Book of the Courtier, Done into English by Sir Thomas Hoby Anno 1561.* London: E. P. Dutton, n.d.

Cecil, Robert. *The Execution of Justice in England.* London: C. Barker, 1583.

Certaine Sermons or Homilies. London: John Bill, 1623.

Cicero, Marcus Tullius. *De Oratore*. Trans. E. W. Sutton and H. Rackham. 3 vols. Cambridge, Mass.: Harvard Univ. Press, 1942.

Copley, A. A. *Another Letter of Mr. A. C. to his dis-iesuited kinseman*. London: n.p., 1602.

Cradocke, Edwarde. *The shippe of assured safety . . . , a discourse of Gods Providence*. London: H. Bynneman, 1572.

A Critical Anthology of English Recusant Devotional Prose, 1558–1603. Ed. John R. Roberts. Duquesne Philological Series, 7. Pittsburgh: Duquesne Univ. Press, 1966.

Crowley, Robert. *The Voyce of the laste trumpet, blowen bi the seuenth Angel . . . calling all estates of men to the ryght path*. London: R. Crowley, 1550.

Daneau, Lambert. *A Fruitful Commentary upon the Twelve Small Prophets*. Trans. J. Stockwood. Cambridge: J. Legatt, 1594.

Daunce, Edward. *A Briefe Discourse of the Spanish State*. London: Richard Field, 1590.

Dent, Arthur. *A Sermon of Repentence*. London: John Harrison, 1583.

Deringe, Edward. *XXII Lectures or Readings*. London: Lucas Harrison, 1576.

Downame, John. *Spiritual Physicke to Cure the Diseases of the Soule*. London: G. Simson f. W. Jones, 1600.

Drant, Thomas. *Horace: his Arte of Poetrie, Pistles, and Satyres Englished*. Intro. Peter E. Medine. Delmar, N.Y.: Scholars' Facsimiles and Reprints, 1972.

———. *A medicinall moral, that is the two books of Horace his satyrs Englished: The Waylyngs of Hieremiah*. London: T. Marsh, 1566.

———. *Three godly and learned Sermons*. London: W. Jaggard, 1584.

Elizabethan Critical Essays. Ed. G. Gregory Smith. 2 vols. London: Oxford Univ. Press, 1904.

The Epic of the Beast, Consisting of English Translations of "Reynard the Fox" and Physiologus. Trans. John Carlill. Ed. William Rose. London: George Routledge, n.d.

Erasmus, Desiderius. *The Enchiridion*. Trans. Raymond Himelick. Bloomington: Indiana Univ. Press, 1963.

———. *The Praise of Folly*. Trans. Clarence H. Miller. New Haven, Conn.: Yale Univ. Press, 1979.

Gibson, Thomas. *A Fruitful Sermon Preached at Occham*. Mauldon: Robert Waldegrave, 1584.

Gifford, George. *A Plaine declaration that our Brownists be full Donatists*. London: [T. Orwin] f. T. Cooke, 1590.

———. *A Short Treatise against the Donatists of England, whome we call Brownists*. London: J. Windet f. T. Cooke, 1590.

Glass of Mans Folly, and Means to Amendment of Life. London: John Wolfe, 1587.

Gosson, Stephen. *Markets of Bawdrie: The Dramatic Criticism of Stephen Gosson*. Ed. Arthur F. Kinney. Salzburg: Univ. of Salzburg, 1974.

Granada, Luis de. *Of Prayer, and Meditation*. Trans. Richard Hopkins. Paris: T. Brumeau, 1582.

Gratarolus, Gulielmus. *The Castel of Memorie*. Trans. William Fulwood. London: R. Hall, 1562.

Greenham, Richard. *Works*. London: F. Kingston, 1599.

Guilpin, Everard. *Skialetheia*. Ed. D. Allen Carroll. Chapel Hill: Univ. of North Carolina Press, 1974.

Hall, Joseph. *Poems*. Ed. Arnold Davenport. Liverpool: Liverpool Univ. Press, 1969.

Harrison, William. *The Description of England*. Ed. Georges Edelen. Ithaca, N.Y.: Cornell Univ. Press, 1968.

Hemmingsen, Nicholas. *The Preacher, or the methode of Preaching.* Trans. "I. H." London: T. Marsh, 1576.

Hill, Adam. *The crie of England.* London: Ed Allde f. B. Norton, 1595.

Hooper, John. *Early Writings.* Ed. Samuel Carr. Parker Society. Cambridge: Cambridge Univ. Press, 1843.

———. *Later Writings of Bishop Hooper, together with his Letters and Other Pieces.* Ed. Charles Nevinson. Parker Society. Cambridge: Cambridge Univ. Press, 1852.

Horatius Flaccus, Q. *Poemata omnis doctissimis scholis illustrata. Iunii Iuuenalis satyrae.* London: N. Norton and A. Hatfield, 1574, 1585.

———. *Satires, Epistles and Ars Poetica.* Trans. H. Rushton Fairclough. Cambridge: Harvard Univ. Press, 1926.

Hoskyns, John. *Directions for Speech and Style.* Ed. H. H. Hudson. Princeton, N.J.: Princeton Univ. Press, 1935.

Hutchinson, Roger. *Works.* Ed. John Bruce. Parker Society. Cambridge: Cambridge Univ. Press, 1842.

Ignatius, Loyola, Saint. *The Spiritual Exercises.* Trans. W. H. Longridge. London: A. R. Mowbray, 1919.

Jewel, John. *Works.* Ed. John Ayre. Parker Society. Cambridge: Cambridge Univ. Press, 1845.

Jonson, Ben. *Ben Jonson.* Ed. C. H. Herford and Percy Simpson. 11 vols. Oxford: Clarendon, 1925–52.

Joye, George. *A contrarye (to a certain man's) consultacion: that adulterors ought to be punished wyth death.* London: G. Joye, [1549?].

Juvenalis. *Juvenal and Persius.* Trans. G. G. Ramsey. Rev. ed. Cambridge, Mass.: Harvard Univ. Press, 1940.

———. *J. Juvenalis et A. Persii Flacci satyrae.* London: R. Field, 1612.

———. *Satires.* Ed. Richard E. Braun. Ann Arbor: Univ. of Michigan Press, 1965.

Keckermann, Bartholomaus. *Rhetoricae Ecclesiasticae.* Hanover: n.p., 1606.

Kethe, William. *A Sermon Made at Blandfor Farm.* London: John Daye, 1571.

King, John. *Lectures Upon Jonah, delivered at Yorke, in the Year of Our Lord 1594.* Oxford: Joseph Barnes, 1597.

Lactantius. *Minor Works.* Trans. Sister Mary Francis McDonald. Washington, D.C.: Catholic Univ. Press, 1965.

La Primaudaye, Pierre de. *The French Academie.* Trans. "T. B." London: Edmund Bollifant f. R. Newberry, 1586.

Lauatere, Lodovicke. *Three Christian Sermons.* Trans. W. Barlow. London: Thomas Creede, 1596.

L[ea], J[ames]. *A True and perfecte description of a straunge Monstar borne in the City of Rome in Italy, in the yeare of Salvation: 1588.* London: John Wolfe f. Walter Dight, 1590.

———. *The Birth, Purpose, and Mortall Wound of the Romish holie League.* London: [T. Orwin] f. Thomas Cadman, 1589.

Marston, John. *Poems.* Ed. Arnold Davenport. Liverpool: Liverpool Univ. Press, 1961.

Milton, John. *Complete Prose Works.* Ed. Don M. Wolfe et al. New Haven, Conn.: Yale Univ. Press, 1953.

Nashe, Thomas. *Works.* Ed. R. B. McKerrow. 5 vols. London: Sidgwick and Jackson, 1904.

Paracelsus. *The Hermetic and Alchemical Writings*. Ed. Arthur Edward Waite. 2 vols. London: James Elliott, 1894.

Paré, Ambroise. *Les Oeuvres*. Paris: G. Buon, 1598.

Philo Judaeus. *Philo*. Trans. F. H. Colson and G. H. Whitaker. 11 vols. Cambridge, Mass.: Harvard Univ. Press, 1929.

Philpot, John. *The Examination and Writings*. Ed. Robert Eden. Parker Society. Cambridge: Cambridge Univ. Press, 1842.

Pilkington, James. *Aggeus and Abdias, Prophetes, the one corrected, the other newly added, and both at large declared*. London: W. Seres, 1562.

———. *Works*. Ed. James Sutherland. Parker Society. Cambridge: Cambridge Univ. Press, 1842.

Playfere, Thomas. *The Meane in Mourning*. London: Widow Orwin f. Andrew Wise, 1596.

Pope, Alexander. *The Complete Works of Alexander Pope*. Ed. William Warburton. London: J. & P. Knapton, 1751.

———. *Imitations of Horace*. Ed. John Butt. Twickenham Edition of the Poems of Alexander Pope, vol. 4. New Haven, Conn.: Yale Univ. Press, 1939.

Puente, Luis de la. *Meditations upon the Mysteries of our Holie Faith, with the Practise of Mental Prayer touching the same*. Trans. R. F. Gibbons. 2 vols. St. Omer: J. Heigham, 1610, 1619.

Ralegh, Sir Walter. *The History of the World*. Ed. C. A. Patrides. Philadelphia: Temple Univ. Press, 1972.

Remains of Old Latin. Trans. E. H. Warmington. 4 vols. Cambridge, Mass.: Harvard Univ. Press, 1938.

Rogers, Thomas. *The Catholic Doctrine of the Church of England*. Ed. J. J. S. Perowne. Parker Society. Cambridge: Cambridge Univ. Press, 1854.

The Sacrum Missal (in English). Trans. Frederick E. Warren. Ed. Vernon Staley. London: De La More Press, 1911.

Sandys, Edwin. *The Sermons of Edwin Sandys*. Ed. John Ayre. Parker Society. Cambridge: Cambridge Univ. Press, 1841.

Silver, George. *Paradoxes of Defense*. London: E. Blount, 1599.

Skene, Gilbert. *Ane Breve Description of the Pest*. Edinburgh: Robert Kekprevite, 1568.

Smith, Henry. *The Sermons of Master Henry Smith gathered in one volume*. London: T. Orwin f. Thomas Mann, 1592.

Some, Robert. *A Godly Treatise*. London: G. B[ishop], 1589.

Somers Tracts. 13 vols. London: T. Cadell and W. Davies, 1809–15.

Southwell, Robert. *An Humble Supplication to Her Maiestie*. Ed. R. C. Bald. Cambridge: Cambridge Univ. Press, 1953.

———. *Spiritual Exercises and Devotions*. Trans. P. E. Hallett. London: Sheed and Ward, 1931.

Spence, Joseph. *Anecdotes*. Ed. S. W. Singer. Carbondale: Southern Illinois Univ. Press, 1964.

Stockwood, John. *A Sermon Preached at Paules Crosse*. London: Henry Bynneman, 1578.

Strype, John. *Annals of the Reformation*. 4 vols. New York: B. Franklin, 1968.

Tertullian. *Disciplinary, Moral and Ascetical Works*. Trans. Sister Emily Joseph Daly and Edwin A. Quain. Ed. Roy J. Defferrari. New York: Fathers of the Church, 1959.

Topsell, Edward. *Historie of Foure-Footed Beastes*. London: W. Jaggard, 1607.

————. *Times Lamentation: An Exposition of the Prophet Ioel.* London: John Windet, 1596.

Tossanus, Daniel. *The Lamentations and holy mourninge of the Prophete Ieremiah.* Trans. Thomas Stocker. London: John Windet, 1587.

Tudor Royal Proclamations. Ed. Paul L. Hughes and James Francis Larkin. 5 vols. Oxford: Clarendon, 1964–73.

Tymme, Thomas. *A Plaine discourse of ten English Lepers.* London: P. Short, 1592.

————. *A preparation against the prognosticated dangers of this yeare 1588.* London: J. Wolfe, 1587.

Tyndale, William. *Doctrinal Treatises and Introductions to Different Portions of the Holy Scriptures.* Ed. Henry Walter. Parker Society. Cambridge: Cambridge Univ. Press, 1848.

Tyrer, Thomas. *Five Godly Sermons.* London: J. H. f. John Harrison, 1602.

Udall, John. *Amendment of life: three sermons.* London: f. T. Mann, 1594.

————. *A commentarie vpon the lamentations of Jeremy.* London: Widdow Orwin f. T. Mann, 1593.

Veron, Jean. *The Huntynge of Purgatorye to death, made Dialogowyse.* London: John Tysdale, 1561.

White, Thomas. *A sermon preached at Paules Crosse on Sunday the third of November 1577.* London: Francis Coldock, 1578.

Whitney, Geoffrey. *A Choice of Emblems.* Ed. Henry Green. New York: Benjamin Blom, 1967.

Wilson, Thomas. *The Arte of Rhetorique.* Ed. G. H. Mair. Oxford: Clarendon, 1909.

Wright, Leonard. *A Summons for Sleepers.* London: Henry Bynneman, 1596.

Wright, Thomas. *The Passions of the Minde in general.* Ed. Thomas O. Sloan. Urbana: Univ. of Illinois Press, 1971.

Wybarne, Joseph. *New Age of Old Names.* London: J. Windet f. W. Barret and H. Fetherstone, 1609.

Zepheria. London: Widdowe Orwin, for N. L. and John Busbie, 1594.

SECONDARY WORKS

Aden, John. *Something Like Horace.* Nashville: Vanderbilt Univ. Press, 1969.

Alden, Raymond. *The Rise of Formal Verse Satire in England Under Classical Influence.* University of Pennsylvania Studies in Philology, Literature, and Archaeology, VII, 2. Philadelphia: Univ. of Pennsylvania Press, 1899.

Allen, Don Cameron. *Doubt's Boundless Sea: Skepticism and Faith in the Renaissance.* Baltimore: Johns Hopkins Press, 1964.

————. "The Renaissance Antiquarian and Allegorical Interpretation." In *Medieval and Renaissance Studies 1967.* Ed. John M. Headley. Chapel Hill: Univ. of North Carolina Press, 1968, pp. 3–20.

Anderson, W. S. "Anger in Juvenal and Seneca." *University of California Publications in Classical Philology,* 19 (1964), 127–95.

————. "Horace, the Unwilling Warrior: *Satire I, 9.*" *American Journal of Philology,* 77 (1956), 148–66.

————. "Imagery in the Satire of Horace and Juvenal." *American Journal of Philology,* 81 (1960), 242–44.

————. "Juvenal and Quintilian." *Yale Classical Studies,* 17 (1961), 1–93.

————. "The Programs of Juvenal's Later Books." *Classical Philology*, 57 (1962), 145–60.

————. "Studies in Book I of Juvenal." *Yale Classical Studies*, 15 (1957), 31–90.

Andreasen, N. J. C. "Theme and Structure in Donne's *Satyres*." *Studies in English Literature*, 3 (1963), 60–66.

Atkins, S. H. "Banks' Horse." *Notes and Queries*, 179 (1934), 28–30.

Auerback, Erich. *Literary Language and Its Public in Late Latin Antiquity*. Trans. Ralph Manheim. Bollingen Series 74. New York: Pantheon, 1965.

Baker, Herschel. *The Wars of Truth: Studies in the Decay of Christian Humanism in the Earlier Seventeenth Century*. Cambridge, Mass.: Harvard Univ. Press, 1952.

Bald, R. C. *John Donne: A Life*. Oxford: Oxford Univ. Press, 1970.

Baldwin, Francis Elizabeth. "Sumptuary Legislation and Personal Regulation in England." *Johns Hopkins University Studies in Historical and Political Science*, 44 (1926), 1–282.

Battenhouse, Roy. "The Grounds of Religious Toleration in the Thought of John Donne." *Church History*, 11 (1942), 217–48.

————. *Marlowe's Tamburlaine: A Study in Renaissance Moral Philosophy*. Nashville: Vanderbilt Univ. Press, 1941.

Beck, Richard. "Urim and Thummim." *Notes and Queries*, n.s. 4 (1957), 27–30.

Bellette, A. F. "The Originality of Donne's *Satires*." *Univ. of Toronto Quarterly*, 44 (1974–75), 130–40.

Berrey, Caryl K., and Clarence H. Miller. "The Structure of Integrity: The Cardinal Virtues in Donne's *Satyre III*." *Costerus*, 1 (1974), 27–45.

Blench, J. W. *Preaching in England in the Late Fifteenth and Sixteenth Centuries: A Study of English Sermons*. New York: Barnes & Noble, 1964.

Bross, Addison C. "Alexander Pope's Revisions of John Donne's *Satyres*." *Xavier University Studies*, 5 (1966), 133–52.

Bruns, Gerald L. "Allegory and Satire: A Rhetorical Meditation." *New Literary History*, 11 (1979), 121–32.

Burrage, Champlin. *The Early English Dissenters*. 2 vols. Cambridge: Cambridge Univ. Press, 1912; rpt. New York: Tudor, 1927.

Calder, W. M. "Philadelphia and Montanism." *Bulletin of the John Rylands Library*, 5 (1922–23), 309–54.

Calderwood, James L. *Metadrama in Shakespeare's Henriad*. Los Angeles: Univ. of California Press, 1979.

Camden, Carroll, ed. *Literary Views*. Chicago: Univ. of Chicago Press, 1964.

Cave, Terence C. *Devotional Poetry in France c. 1570–1613*. Cambridge: Cambridge Univ. Press, 1969.

Chandler, S. Bernard, and J. A. Molinaro, eds. *The World of Dante: Six Studies in Language and Thought*. Toronto: Univ. of Toronto Press, 1966.

Chew, Samuel C. *The Pilgrimage of Life*. New Haven, Conn.: Yale Univ. Press, 1962.

Christiansen, Paul. *Reformers and Babylon*. Toronto: Univ. of Toronto Press, 1978.

Clancy, Thomas H. *Papist Pamphleteers: The Allen-Persons Party and the Political Thought of the Counter-Reformation in England, 1572–1615*. Chicago: Loyola Univ. Press, 1964.

Cobb, Lucille E. "Donne's 'Satyre' II: 49–57." *Explicator*, 15 (1956), item 8.

Colie, Rosalie. *Paradoxia Epidemica: The Renaissance Tradition of Paradox*. Princeton, N.J.: Princeton Univ. Press, 1966.

————. *The Resources of Kind: Genre-Theory in the Renaissance*. Berkeley and Los Angeles: Univ. of California Press, 1973.

Colish, Marcia L. *The Mirror of Language: A Study of the Medieval Theory of Knowledge*. New Haven, Conn.: Yale Univ. Press, 1968.

Collmer, Robert. "The Meditation on Death and its Appearance in Metaphysical Poetry." *Neophilologus*, 45 (1961), 423–33.

Crampton, Georgia Ronan. *The Condition of Creatures: Suffering and Action in Chaucer and Spenser*. New Haven, Conn.: Yale Univ. Press, 1974.

Cruttwell, Patrick. "The Metaphysical Poets and Their Readers." *Humanities Association Review*, 28 (1977), 20–42.

Decker, Josue de. *Juvenalis declamans*. Ghent: E. van Goetham, 1913.

Demetz, Peter, Thomas Greene and Lowry Nelson, eds. *The Disciplines of Criticism: Essays in Literary Theory, Interpretation, and History*. New Haven, Conn.: Yale Univ. Press, 1973.

DeNeef, A. Leigh. "'Who now doth follow the foule Blatant Beast': Spenser's Self-Effacing Fictions." *Renaissance Papers 1978*. Ed. DeNeef and Hester. Durham, N.C.: Southeastern Renaissance Conference, 1979, pp. 11–21.

Dick, Bernard F. "Seneca and Juvenal 10." *Harvard Studies in Classical Philology*, 73 (1969), 237–46.

Dugmore, C. W. *The Mass and the English Reformers*. London: Macmillan, 1958.

Duncan, E. H. "Donne's Alchemical Figures." *ELH*, 9 (1942), 257–85.

Edwards, Lowell. "Juvenal's Thirteenth Satire." *Rheinisches Museum für Philologie*, 115 (1972), 59–73.

Eicholz, D. E. "The Art of Juvenal and his Tenth Satire." *Greece and Rome*, 2nd series, 3 (1956), 61–69.

Elliott, Emory. "The Narrative and Allusive Unity of Donne's *Satyres*." *Journal of English and Germanic Philology*, 75 (1976), 105–16.

Elliott, Robert. *The Power of Satire: Magic, Ritual, Art*. Princeton, N.J.: Princeton Univ. Press, 1960.

Fink, Z. S. "Jaques and the Malcontent Traveler." *Philological Quarterly*, 14 (1935), 237–52.

Finkelpearl, Philip J. *John Marston of the Middle Temple: An Elizabethan Dramatist in His Social Setting*. Cambridge, Mass.: Harvard Univ. Press, 1969.

Fiore, Peter Amadeus, ed. *Just So Much Honor: Essays Commemorating the 400th Anniversary of the Birth of John Donne*. University Park: Pennsylvania State Univ. Press, 1972.

Flynn, Dennis. "Donne's Catholicism." *Recusant History*, 13 (1975), 1–17, 178–95.

Foster, Richard. "Hamlet and the Word." *Univ. of Toronto Quarterly*, 30 (1960–61), 229–45.

Frankel, Edmund. *Horace*. Oxford: Clarendon, 1957.

Freccero, John. "Dante's Pilgrims in a Gyre." *PMLA*, 76 (1961), 168–81.

————. "Donne's 'Valediction: Forbidding Mourning.'" *ELH*, 30 (1963), 335–76.

Fredericks, S. C. "Calvinus in Juvenal's Thirteenth Satire." *Arethusa*, 4 (1971), 219–31.

————. "Irony of Overstatement in the Satires of Juvenal." *Illinois Classical Studies*, 4 (1979), 178–91.

Freeman, Rosemary. *English Emblem Books*. London: Chatto & Windus, 1948.

Friedman, Lila Hermann. "Satiric Personae: A Study of Point of View in Formal Verse Satire in the English Renaissance from Wyatt to Marston." Ph.D. dissertation, University of Wisconsin, 1955.

Giamatti, A. Bartlett. "Marlowe: The Arts of Illusion." *Yale Review*, 61 (1971–72), 530–43.

Gill, R. B. "A Purchase of Glory: The Persona of Late Elizabethan Satire." *Studies in Philology*, 72 (1975), 408–18.

Gransden, K. W. *Tudor Verse Satire*. London: Athlone, 1970.

Grant, Patrick. *Images and Ideas in Literature of the English Renaissance*. Amherst: Univ. of Massachusetts Press, 1979.

Hamilton, A. C. *Sir Philip Sidney: A Study of His Life and Works*. London: Cambridge Univ. Press, 1977.

Hardison, O. B. "The Orator and the Poet: The Dilemma of Humanist Literature." *Journal of Medieval and Renaissance Studies*, 1 (1970), 33–44.

Harris, Bernard. "Dissent and Satire." *Shakespeare Survey*, 17 (1964), 120–37.

Harris, Victor. *All Coherence Gone*. Chicago: Univ. of Chicago Press, 1949.

Harrison, Thomas P., ed. *Studies in Honor of DeWitt T. Starnes*. Austin: Univ. of Texas Press, 1967.

Haydn, Hiram. *The Counter-Renaissance*. New York: Scribner's, 1950.

Heatherington, Madelon E. "'Decency' and 'Zeal' in the Sermons of John Donne." *Texas Studies in Literature and Language*, 9 (1967), 307–16.

Henricksen, Bruce. "The Unity of Reason and Faith in Donne's Sermons." *Papers on Language and Literature*, 11 (1975), 18–30.

Hester, M. Thomas. "Henry Donne, John Donne, and the Date of *Satyre II*." *Notes and Queries*, n.s. 24 (1977), 524–27.

———. "Donne's 'Hill of Truth.'" *English Language Notes*, 14 (1976), 100–105.

Hill, Christopher. *Antichrist in Seventeenth-Century England*. London: Oxford Univ. Press, 1971.

Holden, William P. *Anti-Puritan Satire 1572–1642*. New Haven, Conn.: Yale Univ. Press, 1954.

Howard, Donald R. *The Idea of the Canterbury Tales*. Los Angeles: Univ. of California Press, 1976.

Hughes, Richard. *The Progress of the Soul: The Interior Career of John Donne*. New York: William Morrow, 1968.

Hunt, Clay. *Donne's Poetry: Essays in Literary Analysis*. New Haven, Conn.: Yale Univ. Press, 1954.

Jack, Ian. "Pope and 'The Weighty Bullion of Dr. Donne's Satires.'" *PMLA*, 66 (1951), 1009–22.

Janson, H. W. *Apes and Ape Lore in the Middle Ages and the Renaissance*. London: Warburg Institute, 1952.

Jensen, Ejner J. "The Wit of Renaissance Satire." *Philological Quarterly*, 51 (1972), 394–409.

John Donne: The Critical Heritage. Ed. A. J. Smith. London: Routledge & Kegan Paul, 1975.

John Donne: Essays in Celebration. Ed. A. J. Smith. London: Methuen, 1972.

Johnson, S. F. "Donne's Satires, I." *Explicator*, 11 (1953), item 53.

Jones, Richard Foster, ed. *The Seventeenth Century: Studies in the History of English Thought and Literature from Bacon to Pope*. Stanford, Calif.: Stanford Univ. Press, 1951.

Jorgensen, Paul A. "Elizabethan Religious Literature for Time of War." *Huntington Library Quarterly*, 37 (1973–74), 1–17.

Kermode, Frank. *The Sense of an Ending: Studies in the Theory of Fiction*. New York: Oxford Univ. Press, 1967.

Kernan, Alvin. *The Cankered Muse: Satire of the English Renaissance*. New Haven, Conn.: Yale Univ. Press, 1959.

———. "The Dunciad and the Plot of Satire." *Studies in English Literature*, 2 (1962), 260–66.

Kerrigan, William. "The Fearful Accommodations of John Donne." *English Literary Renaissance*, 4 (1974), 337–62.

———. *The Prophetic Milton*. Charlottesville: Univ. of Virginia Press, 1974.

Knox, Norman. *The Word Irony and Its Context, 1500–1755*. Durham: Duke Univ. Press, 1961.

Kranidas, Thomas. "Milton and the Rhetoric of Zeal." *Texas Studies in Literature and Language*, 6 (1965), 423–32.

LaFleur, Richard A. "*Amicitia* and the Unity of Juvenal's First Book." *Illinois Classical Studies*, 4 (1979), 158–77.

Lauritsen, John R. "Donne's *Satyres*: The Drama of Self-Discovery." *Studies in English Literature*, 16 (1976), 117–30.

Lawall, Gilbert. "*Exempla* and Theme in Juvenal's Tenth Satire." *Transactions of the American Philological Association*, 89 (1958), 25–31.

Leishman, J. B. *The Monarch of Wit: An Analytical and Comparative Study of the Poetry of John Donne*. New York: Harper & Row, 1965.

Levin, Harry. *The Myth of the Golden Age in the Renaissance*. Bloomington: Indiana Univ. Press, 1969.

Lewalski, Barbara Kiefer. *Donne's Anniversaries and the Poetry of Praise: The Creation of a Symbolic Mode*. Princeton, N.J.: Princeton Univ. Press, 1973.

Louthan, Doniphan. *The Poetry of John Donne: A Study in Explication*. New York: Bookman, 1951.

McGrath, Lynette. "Studies in the Norms and Techniques of Sixteenth-Century Satire from Skelton to Donne." Ph.D. dissertation, Univ. of Illinois, 1968.

McLuhan, Marshall. "Cicero and Renaissance Training for Prince and Poet." *Renaissance and Reformation*, 6 (1970), 38–42.

———. "Edgar Poe's Tradition." *Sewanee Review*, 52 (1944), 24–33.

Maitland, F. W. *Historical Essays*. Cambridge: Cambridge Univ. Press, 1957.

Maresca, Thomas E. *Pope's Horatian Poems*. Columbus: Ohio State Univ. Press, 1966.

Martz, Louis. *The Poem of the Mind: Essays on Poetry, English and American*. New York: Oxford Univ. Press, 1966.

———. *The Poetry of Meditation*. Rev. ed. New Haven, Conn.: Yale Univ. Press, 1962.

Mattingly, Garrett. *The Armada*. Boston: Houghton Mifflin, 1959.

Mazzeo, Joseph A. "Notes on John Donne's Alchemical Imagery." *Isis*, 48 (1957), 103–23.

Medine, Peter E. "Contexts of Renaissance Verse Satire: Moralistic and Moral." Ph.D. Dissertation, University of Wisconsin, 1970.

———. "Praise and Blame in Renaissance Verse Satire." *Pacific Coast Philology*, 7 (1972), 49–53.

Merrill, Thomas F. "John Donne and the Word of God." *Neuphilologische Mitteilungen*, 69 (1968), 597–616.

Miner, Earl. *The Metaphysical Mode from Donne to Cowley.* Princeton, N.J.: Princeton Univ. Press, 1969.

Moore, Thomas V. "Donne's Use of Uncertainty as a Vital Force in *Satyre III.*" *Modern Philology*, 67 (1969), 41–49.

Morford, Mark. "Juvenal 13." *American Journal of Philology*, 94 (1973), 26–36.

Morris, John. "The Martyrdom of William Harrington." *The Month*, 20 (1874), 411–23.

Mroz, Sister Mary Bonaventura. *Divine Vengeance.* Washington, D.C.: Catholic Univ. Press, 1941.

Mueller, Janel. "The Exegesis of Experience: Dean Donne's *Devotions Upon Emergent Occasions.*" *Journal of English and Germanic Philology*, 67 (1968), 1–19.

Mueller, William R. *The Anatomy of Robert Burton's England.* Los Angeles: Univ. of California Press, 1952.

Mullaney, Steven. "Lying Like Truth: Riddle, Representation and Treason in Renaissance England." *ELH*, 47 (1980), 32–47.

Murray, W. A. "Donne and Paracelsus." *Review of English Studies*, 25 (1949), 11–23.

Neale, J. E. *The Age of Catherine de Medici and Essays in Elizabethan History.* London: Jonathan Cape, 1963.

———. *Elizabeth I and her Parliaments.* 2 vols. London: Jonathan Cape, 1953, 1957.

Newton, Richard C. "Donne the Satirist." *Texas Studies in Literature and Language*, 16 (1974), 427–45.

Owst, Gerald Robert. *Literature and Pulpit in Medieval England.* Cambridge: Cambridge Univ. Press, 1933

———. *Preaching in Medieval England: An Introduction to Sermon Manuscripts of the Period c. 1350–1450.* Cambridge: Cambridge Univ. Press, 1926.

Panofsky, Erwin. *Studies in Iconology.* New York: Harper & Row, 1962; rpt. of 1939 edition.

Parker, Barbara L., and J. Max Patrick. "Two Hollow Men: The Pretentious Wooer and the Wayward Bridegroom of Donne's 'Satyre I.'" *Seventeenth-Century News*, 23 (1975), 10–13.

Parks, George B. "The First Italianate Englishman." *Studies in the Renaissance*, 8 (1961), 197–216.

Patrides, C. A. *The Grand Design of God.* Toronto: Univ. of Toronto Press, 1972.

———. "*Paradise Lost* and the Theory of Accommodation." *Texas Studies in Literature and Language*, (1963–64), 58–63.

———. "Renaissance and Modern Thought on the Last Things: A Study in Changing Concepts." *Harvard Theological Review*, 51 (1951), 169–85.

Patterson, Annabel M. *Hermogenes and the Renaissance: Seven Ideas of Style.* Princeton, N.J.: Princeton Univ. Press, 1970.

Paulson, Ronald. *The Fictions of Satire.* Baltimore: Johns Hopkins Press, 1967.

Pelikan, Jaroslav. *The Shape of Death.* New York: Abingdon, 1961.

Pepperdene, Margaret W., ed. *That Subtle Wreath: Lectures Presented at the Quartercentenary Celebration of the Birth of John Donne.* Atlanta: Agnes Scott College, 1973.

Pope, Elizabeth Marie. *Paradise Regained: The Tradition in the Poem.* New York: Russell and Russell, 1962.

Quinn, Dennis. "Donne's Christian Eloquence." *ELH*, 27 (1960), 276–97.

———. "John Donne's Principles of Biblical Exegesis." *Journal of English and Germanic Philology*, 61 (1962), 313–29.

Randolph, Mary Claire. "The Medical Concept in English Renaissance Satiric Theory: Its Possible Relationships and Implications." *Studies in Philology*, 38 (1941), 127–62.

———. "The Structural Design of the Formal Verse Satire." *Philological Quarterly*, 21 (1942), 368–84; rpt. in *Essential Articles for the study of English Augustan Backgrounds*, ed. Bernard N. Schilling. Hamden, Conn.: Archon, 1961.

———. "Thomas Drant's Definition of Satire, 1566." *Notes and Queries*, 180 (1941), 416–18.

Reckford, Kenneth. *Horace*. New York: Twayne, 1969.

Rice, Eugene. *The Renaissance Idea of Wisdom*. Baltimore: Johns Hopkins Press, 1958.

Richmond, Hugh. *Shakespeare's Sexual Comedy: A Mirror for Lovers*. New York: Bobbs-Merrill, 1971.

Roberts, John R. "Donne's *Satyre III* Reconsidered." *College Language Association Journal*, 12 (1968), 105–15.

Rose, Elliott. *Cases of Conscience: Alternatives Open to Recusants and Puritans under Elizabeth I and James I*. Cambridge: Cambridge Univ. Press, 1975.

Rudd, Niall. "Donne and Horace." *Times Literary Supplement*, 23 March 1963, p. 208.

Sackton, Alexander. "Donne and the Privacy of Verse." *Studies in English Literature*, 7 (1967), 67–82.

Sanders, Wilbur. *John Donne's Poetry*. Cambridge: Cambridge Univ. Press, 1971.

Schleiner, Winfried. *The Imagery of John Donne's Sermons*. Providence: Brown Univ. Press, 1970.

Selden, Raman. *English Verse Satire 1590–1765*. London: George Allen & Unwin, 1978.

Sellin, Paul R. "The Proper Dating of Donne's 'Satyre III,'" *Huntington Library Quarterly*, 43 (1979–80), 275–312.

Shero, Lucius. "The Satirist's Apologia." *Classical Studies in Language and Literature*, Series II, University of Wisconsin Studies in Language and Literature, No. 15. Madison: Univ. of Wisconsin Press, 1922.

Sicherman, Carol. "The Mocking Voices of Donne and Marvell." *Bucknell Review*, 17 (1969), 38–40.

Simpson, Evelyn M. *A Study of the Prose Works of John Donne*. Oxford: Oxford Univ. Press, 1924.

Singleton, Charles S. *Dante Studies 2: Journey to Beatrice*. Cambridge, Mass.: Harvard Univ. Press, 1958.

Slights, Camille. "'To Stand Inquiring Right': The Casuistry of Donne's *Satyre III*." *Studies in English Literature*, 12 (1972), 85–101.

Sloan, Thomas O. "The Persona as Rhetor: An Interpretation of Donne's *Satyre III*." *Quarterly Journal of Speech*, 51 (1965), 14–27.

Smith, A. J. "Donne in his Time: A Reading of 'The Extasie.'" *Revista di Letterature Moderne e Comparate*, 10 (1957), 260–75.

———. "The Poetry of John Donne." *English Poetry and Prose 1540–1674*. Ed. Christopher Ricks. London: Barrie and Jenkins, 1970.

Smith, Hallett. *Elizabethan Poetry: A Study in Conventions, Meaning and Expression*. Cambridge, Mass.: Harvard Univ. Press, 1952.

Smith, R. E. "The Law of Libel at Rome." *Classical Quarterly*, n.s. 1 (1951), 169–79.

Soens, A. L. "Criticism of Formal Verse Satire in the Renaissance." Ph.D. dissertation, Princeton University, 1957.

Startzman, Louis Eugene. "Images of Evil in the Formal Verse Satire of Joseph Hall, John Marston, John Donne and Alexander Pope." Ph.D. dissertation, Ohio University, 1970.

Stein, Arnold. "Donne's Harshness and the Elizabethan Tradition." *Studies in Philology*, 41 (1944), 390–409.

———. "Donne's Obscurity and the Elizabethan Tradition." *ELH*, 3 (1946), 98–118.

———. "The Second English Satirist." *Modern Language Review*, 28 (1943), 273–78.

Stroup, Thomas B. *Microcosmos: The Shape of the Elizabethan Play*. Lexington: Univ. of Kentucky Press, 1965.

Sullivan, J. P., ed. *Critical Essays on Roman Literature: Satire*. London: Routledge and Kegan Paul, 1963.

Teijeiro, J. S. C. "Apostillas jurisdicas a una satira de Horacio." *Arbor*, 31 (1955), 65–76.

Thompson, Sister M. Geraldine. "Donne's *Notitia*: The Evidence of the Satires." *Univ. of Toronto Quarterly*, 36 (1966), 24–36.

———. "John Donne and the Mindes Indeavours." *Studies in English Literature*, 5 (1965), 115–31.

———. *Under Pretext of Praise: Satiric Mode in Erasmus' Fiction*. Toronto: Univ. of Toronto Press, 1973.

Voss, A. E. "The Structure of Donne's *Anniversaries*." *English Studies in Africa*, 12 (1969), 1–30.

W., E. "The Crucifixion of Haman." *Journal of Warburg and Courtauld Institutes*, 1 (1938), 245–48.

Waddington, Raymond B. *The Mind's Empire: Myth and Form in George Chapman's Narrative Poems*. Baltimore: Johns Hopkins Press, 1974.

Wallerstein, Ruth. "Studies in Donne by Ruth Wallerstein." Ed. Barbara Hillyer Davis. Ph.D. dissertation, University of Wisconsin, 1962.

Waters, D. Douglas. *Duessa as Theological Satire*. Columbia: Univ. of Missouri Press, 1970.

Watts, Michael R. *The Dissenters*. Oxford: Clarendon, 1978.

Webber, Joan. *Contrary Music: The Prose Style of John Donne*. Madison: Univ. of Wisconsin Press, 1963.

Weinberg, Bernard. *A History of Literary Criticism in the Italian Renaissance*. 2 vols. Chicago: Univ. of Chicago Press, 1961.

Weiner, Carol Z. "The Beleagured Isle: A Study of Elizabethan and Early Jacobean Anti-Catholicism," *Past and Present*, 51 (1971), 27–62.

White, Helen. *Social Criticism in Popular Religious Literature of the Sixteenth Century*. New York: Macmillan, 1944.

Williams, Aubrey L. *Pope's Dunciad: A Study of Its Meaning*. London: Methuen, 1955.

———. Rev. of *Satires Against Man: The Poems of Rochester*, by Dustin H. Griffin. *Seventeenth-Century News*, 33 (1975), 28–29.

Yates, Francis A. *The Art of Memory*. Chicago: Univ. of Chicago Press, 1966.

———. "Queen Elizabeth as Astraea." *Journal of Warburg and Courtauld Institutes*, 10 (1947), 27–82.

Yunck, John A. "The Venal Tongue: Lawyers and the Medieval Satirists." *American Bar Association Journal*, 46 (1960), 277–80.

INDEX

Absentia recti, sin as, 13, 47, 79–81
Accommodation, theory of, 105–107, 108–116 *passim*, 156
Acts of Parliament, 40, 127, 144, 146, 151, 152, 158. *See also* Religious controversy, statutes
Adam, 23, 80–83, 110, 141
Aden, John, 147
Adultery, concept and images of, 21, 22–5, 28, 141
Aesop, 107, 115–16, 157
Alden, Raymond, 136
Alison, Richard, 121
Allen, Don Cameron, 120
Allen, Robert, 22–23
Anabaptists. *See* Religious controversy, sects
Anderson, William S., 56, 77, 100, 103, 108, 131, 144, 146–47, 148, 151, 156
Andreasen, N. J. C., 140, 147
Animals, 26–28, 43–44, 80, 146
Antichrist, 43–49 *passim*, 80–83, 122–26 *passim*, 146, 152, 154
Apocalypse. *See* Millenarianism
Apologiae, Roman, 36–37, 143–44
Apparel, concept and images of, 22–25, 26, 28, 50, 53, 140–141
Aquinas, (Saint) Thomas, 10, 25, 59, 67, 144, 148, 149
Aretino, Pietro, 87, 153–54
Ariosto, Lodovico, 106, 112
Aristotle, 67, 148
Armada, Spanish, 41–43 *passim*, 137, 145
Ascham, Roger, 80, 95, 152
Askaparts, 90, 132
Astraea, Queen Elizabeth as, 111
Atheism, 119–127 *passim*
Atkins, S. H., 141
Auerbach, Erich, 153
Augustine, Aurelius, (Saint), 10, 22, 29, 47, 49, 55, 59, 63, 85, 105, 107, 144, 149, 150, 154
Azor, John, 150

Babington, Gervase, 22
Baker, Herschel, 136
Bald, R. C., 73, 99, 144, 155–56

Baldwin, Francis Elizabeth, 141
Barker, Arthur, 136
Baro, Peter, 142
Barrow, Henry, 121, 122–27, 158. *See also* Religious controversy, sects
Barrowists. *See* Religious controversy, sects
Batman, Stephen, 7
Battenhouse, Roy, 6
Beard, Thomas, 7
Beck, Richard, 157
Becon, Thomas, 8, 14, 22, 139
Bedford, Countess of, 71, 139
Bellette, A. F., 138
Bernard, (Saint), 54, 55, 59, 60, 61, 62, 147, 148
Berrey, Caryl K., 147
Bevis, Sir, 90, 92, 132
Beza, Theodore de, 12
Bible, books of: Daniel, 61, 148–49; Esther, 107, 115; Exodus, 114; Genesis, 80, 110; Hebrews, 89; Isaiah, 107, 114, 157; John, 64; II Maccabees, 90–92, 132, 154; Matthew, 106, 112, 154; Micah, 107, 114, 157; Numbers, 107, 114; Psalms, 68, 89, 106, 107, 112, 137; Revelations, 49; I Samuel, 114; Titus, 89
Blench, J. W., 136
Bona carmina, 50–52
Bonaventura, (Saint), 62, 149, 153
Book of Common Prayer, 14
Book of Homilies. See *Certaine Sermons*
Book of Nature, 26, 27, 38, 47–49, 60, 62, 69–71, 146
Books, divine. *See* Bible; Book of Nature; Language
Bowman, Christopher, 126
Bradford, John, 141, 155
Braum, Richard E., 159
Bross, Addison C., 151
Brownists. *See* Religious controversy, sects
Bruns, Gerald R., 159
Bull, Henry, 25
Bullough, Geoffrey, 99
Burton, Robert, 120, 121

Calder, W. M., 158

M. Thomas Hester, Associate Professor of English at North Carolina State University, is Co-Editor of *John Donne Journal: Studies in the Age of Donne*. Twice an NEH Fellow, he has also been Co-Editor of *Renaissance Papers* since 1978. His numerous essays on Renaissance literature have appeared in *Genre*, *Studies in English Literature*, *Texas Studies in Literature and Language*, *Papers on Language & Literature*, and other journals. He is working presently on the satires volume of The Variorum Edition of the Poetry of John Donne.

Books of related interest

Spenser and the Motives of Metaphor
A. Leigh DeNeef

"This Poetick Liturgie"
Robert Herrick's Ceremonial Mode
A. Leigh DeNeef

Gentle Flame
The Life and Verse of Dudley Fourth Lord North
Dale B. J. Randall

Jonson's Gypsies Unmasked
Background and Theme of "The Gypsies Metamorphos'd"
Dale B. J. Randall

*Studies in the Continental Background
of Renaissance English Literature*
Essays Presented to John L. Lievsay
Edited by Dale B. J. Randall *and* George W. Williams

The Golden Tapestry
A Critical Survey of Non-chivalric Spanish Fiction
in English Translation
Dale B. J. Randall